To Darin
Thanks for Coming to Tara

Michal Harari

Jan 13, 2000

SHOWJUMPING LEGENDS

IRELAND 1868–1998

This book is published with the kind support of
The Show Jumping Association of Ireland
and the Irish Horse Board

ACKNOWLEDGEMENTS

This book would not have been possible without the unstinting help of people from all round the country who gave their time and shared both their memories and archives with me. I name them in the order in which I spoke to them — Jim Bryson, Billy McCully, Eileen Parkhill, Doreen McDowell, Ado Kenny, Elsbeth Gailey, Frank Kernan, Frank McGarry, Francie Kerins, Iris Kellett, Maurice Bamber, Roberta Malcolmson, Members of the SJAI Limerick/Clare Branch, Tommy Brennan, Leslie Fitzpatrick, Donal Corry, Colonel Billy Ringrose, Patricia Nicholson and Maeve Dowdall. I also wish to express my gratitude to the Army Equitation School and its members, past and present, for their help and interest.

There would have been no book at all without the initial encouragement of the Chairman of the Show Jumping Association of Ireland, Dr Alec Lyons, and Irish Horse Board Director General, Dermot Ryan, along with the sponsorship provided by both of these organisations. Neither could it have been completed without the co-operation of SJAI Director General, Tony Kelly, and his staff, in making historical material available. Margaret Lynch was also more than generous in allowing access to the archive of her late husband, Stanislaus Lynch.

Thanks also to colleagues, Grania Willis at *The Irish Field*, and Quintan Doran-O'Reilly at the *Irish Farmer's Journal*, who answered my every request for help.

Research could not have progressed without the unfailing help of Mary Kelleher and Gerard Whelan at the RDS Library where a host of showjumping treasures lie. Again, no request for help went unanswered at this most valuable division of the Royal Dublin Society. In particular, the assistance of Niamh Kelly of the Marketing Department was much appreciated, as were the input and contributions offered by David Gray.

My thanks to the many photographers who put the fruit of their art at our disposal — Maymes Ansell of Horseman Photography, Tony Parkes, Ann Hughes, Joe Kirkpatrick, Siobhán English, Ruth Rogers, Patrick Casey and Susan Kennedy of Lensmen Photography. Gratitude as well to Michael Slattery of Castle Freight for making some of the colour reproductions possible.

Thanks to David Houlden of Wolfhound Press for his patient guidance as editor of this work.

SHOWJUMPING LEGENDS

IRELAND 1868–1998

Michael Slavin

foreword by Frank McGrourty

WOLFHOUND PRESS

Preliminary Pages — Illustrations

First Page:
Rockbarton Sculpture (Tara China)

Acknowledgements Page:
Painting of the 1926 Dublin Horse Show by Sir John Lavery now hanging in the Members Club at the RDS (RDS Archive)

Title Page:
Detail from RDS advertising card (David Gray/RDS Archive)

This Page:
Top Left — Trevor Coyle on Cruising
(Fotograf Jan Gyllensten AB)
Bottom Right — Army Band Drummer
 (Susan Kennedy/Lensmen)

Table of Contents:
Top — Detail from RDS advertising card for the 1934 Dublin Horse Show (David Gray/RDS Archive)
Bottom — RDS advertising card for the 1955 Dublin Horse Show (David Gray/RDS Archive)

Page Opposite Introduction:
Drawing depicting scenes from the 1881 RDS Dublin Horse Show (Dr Alec Lyons — originally used for *London Illustrated News* in 1881)

Introduction Page:
Detail from RDS advertising card for the 1937 Dublin Horse Show (David Gray/RDS Archive)

First published by
WOLFHOUND PRESS Ltd
68 Mountjoy Square
Dublin 1
Tel: (353-1) 874 0354
Fax: (353-1) 872 0207

© 1998 Michael Slavin

The Arts Council
An Chomhairle Ealaíon

Wolfhound Press receives financial assistance from The Arts Council/An Chomhairle Ealaíon, Dublin, Ireland.

British Library Cataloguing in Publication Data
A catalogue record for this book is available from the British Library.

ISBN: 0 86327 657 1

10 9 8 7 6 5 4 3 2 1

Front cover photograph: Elizabeth Furth
Cover Design: Estresso
Typesetting: Wolfhound Press
Printed in Scotland by Caledonian Book Manufacturing
Colour Separations: Reprolink

TABLE OF CONTENTS

FOREWORD

The story of the human and horse heroes and heroines of Irish showjumping is chronicled by Michael Slavin in the pages of this book. It is a story interlaced with politics and culture, unfettered fervour and proud traditions; zeniths of glory and lows of disappointment, utter determination and superb vision of the people involved. It proudly proclaims the unique relationships between those great legends of showjumping and the Irish horse. It opens a window on the socio-political environment of the times and conveys, through these momentous achievements in the arenas of the world a historical perspective on the developments of Irish showjumping.

Michael Slavin is the authoritative communicator on the subject of Irish showjumping. His professional work as an equestrian journalist has always carried the hallmark of sustained effort to stimulate in others an incredible love and passion for the sport. In this book, his in-depth knowledge of the riders, the horses and the showjumping world, accumulated over decades of action-based research, is sensitively crafted in a way that communicates the infectious enthusiasm to the reader. Some accounts of the great riders and their mounts of the past interact so intimately with the reader that one feels part of the action. The gripping power of this book is demonstrated in his vivid description of the first ever Irish Nations' Cup win by the Army team in the Aga Khan Trophy Competition at the RDS in 1928 or the superb win for Gerry Mullins on Lismore in the first indoor Derby at Millstreet in 1991.

The style of writing is easy and relaxed and catches both the individual fervour and the prevailing economic conditions of the era. The casual but very touching commentaries on personalities and events down the years lend a sense of intrigue, humanity and admiration for the resilient and resourceful nature of people who are committed to the sport. His portrayal of how Ado Kenny, organiser of the Strokestown Horse Show, silenced the powers of world equestrianism in 1972 through use of the Irish language, or the efforts of Elizabeth Gaily, later an RDS judge, to get riding lessons in Dublin in the mid 1940s, and the 'discovery' of Dundrum by James Wade, are just a few of the jewels from Irish showjumping lore encapsulated in this book.

Neither was the new sport of showjumping devoid of political interest and concerns. This narrative expertly and sensitively leads the reader through the labyrinths of national and international political agendas that have permeated the sport. Particularly in the 1940s and 1950s, practical and organisational difficulties for the sport were enormous. Showjumping had come a long way from the first 'lepping' competitions held on Leinster Lawn in 1868. Rules for the sport had to be devised, written, refined and agreed at a very difficult time in Irish history. Agreement had to be reached on the composition, flag, anthem, emblems and colours of our international teams. The logistics and economic difficulties of competing, both at national and international venues, were daunting. All of this is chronicled here in these pages.

Notwithstanding the skill and determination of the riders and their wonder horses through the decades from the 1920s to the 1960s, the major hero of the sport of showjumping in those times must be Dublin-born and Derry-reared Judge Wylie. It was under his powerful direction leadership and vision that showjumping, despite all of the obstacles, managed to flourish. His unquestionable love of the sport, combined with the highest levels of diplomatic skill and tact, enabled him to make the seemingly impossible happen through the brilliant use of compromise. He was to Irish showjumping what United States Senator George Mitchell is to Irish politics today. The monument to his work is the current healthy state of the sport. This monument bears the inscriptions of those famous riders and their mounts who, through his work, were enabled to reach the pinnacle of excellence in their sport, bringing honour and glory to their country and joy and pleasure to millions of people world-wide.

This book enables you to meet with the great Irish showjumping riders of yesterday, interact with Captain Paul Rodzianko of the Army Equitation School and stroll with our great teacher, Iris Kellett. You will meet heroes of today, Paul Darragh, Gerry Mullins, Jessica Chesney, James Kernan, Eddie Macken, and so many more. You are invited to share with the riders those moments of glory on the great and immortal wonder horses that have made this story possible. In the words of the author, 'I hope you enjoy their company.'

Francis J. McGrourty
Course Director, Equine Studies, University of Limerick

THE JUMPING GROUND

General view of Building from Rock road

INTRODUCTION

In the well-known Irish legend of Oisín, this warrior rode the great white horse of Manannan Mac Lir out from Ireland over the sea to Tír na nÓg — Land of the Ever Young — Land of Victories. On his return, many years later, he was warned not to dismount from the magic horse — for if he did, he would never travel to the land of victories again.

With poignant accuracy, the story of Irish showjumping mirrors this mythic legend of Oisín. Like him, generations of Ireland's ingenious and intrepid horsemen and horsewomen have ventured out in search of elusive victories in lands beyond the waves.

Their success has depended totally on having horses with the ability to match both their dreams and their talents. The jumping power of a willing and athletic mount has been their passport to glory — without it, like Oisín, these riders were bound to earth in the same way as the rest of Erin's favoured mortals.

It is right that Ireland should be accorded the title *birthplace* of world showjumping. It is part of the very sinew of our countryside; and ever since the innovative first 'lepping' competitions were held on Leinster Lawn, in the heart of Dublin, back in 1868, the sport has thrived here in a unique way.

Roscommon sheepfarmer Richard Flynn was the world's very first showjumping champion on that occasion. Since then each generation has yielded its own crop of great stars — jumping legends of their time: Nat Morton, Sam Bailie and Mrs Binty Marshall in the early years; Army heroes, Dan Corry and Ged O'Dwyer in the 1930s; Iris Kellett and Seamus Hayes who swept to stunning British victories after the Second World War; Billy Ringrose, Tommy Brennan and Tommy Wade, who became household names of the 1960s.

Then came the four great horsemen of the 1970s — the booming era of Eddie Macken, Paul Darragh, Con Power and James Kernan, who delivered unprecedented Irish success around the world. Maintaining our place of honour in the great arenas of the world in more recent times have been riders such as Gerry Mullins, John Ledingham, Francis Connors, Robert Splaine, Marion Hughes, Jessica Chesney, Trevor Coyle, Peter Charles, Harry Marshall, Gerry Flynn and Eric Holstein.

While trying to catch the flavour and the fervour of these successive eras, I also attempt to outline the coming into being of the Irish Show Jumping Association as it hesitantly and gingerly grew out of the sport's burgeoning needs on both sides of the Irish border in the 1940s and 1950s. Its evolution fascinatingly prefigures some of the current political developments of our divided island.

I prefer to look on this work as a record of legends rather than a history of the sport here, for its participants — its *dramatis personae* — always appear just that bit bigger than life as they perform feats at home and abroad that even they themselves marvel at.

More than anyone else, these fleeting heroes have known that their moments of glory were not exclusively theirs, but rather experiences that were shared with the great wonder horses that did great and inimitable things. Meta, Red Hugh, Limerick Lace, Snowstorm, Rusty, Loch an Easpaig, Goodbye, Dundrum, Boomerang, Rockbarton, Kilbaha, Diamond Exchange, La Ina, Cruising — these are the great and immortal ones that have made the legends possible in this story of Irish showjumping — I hope you enjoy their company.

𝕽𝖔𝖞𝖆𝖑 𝕯𝖚𝖇𝖑𝖎𝖓 𝕾𝖔𝖈𝖎𝖊𝖙𝖞.

LIST OF PRIZES

OFFERED AT THE SOCIETY'S

GREAT ANNUAL HORSE SHOW,

1868,

TO BE HELD ON THE PREMISES,

KILDARE-STREET, DUBLIN,

ON TUESDAY, THE 28TH OF JULY,

AND TWO FOLLOWING DAYS.

OPEN TO COMPETITORS FROM ALL PARTS OF THE UNITED KINGDOM.

☞ Applications (including postage stamp) for Forms of Entry should state the CLASS for which the Form is required, and be sent to MR. A. CORRIGAN, Superintendent, Agricultural Office, Royal Dublin Society, Dublin; and, when filled, must be lodged, on or before Monday, 29th June, with the ASSISTANT SECRETARY, together with the amount of Entrance Fees; if by Drafts or Post-office Orders, in all cases made payable to HENRY C. WHITE, Esq., Registrar, Royal Dublin Society, without which the Entry Forms will be returned.

NOTE.—The last day for receiving Notice of Entry will be 29th June; and Entries on payment of Double Fees will be received up to Monday, 13th July, and none will be received after that day.

DUBLIN:

PRINTED BY M. H. GILL,

PRINTER TO THE ROYAL DUBLIN SOCIETY.

1868.

Programme cover for the very first Dublin Horse Show run by the Royal Dublin Society at its then headquarters – Leinster House on Kildare Street. A total of 125 Horse Shows have been run by the Society from then until 1998. The advertised programme made special reference to the first jumping competitions. (RDS Library Archive)

CHAPTER ONE

BIRTHPLACE

It would prove expedient to offer prizes for jumping as such a course
will add considerably to the attraction of the Horse Show.
— proceedings of Royal Dublin Society, 1868[1]

Natural as the grass that makes Ireland the most horse-friendly place in the world, the sport of showjumping grew out of our land. While other places like France and Britain have been given some credit for its origins, nowhere is its birth as an entertainment sport better documented than it is here.

It is recorded that in Paris, in 1866, an effort was made to test the jumping ability of carriage horses over some rustic fences; also around the same time in Islington, near London, an obstacle was used to assess the jumping skills of hunters. However, nowhere was there such a concerted and continued evolution of this new phase of equestrian sport than at the early horse shows run by the Royal Dublin Society from 1868 onwards. Rightfully, *The Guinness Book of Showjumping Records* accords these events full credit for giving birth to the international sport we know today.[2]

The birthplace was Leinster Lawn in the heart of Dublin. The person behind the idea was a dedicated and innovative horseman named Lord Howth. He, like many others of the time, knew that the role of the horse in human affairs was changing dramatically. As was tragically proven at places of death like the Balaclava Charge of the Light Brigade in 1854 or at Solferino in northern Italy five years later, lethal firepower and not flesh and blood horsepower was the future stuff of war. The demand for remounts was declining and so, in fact, was the horse population in Ireland at the time — during the 1860s their number in the Irish countryside dropped by over 100,000. Although the Ferguson tractor had not yet arrived, there were enough signs around for people like Lord Howth to know that leisure riding was the future role of the horse. For example, during the second half of the nineteenth century, fifteen new Irish riding and hunting clubs were added to the twenty or so already in existence.

Lord Howth was an avid cross-country rider. He was familiar with the ditches and banks of Meath, the hedges and drains of Kildare and the stone walls of Galway — a county for which he served as Liberal MP from 1863 to 1874. He knew too what kind of jumping power was required from a horse if it was to stay up with the field over the increasing number of division borders that were then more and more becoming part of Ireland's landscape. The question was no longer whether this horse would make a cavalry charger, but whether it could jump. Therein lay the genesis of showjumping.

Adding the word 'show' to the equation was the Royal Dublin Society (RDS). In both 1864 and 1866 it had lent its premises at Kildare Street — Leinster House (present home of Ireland's parliament, the Dáil) — to its sister organisation, The Royal Agricultural Society of Ireland (RASI), for the running of two annual horse shows. In 1867 the RASI moved this new event into St Stephen's Green.

In the meantime, Lord Howth suggested that the Royal Dublin Society run its own annual horse show at Leinster House.[3] Up to that point, worries had been expressed at Agricultural Society Council meetings regarding how such a new venture would be financed. However, at a Council meeting in August 1867, the proposal was accepted and 28 July 1868 was set as the opening day of the first Dublin Horse Show run by the Royal Dublin Society itself. Thus, Sir William Ulick Tristam Gaisford-St Laurence, Fourth Earl of Howth, has to be accorded the title Father of Showjumping for Ireland and the rest of the world. He took a simple test of jumping ability which had previously been used at Islington, and turned it into a unique competitive contest that evolved into a fascinating spectacle as the years went on.

It appears that Howth put up the prize-money himself for these first shows on Leinster Lawn — High Leap, Wide Leap and Stone Wall. In contrast to the complex twelve-to fourteen-fence courses of today, riders at the first horse show at Leinster House in 1868, faced just one fence each day:

Day One: High Leap — over hurdles trimmed with gorse

Day Two: Wide Leap — a gorse-filled hurdle and tank of water 12 feet long

Day Three: Stone Wall — built of loose stones which got progressively narrower near the top

In further contrast to modern competitions, the total of the prizes put up by Lord Howth amounted to £55, as compared with over £200,000 at the Kerrygold Horse Show today.

Lord Howth — 1827–1909 (above) can be accorded the title Father of World Showjumping. As the hand-written 1864 minute (right) from the Royal Agricultural Society of Ireland indicates, he first convinced this sister group of the RDS to run a horse show at Leinster Lawn. This did not include showjumping. However, in 1968 he persuaded the RDS itself to take on the Horse Show and make showjumping part of the programme.
The prize money was £55. That of the 1998 Kerrygold Horse Show event was £200,000.
(RDS Library Archive)

the Horse breeding Committee and stated that the Council of the Dublin Society had offered the use of their premises in Kildare street for the purpose of holding a National Horse Show, provided it was under the auspices of the Royal Agricultural Society of Ireland

The following resolution proposed by Lord Talbot de Malahide and seconded by Major Scott was unanimously adopted viz: "That the Council have heard with much gratification the statement made by Lord St Laurence that a Horse Show will be held in Dublin in the month of April, and that "it be referred to the Horse Committee to arrange the details".

The Royal Dublin Society of the time was no novice in the art of running shows, it had inaugurated its own Spring Show at Leinster Lawn in 1831. It also hosted a Great Exhibition there in 1853. Furthermore, its members were familiar with unforeseen problems associated with such events at which the elements often played their part. For example, the Spring Show of 1850 was hit by a violent hailstorm and a mini-tornado that tore to shreds the temporary housing for cattle and Spanish Asses and let the animals loose in the courtyard. It may be that the antics of the Spanish Asses on that occasion helped implant the idea that a bit of lepping would make a good public attraction.

Weather did not serve the opening of the RDS's first Dublin Horse Show any better but, in the end, this fact simply proved just what an attraction the new jumping competitions could be. As it turned out, the year of 1868 was unprecedented for drought and heat. This hot spell continued right through the months of May, June and July. However, on the very morning that the show was to open, the pent-up rain lashed down on the city. According to a report in the *News Letter* on Wednesday, 29 July 1868:

> ...the proceedings in the extemporised circus in the courtyard for trying the horses were considerably marred by a heavy downpour which commenced about twelve o'clock and continued almost without intermission up until four o'clock. The matter laid down on the surface became trodden into a boggy substance. Jumping, though spirited, might have been better but for this impediment.[4]

One is reminded of the first Irish Showjumping Derby in Millstreet some 120 years later which had a similarly inauspicious start when Noel C. Duggan's new Green Glens arena was almost washed away. Such have been the challenges facing Irish showjumping from the beginning and in just about every instance the skies eventually cleared. On that opening day back on 28 July 1868 the rain did stop and the report in the *News Letter* concluded:

> ...notwithstanding a very high entrance fee — ten shillings — there was a very numerous assembly of visitors on the first day and very considerable interest was manifested in the proceedings, especially the exercise and jumping of the horses.[5]

Under the personal supervision of Lord Howth, the jumping ring had been formed in the courtyard of Leinster House on the Kildare Street side of the building. In *The Horse Show Annual of 1900* an onlooker described the scene thus:

Series of early jumping pictures
(RDS Archive)

*Leinster House — site of the world's first show-
jumping event. In this panoramic view of Leinster
House dating from the late 1890s, the National
Library (left) had already been built. It was not
there when the first jumping was held in 1868 in
what was then called the courtyard. One of the
jumps was positioned exactly where the library
steps now are.*
(RDS Library Archive)

> *...the trials were over timber at 4 or 4.5 feet, a stone wall of
> Welsh sets, topped with round bouldering, erected straight
> in front of the old lodge. A water jump, or hedge and ditch,
> composed of furze bushes piled up to five feet, with a water
> tank beyond, the distance to be cleared being 16 feet, was
> placed where the granite steps now rise to the entrance of
> the New National Library.*[6]

Other problems were encountered on opening day. For one thing,
the addition of live music from the Constabulary Band caused some
consternation. The *News Letter* noted that in the competitions, 'the cases
of baulking were more numerous than pleasant' — the first indication
that refusals would play a part in the new sport. So too would the art of
judging. According to the rules laid down by Lord Howth the decision
refusals would play a part in the new sport. So too would the art of
judging. According to the rules laid down by Lord Howth, the decision of the judges would be based on 'the superiority of form and
style' over the fences. Not surprisingly, on that first day it was reported that they found great difficulty in arriving at decisions and in
some cases objections were lodged. However, it was also stipulated
that any discourtesy or disobedience shown to the officials would
result in disqualification from further trial. There can be no doubt that
this was a competition and that those taking part were out to win.

The very first red rosette in jumping at that inaugural Dublin
Horse Show went to Damson A. Millard of Tullagher, New Ross,
County Wexford, on Benzigue. He won £10. for clearing 4 feet 6 inches
in the High Leap.

The following day both the weather and the crowd improved. *The
Horse Show Annual* records that,

> *...a large field was entered for the water jump and attracted
> spectators from all corners of the show. One Richard Flynn
> of Strokestown, County Roscommon won the Wide Leap
> with the unaptly named Bashful Boy.*

Those that had cleared 4 feet 6 inches of timber on the Wednesday were allowed take on the stone wall on the Thursday. According to the *Irish Farmer's Gazette* of the time, '...the rumour of a six-foot wall to be ridden over, collected a very large concourse of persons.'[7] Nine challengers were through and in the first round the favourite, a little mare from Tipperary decided she had had enough and would have nothing to do with the wall. Two other horses stopped dead and somersaulted their riders over the formidable obstacle. Six survived but when the wall was raised, three more went out in the next round. The three remaining contenders were Richard Flynn, this time with Shaun Rhue; Michael Hanlon from Kildare on George; and the young son of Lord Power from Kilkenny on a gelding credited in the press reports with giving, '...a sustained effort in this very animated struggle.'[8] *The Irish Times* noted that the utmost enthusiasm prevailed and a huge crowd of onlookers used platforms of every description as vantage points to see the struggle unfold. It appears that an extra day had to be added to resolve the matter.

Before what was called 'a further augmented crowd' on the Saturday, Richard Flynn emerged as the eventual winner. Sheep-farmer Flynn of Strokestown owned Shaun Rhue himself and must have gone back to Roscommon a very satisfied man indeed. He sold the gelding for a reported £1,000 (*The Horse Show Annual 1901*) — an excellent price at the time. The buyer was Thomas Conolly of Castletown House, County Kildare — an ancestor of Diana Conolly-Carew, who was to become a famous Irish showjumper almost one hundred years later, and also of Patrick Conolly-Carew, who became an international three-day-event rider and an official of the Equestrian Federation of Ireland (EFI) and the Fédération Équestre Internationale (FEI).

Patrick Conolly-Carew
Lord Carew appears later in the story of Irish showjumping. His ancestor Thomas Conolly of Castletown House bought the first showjumping champion on Leinster Lawn for a reported £1,000. Patrick's sister Diana won the Dublin Grand Prix in 1966.
(Horseman Photography)

Strokestown

It is interesting that Strokestown, home of Richard Flynn, who was the first ever champion at the Dublin Horse Show, has remained faithful to the sport of showjumping down through the years and no small amount of innovation has come out of this area. In the 1970s Ado Kenny, who for many years ran the Strokestown Show, defied the international authorities in order to give a car to the winner of his Grand Prix competition. He was informed by the then world president of the International Equestrian Federation, Prince Philip, that such a prize was not allowed. Told that he had to give special details of the proposed event, Ado sat down and wrote a long letter to the Prince — in Irish. He never heard another word back.

Lord Howth must also have been well satisfied with the outcome of this inaugural event. He had taken a great gamble on both the show and the leaping competitions. As it turned out, over 6,000 people visited the show, 389 horses and ponies were entered and it made a profit of £531. In the *RDS Proceedings* for that year it was declared:

Richard Flynn
Sheepfarmer Richard Flynn of Strokestown — the world's first showjumping champion — shown in this rare picture on Shaun Rhue on which he not only won the high leap but the overall championship after four days of jumping (the last being an added day to sort out a tie for first place). Shaun Rhue is reported to have been sold for the then massive sum of £1,000.
(RDS Library Archive — with special thanks to Gerard Whelan, who discovered this old photo)

RDS Medal — A John Woodhouse medal used at the early Dublin Horse Shows
(RDS Archive)

...it is believed that this was the largest exhibition of the kind yet held. The quality of the majority of the horses exhibited was pronounced by the judges to be very superior. In addition to the above, special prizes were offered for jumping over hurdles, temporary stone walls and water, which were spiritedly contended for.[9]

They were no longer talking about a test for hunters but a hard-fought contest in its own right which attracted a very interested audience. The sport of showjumping had been born over those four days in the courtyard at Leinster House.

For the next two years, 1869 and 1870, the show was repeated in just about the same format at the Kildare Street venue. However, as entries increased, the RDS began to worry that it would run out of space. It appears that the Society breathed a sigh of relief when the Royal Agricultural Society of Ireland took up the event once more in 1871. The RASI had by this time begun running an annual National Horse Show at various venues around the country — Sligo, Belfast, Ballinasloe and Ennis. In the year 1871 it was the turn of Dublin once more. But this time, instead of going to Leinster House, as it had done in 1864 and 1866, or to St Stephen's Green, as in 1867, the RASI made a far-reaching decision to bring the event out into the then open countryside along the Dodder River at Ballsbridge. Just a twenty-five-minute carriage ride from Kildare Street, on land owned by the Earl of Pembroke, they laid the foundations of a tradition that was to be taken on by the RDS itself exactly ten years after that.

In the meantime, however, showjumping evolved within the confines of the courtyard at Leinster House. In 1869 the crowd had grown to 10,529 during the four days and the profit reached £923.

Fences used in the first Dublin Horse Shows

HIGH LEAP — over hurdles trimmed with gorse — two classes over 4ft 6ins. Hurdles — three classes at 4ft — two at 3ft — and one over 2ft 6ins confined to ponies less than 12 h.h.

WALL JUMP — over a loose stone wall of progressive height, which would not exceed 6ft.

WIDE LEAP — over 2ft 6ins gorse-filled hurdle with 12ft of water on the other side.

SWEEPSTAKE — run on the fourth day over the hurdle fence until there was an outright winner.

For all the adult competitions the riders had to weight out at 12 stone. They were allowed practise each morning from 7 to 9 a.m.[10]

Crowd numbers continued to increase when the event returned from Ballsbridge to Kildare Street in 1872. By the following year the RDS had a specially convened Council meeting to decide on a new rule for the jumping — for the first time it decided that while competition was in progress stewards would be empowered '...to clear and keep the ring and exercise grounds free of all persons whomsoever, whether members of the Society or others....'[11] To tell members they could not walk on their own ground was a bold step but it is clear from this decision that showjumping had begun making its own demands.

Those demands soon included more room for the leaping competitions. In October 1872, the RDS Agriculture Committee, still headed by Lord Howth, urged the council '...to take steps to obtain additional space for the shows....' By 1874 total horse entries at the show had reached 636 — almost double those achieved at the first show. The number of people passing through the newly installed turnstiles was also up 100 per cent to 21,857.

With none other than Sir Arthur Guinness (grandson of the founder of the famous brewery) doing the negotiating with the government, the RDS somehow got £25,000 to help it move the show to larger premises. In 1889 the RASI again brought its National Horse Show to Ballsbridge. Matters moved quickly after that. Early in the following year, negotiations had reached such an advanced state between the RDS and Ballsbridge landowner, the Earl of Pembroke, that the corporate seal of the Society could be affixed to an agreement for the renting of fifteen acres along the Dodder for the most reasonable annual fee of just £180.00. In a further generous gesture, the Earl of Pembroke granted a 500-year lease to the Royal Dublin Society.

The young sport of showjumping could now expand and the developments this allowed were to determine the direction it would take, not only in the land of its birth, but also around the world.

For one thing, riders would no longer be jumping one fixed fence each day. Instead there would be a continuous course, covering some three acres of the newly acquired fields. On 23 March 1880 the RDS Council voted to proceed with the work of making the necessary fences and laying out the ground for jumping.

By November, buildings at the site were reported to be 'in a forward state.' A permanent stand for viewing the jumping that could accommodate 800 people was put in place and in February 1881, the sum of £100 was appropriated for the purpose of buying timber for the fences. All would soon be ready for a new beginning of the leaping game.

Writing some twenty years later in *The Horse Show Annual*, an anonymous author, who obviously experienced the move from Kildare Street to Ballsbridge, summed up its effects in this way:

First Trial Jumping at Ballsbridge 1871
A contemporary drawing of the first trial jumping held at Ballsbridge in the Royal Agricultural Society of Ireland Show there in 1871. Prince Arthur (Duke of Connaught) was in the temporary stand. (RDS Archive)

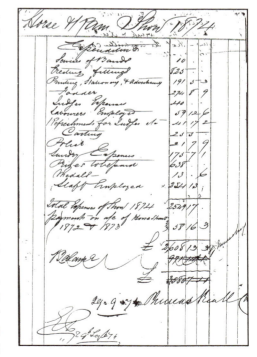

The first RDS Dublin Horse Show made a profit of £531. The draft expenditure sheet for the 1874 show indicates a cost of £2,549.17s.00d. (RDS Archive)

*...since the Royal Dublin Society obtained their spacious
premises at Ballsbridge and moved the yearly celebration to
such enjoyable quarters, old and young, gentle and simple,
peer and peasant, have participated alike in its pleasures
and its glories....*[12]

It was not long before those 'pleasures and glories' spread beyond the
confines of Dublin city to be enjoyed by the entire island of Ireland.

Footnotes to Chapter One

[1]   Meenan, J. and Clarke, D. (eds), *The Royal Dublin Society 1731–1981*, Dublin: Gill
      and Macmillan, 1981: p. 119.
      Proceedings of the Royal Dublin Society, Dublin: Royal Dublin Society, 1967–1968:
      vol. 104, p. 100.
[2]   Dreaper, Judith, *Showjumping Records Facts and Champions*, London: Guinness
      Books, 1987: p. 9.
[3]   *Proceedings of the Royal Dublin Society*, Dublin: Royal Dublin Society, 1866:
      vol. 110, p. 15.
[4]   *The News Letter*, Wednesday, 29 June 1868.
[5]   Ibid.
[6]   *The Horse Show Annual*, Dublin: Royal Dublin Society, 1900: p. 6.
[7]   *Irish Farmer's Gazette*, 21 August 1868.
[8]   *The Irish Times*, Saturday, 1 July, 1868.
[9]   *Proceedings of the Royal Dublin Society*, Dublin: Royal Dublin Society, 1868: vol.
      112, p. 7.
[10] Ibid., 1869, after printed schedule of classes.
[11] Ibid.
[12] Op. cit., *The Horse Show Annual* , p. 7.

CHAPTER TWO

LEAPING INTO A NEW CENTURY

It is difficult to see what saved horse jumping during the years before
the First World War. Perhaps it was the remarkable interest that the
public took in it.

— F.J. Barton: 'One Hundred Years of Showjumping'[1]

Fearful predictions that a move from Kildare Street to the wilds of Ballsbridge would be a disaster were not fulfilled during the first horse show at the new venue in August 1881. Entries numbered 589 horses and sixty-two rams — yes rams, for this was still called The National Horse and Ram Show. The RDS had spent £11,000 on the new premises and over the four inaugural days attendance was 17,756 — up by a third on the 1880 event in the city. Ten years later, it had soared to over 46,000 and continued to grow as the new century approached, totalling 59,176 in 1899. Entries of horses had also increased and had reached a total of 1,397 by that time.

Developments in the jumping arena proceeded quickly in the first few years at the new Ballsbridge grounds. At the opening show there, just three jumps graced the enclosure, which were approached and jumped as follows: a high hurdle with a ditch on either side placed between guide railings, a right-hand U-turn down the middle of the arena to a water jump, a left-hand turn down the south side which led to a stone wall jump. This new continuous course was not used on Tuesday, the opening day of the show. On the Wednesday and Thursday it came into use for the very first time. On these two days those who jumped well, in the opinion of the judges, went forward to a championship on the Friday. The course was only slightly changed in each of the following two years but in 1884, banks were introduced after an extra twelve acres had been added to the show grounds. Demand for seats in that year was so great that places in the grandstand had to be reserved for the first time.

What was to be termed 'the Ballsbridge Course' was introduced in 1885 — hedge, ditch, single bank and stone wall on the line along the grandstand side, followed by a double bank, water jump and hurdle after the turn for home. Amazingly, this course remained unaltered for the next fifty years. Even then the change was minor — a swinging gate, much hated by riders, replaced the hurdle in 1935.

However, showjumping was not developing in isolation at the RDS. Other places both at home and abroad were taking up the new sport and using it to suit their own needs. A report in the *Manchester Courier* of 1877 noted that at the local show there, run by the Royal Agricultural Society, 'A good portion of the afternoon was devoted to hurdle and water-fence leaping which was a good entertainment.'[2] In Ireland, the RASI continued the practice of bringing its National Horse Show to different parts of the country.

Plan of Royal Dublin Society Grounds at Ballsbridge. (RDS Archive)

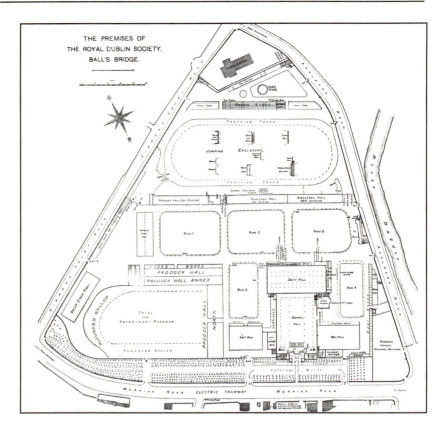

Drawing from The Illustrated London News *of stone wall jumping at the first show run by the RDS in Ballsbridge 1881.* (Dr Alec Lyons)

In 1879 it visited Newry and in 1880 it was run in Clonmel where, according to research done by Colonel W.E. Watson, a local historian, showjumping contests were held over a course that had a bank, stone wall and water jump. An identical event went to Kilkenny in 1884 and to Derry in 1885.

The problems of horse transport undoubtedly hampered the spread of the new sport. It is noted in one newspaper report of the initial show at Leinster House in 1868 that the railway kindly gave a free ride home for any horses that were unsold. After moving to Ballsbridge, the RDS itself paid the railway company to build a siding just across from its Merrion Road premises in order to facilitate the burgeoning entries for the show. This new line was indeed a major help to enthusiastic riders in search of a place to showjump. Right into the new century, even after the advent of motorised transport, there were competitors who would drive to their local railway station, travel to the nearest terminal to the show and then ride their horse to the arena. Others drove to shows with their jumping horses either drawing the trap or following behind, rode in an event and then drove home again in the same manner. The great County Down rider, Jim Bryson from Newry, can recall that in the 1930s and 1940s he would walk his horses 25 miles to Castlewellan the night before the show, stable them there, jump the next day and then walk home again.

Places like Ballymena, in County Antrim, and Loughrea and Ballinasloe, in County Galway, were promoting the growing sport at the end of the last century although attempts at introducing it at these venues were not always successful.

A report in the *Tuam Herald* of the 1900 show in Loughrea noted:

> *...there was supposed to be a competition for cobs. But when brought before the insignificant obstacles set for them they obstinately refused to even look at them.*[3]

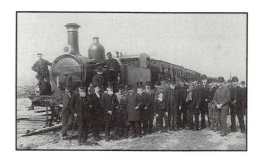

The possibility of transporting horses by rail greatly helped the development of showjumping. Pictured here is the official opening of a special railway siding at the RDS grounds in Ballsbridge in 1893 which facilitated those bringing jumpers to the show for many years to follow. (RDS Archive)

However, later years brought a vast improvement in the performances at this great western venue.

Its neighbour, Ballinasloe, is one of the oldest agricultural shows in Ireland — dating back to the 1840s. It featured the stone wall jump right up to the 1950s when hero of that era Tommy Wade, with the equally famous Dundrum, began a legendary career.

Ballymena initiated its own event in the 1890s and it was from here that one of the best-known early jumping stars emerged — one Nathaniel Morton of Knockanure. During nineteen years of competition at the RDS around the turn of the century, he is credited with having accumulated combined winnings of over £1,000 with forty-four different horses. That was some accomplishment at a time when first prizes generally stood at no more than £25. At the inaugural show run by the Royal Ulster Agricultural Society in its new Balmoral show grounds in 1896, Nathaniel Morton fought a memorable battle in the rain against a Newtownards veterinary surgeon by the name of Sam Bailie, who also had Ballsbridge wins to his credit.

Sam Bailie

Sam Bailie, of Newtownards, can claim credit for being Ireland's first international showjumper as, in the early 1900s, he took a jumping horse off to a show in Holland. The unusual was usual for Sam who adored the horses he kept in his Newtownards yard. One season it all got a bit much for him and he decided to sell sixty of them at public auction in Belfast. With the help of about fifteen men he walked them all the twenty miles to the city. However, when he got there he had a change of heart and simply turned the cavalcade around and headed back for home.

There had been showjumping in Belfast prior to the beginning of the Royal Ulster Society's show in 1896 but at that time the new grounds at Balmoral provided a permanent course that included similar banks to those in Ballsbridge. (RUAS Belfast)

For the contest at Balmoral in 1896, Nathaniel Morton brought Dublin winner Little John into the fray along with Poor Mary Ann, Twist and Duke of Wellington. Bailie had Meta and the mare Idalia. After several rounds of jumping on what was called 'very greasy going' Morton was declared the winner. *The Horse Show Annual* notes that this Ballymena campaigner also had victories in Lisburn, Armagh and in his home town, where it was said, '...the jumping is as good as

Visit by the Prince of Wales to Dublin Show in 1893 (RDS Archive)

at *Dublin or anywhere else in the kingdom.*[4] Both Nathaniel Morton and Sam Bailie were forerunners of a great tradition in Northern Irish showjumping that lasts to this day.

The fences used for that first show at Balmoral were very much a copy of the Ballsbridge course — bank and ditch, double bank, stone wall and water jump. A report of the events printed in *The Whig* noted, '...though only temporary erections they had been built well and careful.' There can be no doubt that all of the shows springing up at the turn of the century, on both sides of the Irish Sea, were using a version of the RDS invention — the only known permanent course existent at the time. In his authoritative essay 'One Hundred Years of Showjumping', F.B. Barton says:

> *In the closing years of the century the sport — for sport it had become — was taken up enthusiastically by local shows in all parts of the country and the Dublin course was reproduced, in part or wholly, in almost every show ground.*[5]

At the Royal Meath Agricultural show, in Navan, they used a double bank, stone wall, water jump and hurdle. At the end of the first decade of the new century a report in the *Meath Chronicle* confirms that these same obstacles were still in use and not everyone had mastered them. Of the open jumping competition the *Meath Chronicle* of 9 August 1910 notes, '...there were a great many scrambles in the first round and no little amusement was afforded.'[6]

During the latter twenty years of the fading century, the sport of showjumping began to take hold across Europe and also in the USA. Annual jumping events came to Paris during the 1880s and it was there, in 1900, that showjumping was first included in the Olympic Games. Prior to that, in 1883, The National Horse Show at Madison Square Garden, in the heart of New York was inaugurated. It went on to be one of the first foreign events visited by Ireland's new army showjumping team formed some forty-three years later in 1926. Holland ran its first competitions in 1883 and Italy held its Concorso Ippico Internazionale in Turin in 1902. The world's first ever Nations' Cup for military teams was run at Olympia, London, in 1909. (This same venue, a baptism of fire for the new Irish team in 1927, was also to be the scene for one of its greatest moments of glory.)

As an indication of just how internationally widespread the sport had become by the turn of the century, that first Nations' Cup at Olympia had teams from Italy, France, Canada, Belgium, Argentina and Britain taking part. All were military sides and this remained the norm until after the Second World War.

Both the USA and Russia took part at Olympia in 1911 for the first time and the very polished Russian squad was a close second to France on that occasion. One of its top performers was one Captain

Paul Rodzianko, who at that time was a very rich man. He was later to come to Ireland, having fled his homeland after the Russian Revolution.

During those early years, rules of the sport evolved very slowly. This was particularly true in Ireland where the basic judging criteria of form and style of jumping fences remained largely unaltered from the very first show in the RDS until about 1920. A minor amendment was introduced in the Dublin show of 1891 to avoid long delays caused by riders, who might circle many times before taking on a fence. It stated that obstacles must be taken at a fair hunting pace.

Minutes of the Royal Agricultural Society, and of the Dublin Horse Show Committee during these formative years of the sport give ample evidence that these guidelines were not sufficient to control the growing sport. Bitter disputes were common and frequent objections were lodged in relation to winners. Adding to the confusion was a huge increase in entries. For example, by 1895 numbers in the four-year-old class at the RDS had topped the 200 mark; in order to cope it was decided to run the competitors off in pairs. This created desperate problems for the judges positioned at the centre of the ring as they tried to award points to two horses at the same time. No wonder there were disputes.

One of those severely treated under this system was a man from Coleraine named William Evelyn Wylie. At a show just before the First World War he entered with a good horse and was paired with a fellow who fell during the round and had to be carried from the ring while his mount walked out lame. However, when the winners of each heat were announced the injured rider was among them and Wylie was eliminated from further participation. In reply to his complaint the judges simply told him, '...we are doing the best we can — the decision stands and we can do nothing for you.' Another time, at a country show, he was in line to win an event when the judges just decided they had had enough, cancelled the competition and arbitrarily awarded prizes.

In a memoir later written for the RDS, Wylie recalled how he made a decision there and then — '...if ever I have sufficient influence my first effort will be to frame some jumping rules.'[7]

Before very long, the then Justice Wylie had a great deal of influence and during the 1920s and 1930s, almost single-handedly, he reinvented Irish showjumping and became the godfather of a newly born international army team.

Just how arbitrary the process of judging the new sport could be can be gleaned from the *Meath Chronicle* report of the Navan show in 1910. In one class, two competitors emerged with equal merit after two rounds. It was then decided to try them again over the double fence jumped in reverse. When that did not sort them out the order was given that they both must jump the original course again.

This handwritten minute for starting what was called the Ballsbridge Course is from an RDS committee meeting of 1881. The course was completed four years later, and became a model for shows all around the country. Its basic lay-out remained largely unchanged for the next fifty years. (RDS Archive)

Advert for 1897 Dublin Horse Show (RDS Archive)

Judge William Evelyn Wylie

Judge Wylie (pictured opposite) was a vastly intelligent and diplomatic man. He bridged gaps between the provinces of Ireland as well as between British rule and the emergence of the infant Irish Free State. His great tact was also apparent when smoothing out difficulties between competitors and the judges' box. He found ways to make what seemed impossible happen through his brilliant use of compromise. Born in Dublin in 1881, he grew up in Coleraine, where his father served as Presbyterian minister. He went on to be an honours law student at Trinity College, Dublin and graduated as a Barrister from the King's Inns also in Dublin. After a number of very successful years at the Bar he was made a judge at a crucial time in Irish history — 1920. Indicative of the respect he could command, he had acted as Law advisor to the British Government in Ireland before the setting up of the Irish Free State, and then after the Anglo–Irish Treaty of 1922 he was appointed by the new Government as judicial Commissioner to the Land Commission. In both those posts his powers of reason and diplomacy were fully tested but never more than in the role he played as a leader in the RDS and the head of Irish showjumping during the next thirty years. It was ironic then, that when he had started his jumping career early in the century, he was unjustly eliminated from a competition in Paris and, despite his protests, was sent home to Coleraine without a rosette. He led a protest against the Ballsbridge judging in 1919 and managed to effect change in 1921. He led showjumping in Ireland for the next thirty-eight years until his retirement as Chairman of the Executive Committee in 1959. He died in 1964. His son John continued the tradition and until the 1980s was the voice of showjumping as the honey-toned announcer in the main arena of the RDS.

During the First World War years (1914–1918), horse shows at the RDS were abandoned and the Ballsbridge show grounds were taken over by the British Army. It is said that the already famous arenas became grazing grounds for mules during this time. However, this interruption at the home ground of showjumping did not hinder growth of the new sport at smaller venues throughout the island as a whole. The First World War, in fact, assisted this growth as a number of small shows were also run to help various charities associated with the global conflict. Horse jumping events aided hospitals and funds for injured soldiers. These meetings added to the shows already in existence and gave even more opportunity for competitions to take place; as will be discussed in a later chapter this period also opened the door for more and more lady riders to take part. In fact, jumping classes for ladies were advertised as features at events in Navan, Castlepollard and other such towns around the country. There was a rule in the RDS right up until 1913, stating that, '...no lady is allowed ride in any jumping competition....' This and perhaps a number of other rules

Following the move to Ballsbridge, demand for grandstand seats was so great that reservations had to be made. Show attendance had reached nearly 60,000 by 1899. (RDS Archive)

In the early 1900s ladies were not allowed jump at the RDS. When this restriction was lifted they took part, riding side-saddle. In 1920 a formidable rider named Binty Marshall, who rode horses for Mount Juliet in Kilkenny, dominated the mixed classes on offer. (Irish Life Magazine)

were ignored at the emerging country shows of the time. The result was a growing competence on the part of lady riders, and in 1919 when shows were resumed at the RDS after the Great War, ladies were allowed compete there for the first time, although only in their own confined class. The following year when they entered open classes they swept the boards against their male counterparts, winning a total of seven events.

Also after the First World War, the RDS had to face up to problems associated with judging — at the heart of this effort was Judge Wylie. Perhaps the incident that most encouraged him to reform the sport happened at the first Dublin Horse Show after the so-called war to end all wars. On that occasion an attempt was made to run one competition on the knock-out principle but the event proved an utter disaster and ended in chaos. In many instances the best horses did not get through to the final, while some with very poor rounds did qualify. When it was over, the riders staged a protest, and at the forefront of an effort to sort the matter out was the diplomat Wylie. He finally got the officials to announce that the next day's competition would be run in the more conventional way. Thus, he brought about a momentary peace but he also knew that the judging problem had to be grasped and knocked into shape. He later wrote:

> Truly, horse jumping must have been a plant of hardy growth to survive and flourish in the conditions that then existed.[8]

Whether by design or coincidence, 1921 saw the birth of two sets of showjumping rules, each of which operated very differently. In that year the Fédération Équestre Internationale (FEI — the international governing body of the sport) introduced a set of rules for showjumping which was to be applied internationally. In the meantime, Judge Wylie's first move to improve judging conditions in Ireland came soon after he was appointed to the RDS Agricultural Committee in 1921. He immediately introduced a new points system for judging each fence, and appointed two official markers to record the decisions of the judges. The use of two markers, usually drawn from Dublin accountancy schools, continued in the judges' box at the RDS right up until the early 1980s. After that, the Showjumping Association of Ireland (SJAI) took up responsibility for the appointment of judging officials. During the first year of this change-over, matters got a bit cramped in the judges' box as the two accountants remained, marking their two large sheets while the new appointee marked a slick new SJAI sheet. However, the matter was soon resolved after that. Traditions often appear to die slowly at the RDS and sometimes this is no great harm.

The two sets of judging rules, which emerged simultaneously, may be outlined as follows:

The Wylie Judging System of 1921

Points for good jumping were to be awarded on the basis of accumulation.

Points were to be awarded for each fence up to a maximum of five per fence.

A maximum of five bonus points could be awarded for rounds of exceptional merit.

Mistakes with the forelegs were to carry more potential faults than those made with the hind legs.

Points awarded by each of the judges were to be recorded by two markers.

The new FEI International System of 1921

In contrast to Wylie, this was a negative system of penalties for mistakes:

A light wooden slat was placed on top of each fence, and dislodging it cost the rider half a penalty.

A knockdown of the fence itself, with the fore or hind legs, cost four penalties.

Refusing or circling before a fence was also penalised.

Judges – The first official judges' rule book was not produced in Ireland until the 1940s. Prior to that time a good deal of confusion reigned. Our picture shows a group of judges from the 1930s at the RDS. (G.A. Duncan)

Judge Wylie's new judging system was at best a stop-gap measure and he was the first to admit it. However, it was to be another ten years before his system was fully upgraded. International standards were imposed on Ireland by the FEI which also came into existence in 1921. The sticking point between the Irish and the international systems was the continued Irish use of banks, stone walls and other natural obstacles. For a time the Irish were allowed continue with their own unique methods, but from the moment international Nations' Cup jumping came to the RDS, in 1926, pressure was exerted for Ireland to join the FEI and conform to its rules.

In 1931 the matter came to a head and, in November of that year, Judge Wylie was dispatched along with Lord Holmpatrick and Captain F.B. Barton to argue the Irish cause at an FEI Bureau meeting in Paris. During the three days of negotiations Wylie's diplomatic powers were tested to the full. After the first two days the sides were deadlocked and it looked as if Ireland would be faced with having all international riders barred from jumping in its proud new Nations' Cup event. Having stayed up until two in the morning discussing the problem, Wylie and the Irish delegation finally came up with a compromise — the new FEI rules of faults would apply to all fences in the Irish arena except those that were considered indigenous to Ireland. The FEI accepted; both sides had saved face and the newly instituted Aga Khan Trophy was secure. The stage was now set for the new Irish showjumping team to make its international entrance.

Footnotes to Chapter Two

[1] Meenan, J. and Clarke, D. (eds), *The Royal Dublin Society 1731–1981*, Dublin: Gill and Macmillan, 1981: p. 123.

[2] *Royal Agricultural Society Proceedings*, Dublin: Royal Dublin Society, 1877.

[3] *The Horse Show Annual*, Dublin: Royal Dublin Society, 1910.

[4] *The Tuam Herald*, Saturday, 26 May 1900.

[5] Op. cit., Meenan, J., Clarke, D. (eds), p. 123.

[6] Ibid.

[7] Ibid.

[8] Ibid.

CHAPTER THREE

THE ARMY HEROES

We were racing and hunting men and we knew nothing about showjumping.
— Major Gerald 'Ged' O'Dwyer on the first recruits to Ireland's new Army Equitation School at McKee Barracks in 1926[1]

They were mounted gods of their time — heroes in uniform, riding out to bring the message of a new nation to the world. From the moment of its tentative founding in 1926, the army jumping team's story reads like the script for a Hollywood film. From that time, some seventy years ago now, the Army Equitation School at McKee Barracks in the Phoenix Park has been at the heart of Irish showjumping and a vital link between the domestic industry and the rest of the equestrian world.

It was Swiss inspiration, and the Irish willingness to have a go at the unknown, that brought about this far-reaching development in the history of Irish showjumping. A former rebel soldier, twenty-seven-year-old John Gerald 'Ged' O'Dwyer of Limerick (quoted above), was one of the young officers called up early in 1926 to take the leap into this previously uncharted territory. Along with him, in that very first group, was another survivor of the Irish War of Independence and the subsequent Civil War, twenty-four-year-old Dan Corry of Loughrea; joining them also was twenty-nine-year-old Cyril Harty, who was from a Limerick racing family.

Like many other things in the history of Irish showjumping, the formation of this first ever team was more a product of chance and pure destiny than the result of any long-term planning.

The Swiss connection came about through a meeting at the Shelbourne Hotel, Dublin, in the Autumn of 1925, between two of their army officers and Judge Wylie of the RDS. Colonels Zeigler and Haccius were in Ireland on a mission to purchase horses. As they chatted with Wylie over coffee, the question was asked why Ireland, a major supplier of mounts for the growing sport of international showjumping, was not taking part in the new Military Nations' Cup competitions that had sprung up during the previous sixteen years in Belgium, Britain, France, the USA, Canada and Switzerland. The colonels wondered whether the running of an international horse show and the formation of an Irish team could be considered. They were talking to the right man because the Judge was not only aware of the developments going on abroad but was also in a position to influence both the RDS and the new Government in this matter. Also at the RDS in 1921, he had been instrumental in organising a competition class confined solely to military riders.

This bit of extra prodding from the Swiss colonels was all it took to have him expand this idea into the world domain. He acted quickly, but not without some misgivings. As he later wrote:

Edward Bohane (left) who, with Judge Wylie, initiated the first international jumping at the RDS in 1926. (Irish Press)

I confess I was at first a bit doubtful of the practicability of the scheme but I undertook to consult Mr. Bohane, Director of the RDS and the Committee.[2]

He goes on to note that Edward Bohane had quite a flair for showmanship and immediately saw the immense entertainment possibilities afforded by the new international competitions.

However, the plan could not work without the full co-operation of the Government, and Wylie had to find a way of convincing them as well. Colonel Zeigler had mentioned to Wylie that between 500 and 1,000 horses each year were purchased out of Ireland by Switzerland alone. It was his contention that this number could be increased through having an international shop window, like the Dublin Horse Show, available to buyers for the growing number of military teams in Europe and the Americas.

From studies already done by the Royal Dublin Society it was clear that its annual horse show did indeed contribute significantly to the number of horses exported from Ireland every year. One report published in 1900 indicated that between 1881, when the show first moved to Ballsbridge, and 1899, the total number of Irish horses annually sold abroad went up from 30,000 to 42,000. The sales figures were also calculated on the number of horses shipped from Dublin Port during the period of the show and the week immediately after it. There were 305 exported in 1884 and 730 sold to the foreign market in 1899.

Thus, when Colonel Zeigler contended that Ireland was losing out on a further increase in sales through not having a top-class international show, Wylie instantly recognised this as a very important argument in favour of the new team proposals. As well as promoting the image of Ireland as a new independent state, there was an added economic benefit to be reaped from horse sales. Such potential income for a hard-pressed exchequer was to be his most useful selling point when, within weeks, he initiated talks with the Department of Agriculture and the Ministry of Defence.

In the RDS he had received a friendly hearing from Edward Bohane. However, he may not have known at the time, that within the Government, he also had a very positive listener in the then President of the Irish Free State, William T. Cosgrave. He was very interested in equestrian matters and as Ged O'Dwyer later found out, gave the idea an early approval. However, as could be expected, not everyone in the new administration could see the value of spending money on horses when so many demands were being made by people in great need. Thus, while it is clear that President Cosgrave was on Wylie's side from September 1925 onward, there appears to have been some foot-dragging within the lower levels of administration after that.

However, Wylie's brilliant diplomatic talents were soon brought into play on such matters. Knowing that he had support at the top, he ignored any stalling tactics he encountered and moved in the one area where he had full support — the RDS. Major Ged O'Dwyer recalls these times in Thomas Toomey's book, *Forgotten Dreams*:

> *Without receiving a definite commitment from the Government, the RDS went ahead with plans for an International Military Jumping Competition. In a sense their action seems to have forced the issue and the Government gave the go ahead, in April 1926, to enter for the competition which was to take place in August. It seems incredible today to contemplate what was being undertaken. In April 1926, when they had neither a rider or a horse to their name they had entered an Army Jumping team to take on the cream of Europe.*[3]

In an interview for the *Irish Farmer's Journal* shortly before his death some seventy years later, Ged further noted:

> *President Cosgrave was a great man for the small farmer and he felt that a better sale for horses would help them in the long run.*[4]

In the end, this fact and a positive attitude from the then Minister for Agriculture, Patrick Hogan, were crucial to a decision that has since had a profound influence on the sport of showjumping both in Ireland and around the world. At a cabinet meeting in mid-April, Minister Hogan's recommendations on the formation of a

McKee Barracks in the Phoenix Park had been home for cavalry units under British rule. When the new recruits arrived at the Army Equitation School in 1926, the only equine animals there were cart horses. However, within months the stables began to fill up with hunters-turned-showjumpers. The unit, which comes under the Transport Command, has used the shoulder flash badge of a horse's head and an olive branch.
(Joan Parker)

showjumping team were accepted, and recruitment began immediately. O'Dwyer, Harty and Corry were the first called. Dan Corry, who throughout his long career maintained a great sense of humour, lived to take part in the sixtieth anniversary of that call-up. Upon the arrival of the three team recruits at McKee Barracks he once noted, '...when we got to the barracks the only horses there were pulling carts in the yard....'

In a very real way, this situation is a miniature picture of the sport's history. In a small country like Ireland, success in the international world of competition was always going to be against the odds. At this time it seemed a mission impossible — a dream realisable only through the miracle quality of the Irish horse and the intense love of things equine that is so much a part of the Irish people's nature.

Both the miracle and the love were fully called upon over the next ten years as these men without mounts grew into an unbeatable force on the international scene. The first innocent strides in that direction were taken over the next three months as the newly appointed Officer Commanding of the Army Equitation School, Major Liam Hoolan, in co-operation with Judge Wylie, gradually brought in some hunters for the young officers to ride. An indication of the ethos and enthusiasm of the time can be gleaned from the names given to the new mounts which were drawn from ancient Irish heroic lore — Cuchulainn, An Craobh Rua, Finghin and Oisin. Later this practice was dropped in favour of naming each horse after its place of origin. Thus Slievenamon, Kilmallock, Blarney Castle, Shannon Power, Rosnaree and Limerick Lace became well-known partners of the army riders.

However, in those early days of the new venture, the heroic names were more appropriate to the patriotic spirit that drove the first recruits — O'Dwyer, Corry, Harty, and National Hunt jockey Tom Mason who soon joined them but never made it onto the international circuit. From the time they arrived at McKee Barracks they had twelve weeks, at the most, to prepare. It was an overwhelmingly demanding test to be ready to take on fences at the RDS that none of them, as far as we know, had ever even seen before. When asked how they coped during those days of learning, Major Ged O'Dwyer replied succinctly — 'it was a struggle'. Nevertheless, in their own way, they were making progress, as evidenced by a creditable performance during their first warm-up show in Bray, County Wicklow. True, it was not a very demanding test, but nonetheless the new team must have gained a moral boost when Captain Dan Corry won their first red rosette in the Over the Course class with Finghin. For good measure, O'Dwyer was second on Oisin and Harty third with Cuchulainn. In the stone wall event Ged and Oisin were in the prizes again, taking third place. After that they were welcome visitors to shows in Dundalk, Tullamore, Ballinasloe and Clones. At the latter fixture most of the other competitors were from Ulster, where the sport was also in the process of continued growth.

Soon their opposition was to be from much further afield as they faced the challenge of the 1926 Dublin Horse Show. There they were up against teams from the most progressive showjumping nations of the era — France, Holland, Belgium, Britain and Switzerland, whose Chef d'Équipe and coach, Colonel Zeigler, had played such a vital role in bringing the RDS event about. Included on the Swiss squad were two of their team silver medalists from the 1924 Olympics in Paris — Captain Van der Weid and Captain Hans Bühler. They were joined by Captain Charles Kuhn who was to take Olympic bronze two years later in Amsterdam.

The first group of recruits at the Army Equitation School in 1926 included Captains Ged O'Dwyer from Limerick (left) and Dan Corry of Loughrea (middle). Fred Ahern of Meath joined them in 1930. Longest serving of the initial intake was Corry, who competed until 1954. He is shown riding Red Hugh. (SJAI Archive)

Massive publicity about Ireland's new venture into international sport ensured a huge and enthusiastic crowd over the four days of the show. Fulfilling Edward Bohane's assumptions about the attraction that military competitions would provide, the attendance was up from 67,000 the previous year, to a new record of close on 100,000. However not all were rooting for the new Irish team. Ged O'Dwyer scoffed at any such notion when recalling the show in the *Irish Farmer's Journal* interview. Not at all forgetting his revolutionary background, he noted, 'I had the strong feeling that at least half of the packed stands on opening day were hoping for a win by Britain.'

He may well have been right since the Royal Dublin Society was deeply rooted in a unionist ethos. The very grounds had emotive associations for a soldier like Ged since it had been a billeting place for the British Army during both the First World War and the War of Independence. It has to be remembered that the Anglo–Irish Treaty of 1922 had been signed only four years previously and that the Civil War had ended even more recently than that. During that conflict both he and Dan Corry played important roles on the Government side along with Michael Collins. Michael had been no great friend of the RDS and was instrumental in its having to move out of Leinster House to make way for the new Dáil.

These facts of history would naturally have created an ambivalent attitude in a number of those attending this historic inaugural event. That same ambivalence was to appear time and time again in the story of Irish showjumping in the following years. We can be thankful that, this and many other aspects of our divided island have always ended up in second place to the spirit of the sport itself, which has played more of a healing and unifying role in Irish society than a derisive one.

In fact, from the first bell of that 1926 show, the power of this international sport took over. The atmosphere is described by Thomas Toomey in *Forgotten Dreams*:

> At 4 o'clock the first International Military Jumping competition began and to tumultuous applause the first two competitors into the arena Captain Gerard O'Dwyer, riding the powerful sorrel Oisin and the Belgian officer Lieutenant Baudouin de Brabandere on a horse called Acrobate, led off.[5]

Dan Corry
Dan was the longest serving of the initial group of army riders. He returned as a riding officer after the war and competed for the next eight years.
(RDS Archive)

A tradition established at McKee was the Military Dinner hosted on the night before the Aga Khan Trophy Competition. At first the Irish recruits did not have dress uniforms. However, they did get them during Colonel Rodzianko's time there.
(RDS Archive)

In the method of the time, the two riders jumped an identical track and were individually judged at each obstacle according to the Irish method of marking. This remained in use at the RDS until the FEI put a partial stop to it in 1931 and completely ruled it out in 1954. Ged had a good round on Oisin that earned him a recall for the second. Also called back was Dan Corry on Finghin. It stands as a credit to those two riders who, just three months previously, knew nothing at all about the art of showjumping.

Corry and O'Dwyer made it through the next round as well and were among the twelve out of a starting list of twenty-six that were invited back for the third round. At the end of that Van der Weid on Royal Gris was declared the winner, with Dan Corry fourth. There was a tie for second place between Ireland's Ged O'Dwyer and Hans Bühler of Switzerland. They had to jump again — an incredibly tense moment that has been played out again and again in home international events since then, as Irish riders battle for honour on their home ground against the best in the world. However, this occasion was uniquely special.

O'Dwyer had been commended for coolness under fire during the Civil War and he had to display that quality once again here in this sporting battle on which so much depended. First of the two to go in the tie-breaking round, he and Oisin returned clear and, to a rousing roar from the crowd, they were given a maximum score by the judges. The Swiss rider was well up to the challenge on Wladimir — clear all the way to the water jump that ended the course — but a slight hesitation there from the Swiss man put Ged ahead. Although it was the second-place rosette he took, the crowd's response was so instantaneous and prolonged that it was as if he had won. It is comparable to a time some seventy years later, when Jackie Charlton's Irish football team drew with Britain through a brilliant last-minute goal and the cry was — 'Ireland won — one all!'

Contrary to some accounts of the event, Ireland achieved a very creditable second once more in the first staging of the Irish Nations' Cup competition for the Aga Khan Trophy, on the Friday of that same historic week.

Attempting to save their mounts for the Cup encounter, the Irish did not feature in competitions on Wednesday or Thursday. On the Thursday night, the Government and the Army Chiefs of Staff hosted an inaugural dinner at McKee Barracks for all the visiting teams. Events were to occur at that function which were to have an important bearing on the destiny of Ireland's showjumpers in the year ahead. During the evening, invitations were extended for Ireland to compete in the British Nations' Cup at Olympia in London, the following June, and at the Swiss equivalent in Lucerne immediately afterwards. Still riding high on the success of opening day and hardly knowing just what a challenge had been presented, the invitations were accepted by the Irish officials.

Also at that same dinner, the young Irish officers initiated contacts with riders from other countries who were to become lifetime friends. Among those present were Irish-born members of the British squad Major Edward T. Boylan, whose son, Eddie, later became a hero for Ireland in the sister sport of three-day-eventing, and Captain Joseph Hume-Dudgeon, whose equestrian school in Dublin was later to become the formative ground for a whole new generation of Irish riders.

The Aga Khan Trophy

How Ireland named its Nations' Cup The Aga Khan Trophy came about through a close association between Ireland and the then holder of the Aga Khan title (the head of the Ismaili Islamic sect). As a youth he had had two Irish tutors, one named Kenny who was an expert in optical matters. (Through Kenny it was discovered that the Iman, or heir to the title, was short-sighted and needed glasses.) After he took up the hereditary title, he visited the Dublin Horse Show on more than one occasion. In the mid-1920s he was living in Switzerland, and having heard through Colonel Zeigler of the RDS plan to run an international team competition in Ballsbridge, offered to put up the trophy. Each time that it has been won outright, the holder of the Aga Khan title at the time has replaced it. The first cup was won outright by Switzerland and it has also been won twice by Ireland and twice by Britain. Although Britain came very close to winning the present Aga Khan Trophy in 1990, when their team was disqualified on a technicality, the sixth version has survived up to now.

His Highness the Aga Khan presenting the current Trophy to RDS Committee members John Carroll and James Meenan in 1980 after Ireland won the previous cup outright in 1979. Britain almost took this one outright in 1990. They were just about to give it to their long-standing Chef d'Équipe Ronnie Massarella when on a technicality they were disqualified from their 1990 win.
(Lensmen Photography)

The effective Irish performance on opening day ensured superb local support for Friday's Nations' Cup. People who had never before visited the RDS or known anything about showjumping were drawn to attend the event at this special time. A throng of 34,000 people packed every viewing space around the arena, and so great was the demand for entrance tickets that the doors had to be locked and barred half an hour before the scheduled start of the competition.

The showmanship of Edward Bohane was clearly brought to bear on the ceremonial parade of teams which has remained unchanged to this day. Making full use of the newly instituted Irish Army bands the organisers created emotive pageantry which is unique in all the world. A carriage first brought President Cosgrave and other dignitaries to the grandstand. Then individual band units led in each team which stood facing the President's Box while their country's national anthem was played. Ireland's team of Dan Corry on Finghin, Ged O'Dwyer on Oisin and Cyril Harty on Cuchulainn were marched in to the tune 'A Nation Once Again' and when the new Irish Free State's anthem, 'The Soldier's Song', rang out, it conjured up a strong emotive meaning. The re-enactment of this beautifully choreographed ceremony each August continues to stir emotion and is still the main highlight of Ireland's showjumping year.

A rare picture of the very first presentation ceremony of the Aga Khan Cup in 1926. It shows the Irish side of Ged O'Dwyer, Dan Corry and Cyril Harty in second place behind Switzerland and ahead of Britain. Some published results of the event used the first-round scores and put Ireland in fourth. (RDS Archive)

In some accounts of the inaugural Aga Khan Trophy competition itself, the team placings after the first round are given as the final result. These left Ireland in what would have been a very disappointing fourth place. However, the scores as recorded in the RDS archives reflect a much more satisfying outcome for the home side (the event was judged by the Wylie system — see Chapter Two).

In the first round Ireland did indeed drop to fourth with a score of 82 points. Switzerland led with a very respectable total of 85.5, France were second on 84 points and Belgium were third with 83, while Britain and Holland stood below Ireland on 79 apiece. So, with less than ten points dividing the sides it was all to be decided in the second round. To the delight of the packed stands, all three Irish team members performed outstandingly. At that time all team members went one after the other, unlike today when one rider from each team jumps in consecutive legs of each round. Dan Corry's only fault occurred at the wall where Finghin dislodged one stone. Both O'Dwyer and Harty returned faultless on Oisin and Cuchulainn for a superb second-round total of 87.5 and an overall score of 169.5 points. Only the well-schooled Swiss side could better that; they had scored 89 in the second round and finally beat Ireland for first place by just five points. When President Cosgrave presented the Aga Khan Trophy, the Swiss got a rousing reception but when it came to the second-placed Irish — as with Ged O'Dwyer on opening day — the applause was of the sort more fitting for champions. The response to Ireland being in the thick of international competition and getting into the prizes was utterly positive and a total justification for the decision of the Government to authorise expenditure on an army jumping team. The sale of seventy-five horses to the Swiss Cavalry at the conclusion of the show was another very positive outcome.

From that time until now, the affection of Irish people for their mounted officers in uniform has never waned. In more recent times one can point to the ecstatic receptions received by riders such as Commandant Gerry Mullins who, on one occasion, had to wait nearly five minutes before the announcement of clear round could be made on the public address, the applause was so intense and prolonged.

It is never forgotten, particularly among the farming community, that the army team will always ride Irish-bred horses and that it was established in the first place to help promote farm incomes. However, this enthusiasm for the institution does not always carry through into the financial decisions of the Government. The Army School has had to fight for its funding year after year since its foundation. It has survived — but only just; their its to buy horses do not always outweigh the demands of the exchequer for hospitals and other human needs. While the riders did not get all they needed, they have always got just enough to keep going, and in each decade since their foundation, have come up with at least one great horse and rider combination that kept their flag flying even in the most difficult of

times. Names of Irish Army horses such as Limerick Lace (Ged O'Dwyer
— 1930s); Ballyneety (Kevin Barry — 1950s), Loch an Easpaig (Billy
Ringrose — 1960s), Garrai Eoin (Ned Campion — 1960s), Coolronan
(Con Power — 1970s), Rockbarton (Gerry Mullins — 1980s) and Kilbaha
(John Ledingham — 1990s) will always be remembered.

There can be no doubt that the good performance at their maiden
international outing in 1926 helped seal the army team's place in the
hearts of Irish followers of equestrian sport. However, it also raised
expectations that in the short term could not be met. In analysing what
happened after that initial burst of success at the RDS, it must be
remembered that the Ballsbridge arena and the judging system in use
there at the time suited the hunting style of the new army riders. The
banks and water jumps posed no great difficulty for their Irish mounts.
For the opposition, particularly from France, Switzerland and Holland,
the Ballsbridge course was a severe test that contrasted sharply with the
continental tracks that were beginning to depend more and more on
obstacles consisting of light timber poles erected on upright standards.

The Irish team was soon to learn just what this new type of course
meant when its members made their first visit to Olympia, London, in
June of 1927. In an effort to prepare themselves, the army men got as
much information as they could from the British riders as to what they
could expect. Friends like Captain Hume-Dudgeon were generous
with their advice and as a result it was possible to build a fairly similar
track at McKee Barracks on which to practise. Unfortunately, it was all
to be of no avail — their preparations proved to be inadequate and the
trip to London was a total disaster. Their mock course at McKee
Barracks had two defects — the fences were too small and they
allowed for too much distance between jumps.

A British riding instructor of the time, Lieutenant Colonel Geoffrey
Brooke, in his book *The Way of a Man With a Horse*, published in 1929,
graphically described what the team was about to face;

> ...an arena like Olympia necessitates a horse that will not
> rush, but can take his fences collectedly and smoothly
> and is ready to push on the pace when extension as
> opposed to elevation is required. Consequently we find at
> Olympia that the consistent winner is an animal with an
> even temperament and readily controlled by the hand and
> leg....[6]

Not the stuff for hunters and cross-country men — when the Irish
arrived in the confines of the indoor arena and faced not only the new
fences but a totally different system of faults judging, everything went
wrong. 'We were kicking poles into the Irish Sea,' Dan Corry noted
ruefully on radio at the time. When discussing the subject during the
course of his interview with the *Irish Farmer's Journal*, a cloud of
sadness came over Ged O'Dwyer's face as he recalled the outcome.

Early parade of military teams for the Aga Khan Trophy with Ireland, Sweden, Germany and Holland. (Show Jumping Association of Ireland)

'We were just plain embarrassed. Our big striding horses just could not cope with the tight distances and we knocked everything in sight.'[7] The Nations' Cup scores tell it all — Britain 5 faults; France 10.5 faults; Italy 20.5 faults; Poland 26.5 faults; Belgium 31.5 faults; Sweden 38.5 faults; Ireland 75.5 faults. The news coming back to Ireland from the event was distressing to many people who had deep hopes in the new team — none more so than the Irish peer The McGillicuddy, who wrote a strong letter to *The Irish Times*, stating in no uncertain terms that the team needed expert training before taking on a task like this. In a reply Judge Wylie took great exception to the views expressed. In this instance one has to disagree with the father of the Irish team and take The McGillicuddy's side.

However, one good thing did emerge from this chastening first Irish visit to Olympia —initial contact was made with the great Colonel Paul Rodzianko. A pure genius of a riding instructor, he was destined to be the Irish showjumping team's mentor throughout the following years. At the time of meeting with the young army team in 1927 this Russian exile was certainly not unfamiliar with Ireland. It appears that he had visited the Dublin Horse Show in the past and had previously competed on an Irish-bred mount. He was coaching some of the riders at the 1927 Olympia show when he made contact with what was, at that point, a very depressed Irish side.

Travelling with the Irish team to London was a Colonel Michael Hogan, who was soon to be appointed Assistant Quartermaster General of the Army. Part of his new responsibilities included arranging finance for the Army Equitation School. He had a very positive attitude towards the new team, but no doubt his convictions, like those of many others, were severely shaken by the poor Irish performance at Olympia. It became very clear to him, after this event, that outside assistance would be needed if the team's efforts were to endure. There is no record of what transpired during Hogan's first meeting with Rodzianko but it is clear that the seed of an idea was germinated.

The months that followed the Olympia disaster were to prove fertile ground for the growth of that idea.

Although knowing they were in serious difficulty, the team travelled on from London to Lucerne to fulfil their invitation from Colonel Zeigler — certainly by this stage, it was a bridge too far. There they encountered courses that were very different from anything they had ever experienced before. At home and to some extent in London, the courses were very much fixed, and the same obstacles were faced in just about every competition. On the Continent, however, matters had moved on considerably, and a great variety of fences were in use, often differing with each class. The euphoria of Dublin was very far away now, and even the depression of London was mild compared to the dispiriting experience of Switzerland.

The team's highest placing during the four days of jumping was twelfth. The Irish were so out of steam by the time it came to the Nations' Cup that they did not participate against the teams from Belgium, Hungary, France and Switzerland. 'We swore we would be back and that things would be different,' Ged O'Dwyer once commented. Writing in the French equestrian journal, *Revue de Cavalerie,* on the subject of Ireland's predicament, a Captain Montergon commented:

> ...it was at Lucerne in 1927 that I saw her competitors for the first time. None of them had any experience in international competitions. How fine the courage of the young Irish Army, thus flinging itself boldly into the water in order to learn to swim.[8]

Matters were not much better on their home ground at the Dublin Horse Show of 1927. In an attempt to update the RDS courses, Judge Wylie had instituted a two-phase track. This comprised an outer course of continental-type obstacles and an inner course that included the traditional Irish banks, water-jump and stone wall. This new development did not work in favour of the home side, which finished a disappointing last behind teams from Switzerland, Britain and Belgium. Neither did the Irish fare any better in the individual contests. It was a rainy week that year in Dublin and Irish team spirits coincided with the dank weather. Something would have to be done to revive the team; training in the new art of equitation was the answer and Colonel Paul Rodzianko was the man to conduct it.

Action was needed and Colonel Michael Hogan didn't waste any time after his appointment as assistant to the Quartermaster General. With the same kind of diplomatic deftness that had characterised Judge Wylie's negotiations for the setting up of the Army Equitation School, Hogan employed Colonel Rodzianko for a three-year contract, starting early in 1928. As Thomas Toomey notes in *Forgotten Dreams,* 'Hogan, it seems, may not even have had any sanction to hire the Russian, but hire him he did....'[9] Rodzianko was reputed to have been earning £50 a week. This would have given him a total salary equal to half of the Army Equitation School's 1931 travel budget for both horses and riders — about fifteen times the wage of an average soldier at that time![10] Hogan's quick move was to be both a salvation and a crucifixion for the young officers. As Ged O'Dwyer recalled:

> He turned us inside out but it hurt. We were in the saddle for six hours a day and while the new seat was easy on the horse, it was very uncomfortable for us. I can remember many nights dragging myself back to our barracks and just about having the energy to undress and get into bed only to wake up sore the next morning. But then it was back into the grind once more — heels down, toes out, knees in, hollow back and light hands — for six more hours.[11]

Rodzianko's arrival at McKee Barracks in 1928 was a new beginning, which turned the fortunes of the Irish Army team around and which brought it to Olympic standard in less than eight years.

Rodzianko

Paul Rodzianko (pictured opposite) was born in the Ukraine to a family with a long and distinguished military history. They owned huge estates — it was said that Ireland would fit within their lands. His father was personal equerry to Tzar Nicholas II. As a young officer Paul was assigned to a Cossack Regiment — the Tzar's Household Cavalry. Since he showed great promise in the saddle, he was sent abroad to study — first under the Scottish innovator Fillis and later with the great Caprilli in Italy. Prior to the First World War he was on the winning Nations' Cup team for his country at Olympia, London, in 1914, on an Irish bred-horse called McGillicuddy Reeks. He served on the Italian front in the First World War but returned home to fight on the White Russian side in the Russian Civil War. In 1920 he was forced to flee abroad and became an instructor at his old school in Italy until Mussolini's Black Shirts had him thrown out. He was based in England when he first came in contact with Irish equestrianism. His first tour to Ireland was from 1928 to 1931. He returned again to instruct both army and civilian riders in the early 1950s, having spent the Second World War serving with the British forces in North Africa and Italy. Upon his return to Ireland, showjumpers of the 1950s, like Elsbeth Gailey and many others, benefited greatly from his genius. Army rider, Commandant J.J. O'Neill, said of Rodzianko:

He was a magnificent instructor with great control and understanding of horses. Despite his years he had great vitality and his enthusiasm was infectious.

Footnotes to Chapter Three

[1]   Taped interview between author and Major 'Ged' O'Dwyer in summer of 1993.

[2]   Wylie, W.E., *The Development of Horse Jumping at the Royal Dublin Society's Shows*, Dublin: Royal Dublin Society, 1952: p 10.

[3]   Toomey, T., *Forgotten Dreams*, Limerick: O'Brien-Toomey, 1995: p. 88.

[4]   Op. cit., Taped interview.

[5]   Op. cit., Toomey, p. 91.

[6]   Brooke, G., *The Way of Man with a Horse*, London: Seeley, Service & Co., 1929: p. 236.

[7]   Op. cit., Taped Interview.

[8]   Op. cit., Toomey, p 114.

[9]   Ibid., p. 98.

[10] *Thoms Directory of Ireland*, Dublin: Alex Thom & Co., 1931: p. 623.

[11] Op. cit., Taped Interview.

CHAPTER FOUR

TAKING ON THE WORLD

*Tip top horses and equally good riders — no team in the world could
beat the Irish.*
— Germany's 1936 Olympic gold medalist Rittmeister Kurt Hasse[1]

During the months after his arrival at McKee Barracks, Colonel Paul Rodzianko kept his work with the team a close military secret. There were no trips abroad and the army riders were absent from local shows around the country. If he was to be successful in turning the squad around, he wanted to take his time and put it on display where and when it really mattered — in the Aga Khan Trophy competition at the RDS.

When the time came, the miracle that the Russian trainer was performing was made very evident. He was indeed recreating both the young riders and their mounts. The pain they were suffering was not evident to the crowd but the results were and that was enough. Sporting people want winners and that was what Rodzianko was going to give them; not only was he going to deliver success, he was going to do it with the very horses that had been going so badly for O'Dwyer, Corry and company before he took over their training.

In the opening event of the 1928 Horse Show, Cuchulainn and Cyril Harty were a close second to Lieutenant General Ganshof of Belgium, and then, in an open class, Ged O'Dwyer won on Lismore. The following day Harty recorded the first military international win by the army team when taking the Puissance on An Craobh Rua, clearing a height of 6 feet 9 inches. These men were riding better than ever and the crowd knew it. In Thursday's main event, Dan Corry kept up the good Irish performance, taking second place on Roisin Dubh. At the military dinner that night, the improvement in Ireland's team was the main topic in speeches made by the visitors. On that same night, the then Minister for Defence announced that in the year ahead, the Irish would contest Nations' Cup events in Belgium, Britain, France and the USA. The revival was taking hold and this fact was very evident the next afternoon when Ireland had its historic first Nations' Cup victory in the Aga Khan Trophy event.

Dan Corry on Finghin, Ged O'Dwyer on Cuchulainn and Cyril Harty with An Craobh Rua led by just two points ahead of Britain after the first round. There was still nothing in it after the first two horses had completed the second round and it was all down to the last rider of the two leading sides — A.M.A. Baillie for Britain and Cyril Harty for Ireland. Baillie gave a cool and near-perfect performance on Grenadier to leave the British with a total score of 272 points. All of the hard work that had happened behind the walls of McKee Barracks during the previous six months was now to be tested. Could Harty match the visitor's round, not only over the familiar banks and ditches, but over the new continental-style outer course as well?

The Irish side of O'Dwyer, Corry and Harty won the Aga Khan cup for the first time in 1928. Home teams have taken it 18 times since then. Winning it is still the high point of any showjumping season and the dream of any young rider. Over the years fewer than 40 Irish riders have had the thrill of competing in it, much less winning it.
(RDS Archive)

The Irish Times report of the event noted that An Craobh Rua became restive at the start of the second track but Harty held his nerve and his team's advantage to put up a winning total of 277 points.[2] The stands rang out their ecstatic response to herald Ireland's true début in the world of international showjumping.

The euphoria of that day was maintained over the next few weeks as the victorious Irish team members visited local shows around the country; particularly in Limerick and Galway, the home counties of O'Dwyer, Harty and Corry. They won at places like Kilmallock and Loughrea but soon they were to face stiff international opposition once more when they headed for their first French Nations' Cup challenge at Biarritz in early October. They planned well for this trip — bringing more horses per rider than on their disastrous first outing to London and Lucerne. They also gave themselves more time between their arrival and the beginning of competition. The team was learning and Rodzianko knew the kind of problems the riders faced when they had to cross an ocean to reach the show involved. To regain their land legs, Rodzianko and the team spent several days with the French Cavalry, the Cadre Noir, in Saumur before travelling south to the Spanish border. Despite some frustrating train delays and a bout of tummy bug that hit Ged O'Dwyer, they still had an excellent outing at Biarritz.

On opening day Dan Corry rode Roisin Dubh to second place in the Grand Military International which had started with fifty-seven competitors. Judge Wylie had bought this little brown mare in Carlow for the Irish Army, and her runner-up prize here earned more than the £70 he had paid for her. Two days later Corry was in the money once more, sharing first place with a Belgian in the jump-off class. Ged O'Dwyer's illness kept him out of action when Ireland came third in the Nations' Cup, his place having been taken by new army recruit Tom Finlay of Laois. Nevertheless, Ged was back in the saddle with a vengeance for the last three days of the show. With Oisin he was through to the jump-off in one event and came second to Captain Lassardierre of France. However, his best shot was still to come in the French championship on Sunday. During his interview with the *Irish Farmer's Journal* some sixty-five years later, Ged was asked to name the most memorable moment of his career. 'I suppose it would have to be my winning of what was called the Loewenstein Cup in France — the first Grand Prix victory in the history of our team.'[3] He went on to recall how Oisin gave him a brilliant jump at a tricky bank to take the championship.

The Irish were back in France for their first show of 1929 when the Nations' Cup moved to Nice. They did not have a very successful outing there and later admitted to missing the presence of their mentor Rodzianko, who was not allowed travel because of the costs involved. Fortunately, the team members were somehow able to persuade the Minister for Defence to have him act as away advisor during the rest of that season. Rodzianko went with them to

Brussels in May and also on their first return visit to Olympia since the disaster of 1927. In Brussels, the first thing he had them do was walk their horses the twelve miles from the city to the show grounds in Genval. The exercise must have helped since over the six days of the show they took a total of 6,000 Belgian francs in prize money. A young horse called Finghin Og, who only a few weeks earlier had been pulling a cart at the Curragh, won the main jump-off class for them.

Their return to Olympia, in June, was all they had hoped it would be when they promised, two years earlier, that they would be back and that matters would be different. This time, over eight days of jumping, they were placed either second or third twenty-six times and won a total of eight first prizes. Their best performance was from Dan Corry who won the prestigious Duke of Connaught Cup on Slievenamon. Instead of last, as on the previous occasion, they were third in the Prince of Wales Cup, finishing behind Britain and France.

Demonstrating the growing horse power of the Irish team, the army men returned home from London to sweep all of the top prizes at the Tipperary show in the first week of July with a group of mounts totally different from those used at Olympia. That strength was again shown the following month at the Dublin Horse Show. After two rounds, in which new team member Tom Finlay was the hero, Ireland was tying with France for first place in the Nations' Cup competition for the Aga Khan Trophy. They were then only narrowly beaten in the jump-off. All of this gave the team the courage to take on its most daunting challenge to date — a trip across the Atlantic for the tough North American winter shows in Boston and New York. With the legendary groom Sergeant Paddy Dunne in charge of the horses, the team sailed in mid-October on what was to be one more important learning mission. They did not win any competitions on that occasion but the trip certainly paved the way for much more successful campaigns in the years that followed. One thing is sure, they received a loving welcome from the emigrant Irish in both cities. This welcome has never changed but in those early days of the new state, the reception was particularly poignant. However, Ged O'Dwyer recalled that one official of Irish descent at the Boston show did not appear to be very friendly towards the idea of the Irish Free State. A couple of years later though, when the army team won the Boston Cup, this same person threw his hat in the air and shouted, 'Hooray for Ireland!' This was just one of many instances where the sport proved capable of healing wounds.

When the Irish returned to North America in the autumn of 1930 they won events in both New York and Toronto. Between 1928 and 1930 they had taken ten individual firsts at shows in France, Belgium, Britain and the Americas but away Nations' Cup wins still eluded them.

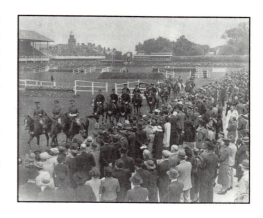

*Ireland at the top of the world
Parade after Ireland had won the 1938 Aga Khan ahead of Germany, France, Britain, Holland and Canada.* (Independent Newspapers)

Paddy Dunne

Early riders in the Army Equitation School at McKee Barracks reserved their highest praise not only for their Officers Commanding or instructors, but also for the great groom, Sergeant Paddy Dunne. In fact, this unique Tipperary man gets almost as much mention in the index of Thomas Toomey's *Forgotten Dreams* as any of the team's stars.

As a young lad he worked for a number of Tipperary stud farms and in addition to his own intuitive knowledge he absorbed a great deal of horse lore from very experienced owners. He joined the Army in 1922 at the age of forty-four, and when the Army Equitation School was formed in 1926, Paddy became part of the groom team. He won particular praise for his uncanny ability to have his horses back in shape after the long boat trip to the USA. Respect for his store of knowledge about horses and their ills grew not only within the Irish Army but also among the international showjumping fraternity. One person who famously turned to him for help was Queen Wilhelmina of the Netherlands. At one show that she attended, a Dutch team horse became inexplicably ill. When veterinary advice failed, the Queen asked Paddy to help out. Mysteriously he found the answer. The Queen later invited all the Irish riders and grooms to her hotel for a drink. During the evening Paddy offered to buy her a drink, 'Whatever you are having yourself', she said — she got a Guinness whether she liked it or not! His great tradition of grooming, combined with good humour, has been carried on within the Irish Army ever since his time. Among well-known names that followed him was Sergeant Major Steve Hickey, who learned course building while travelling with the team, and went on to build the course for the 1982 World Championships in Dublin. There was also Jimmy Doyle or 'Doyler', who groomed the great Rockbarton for both Con Power and Gerry Mullins, and became a top yard manager on the US circuit.

Early in 1931, Colonel Paul Rodzianko parted company with the Irish Army. While he had been close to the riders during his term, it appears that he was never fully accepted by the authorities who may not have understood how he was worth the amount of money they were paying him.

Even so, for those within the world of showjumping, no value could be placed on what he did for the fledgling jumping team and on the foundations he laid for future recruits like Colonel Billy Ringrose, who later said of him:

> He introduced the latest and best developments to the
> School during this period. After his contract terminated,
> his methods were adhered to by the riders he had trained
> and was one of the telling factors in their success.[4]

The success that the Irish really longed for was in away Nations' Cups and that was the glory they hunted in the years following Rodzianko's departure. Major Ged O'Dwyer spelled out their feelings at the time in his interview with the *Irish Farmer's Journal*:

> *...we had grown in confidence but we were no longer satisfied with individual wins ... we wanted to get the maximum publicity for Ireland and the Irish horse that came from winning Nations' Cups. I was put in charge of the team soon after Colonel Rodzianko left and I laid down the priority that we would only go after the most important events on future trips abroad.*[5]

At the beginning of 1931, the School's strength had been increased to nine riding officers; from Meath had come Fred Ahern along with Kerry-man Dan Leonard, George Heffernon of Kildare, Jim Neylon from Clare and Jack Lewis of Limerick. New horses had been added as well, and while Ireland would never match opposing squads like Britain and Germany in terms of re-mount numbers, the team was in a position to bring more equine power into action on future campaigns.

The team's first show without Rodzianko's backing, at Nice in April 1931, proved to be another chastening experience as Ireland finished eighth behind Switzerland, France, Spain, Portugal, Italy, Poland and Belgium.

Matters improved dramatically three weeks later in Brussels, where the team achieved two firsts plus several good placings, earning 11,000 franks in prize money. However, Ireland's most satisfying result came in the Prix des Nations when the team of O'Dwyer, Harty, Leonard and Ahern tied for first place with the Italians — ahead of Belgium, Spain and France. They were narrowly beaten in the jump-off but the event was still a great morale boost.

For the first time, Ireland fielded five riders at Olympia that year but the Prince of Wales Cup eluded them once again. They were lying a good second behind France after the first round but did not fare so well second time out, and they ended up finishing in a disappointing fourth place. Although slightly denting their confidence, this defeat appeared to put them more on their toes for the following outing to Lucerne in July. Upon arriving there, team-leader Ged O'Dwyer got word from Dublin that he had been promoted to Commandant. He celebrated by delivering two superb clear rounds in the Nations' Cup, on Rosnaree, as Ireland swept her way to her very first team victory abroad. Joining Ged in that emotion-packed success were Tom Finlay on Moonstruck, Cyril Harty with Kilmallock and Dan Corry on Finghin, who afterwards won the Puissance there as well. Ireland's winning total after two rounds was twenty-four faults. The home team came a close second with twenty-eight faults, and only O'Dwyer's final clear avoided a jump-off. The Italian team that had beaten Ireland in

Opposite: Dan Leonard
Dan, from Kerry, joined the Army in 1931 and
was a member of a number of winning teams. He
was a keen dresser and delighted in the fact that
the army team was given dress uniforms during
his time. Prior to that, they attended social
functions in their riding gear. (Joan Parker)

Brussels came third, Belgium was fourth, and France and Hungary were joint fifth.

Lucerne was a powerful new beginning for the Irish team and truly put it on the world showjumping map. French expert Captain Montergon, who had been so condescending towards the young Irish team back in 1927, spoke differently now:

> *Ireland has indeed begun to swim and its swimming*
> *master Colonel Rodzianko chose the proper method: short*
> *leathers, firmly seated, and at the same time forward,*
> *watching closely the 'short ones' in a word thoroughly up*
> *to date — we shall see arise in the International sky new*
> *stars or rather a new constellation — the Irish Horse.*[6]

How right he was this time. Later that year Ahern, Corry and O'Dwyer won the Nations' Cup for Ireland at the great Winter Fair in Toronto. Their total over two rounds on Blarney Castle, Shannon Power and Turoe was a mere two penalties — enough to place them first ahead of Britain, the USA, France and the home team, Canada.

These important wins could not have come at a better time as the beginning of 1932 heralded the dramatic coming to power of a Fianna Fáil government. Headed by Eamon de Valera, who just nine years previously had been the sworn enemy of W.T. Cosgrave's administration, it was seen by the team as an unfriendly force. In addition, former IRA Chief of Staff, Frank Aiken, had now been appointed Minister for Defence. There was cause for worry at McKee Barracks since a number of the riding officers there had fought on the opposite side to Aiken in the Irish Civil War of 1922. To his credit, Aiken let the past die and made no obvious move against the Army Equitation School. However, the new situation in Irish politics was an extra spur to Corry, O'Dwyer and company to try even harder in their efforts to publicise the new state through important wins abroad.

On home soil, however, in May 1932, an important bridge-building opportunity was lost. An invite had been received from the Royal Ulster Agricultural Society (RUAS) for the team to compete at its annual show in Balmoral. The response was less than positive. Other commitments were given as the reason for the Irish Free State Team not going north. During the many troubled years since then no Irish Army rider has ever jumped at the RUAS show in Balmoral. (During the IRA cease-fire of the early 1990s two young officers did compete at the Northern Indoor Championships in Eglinton and they received a wonderful and friendly reception.)

It is reasonable to conclude that at all times the riders themselves were the greatest of diplomats but many times, both then and in later years, officials with deep-grained political convictions got in the way of sport and friendship. It appears that such attitudes may have been evident in June of 1932 when the Irish team again visited Olympia in

Departure for USA – a journey into the unknown
for the young army team as they went to compete
in New York, Boston and then Toronto in Canada.
Picture shows Sergeant Major Steve Hickey
leaving Dublin on one of his trips as groom with
the team. (Joan Parker)

Above top: complete with soft hat, Eamon de Valera was on hand to present the Irish trophy to Major Ged O'Dwyer at the 1934 Horse Show. The two men had been on opposite sides in the Civil War but this was a moment of peace between them. Above: Dev did not like the idea of wearing a bowler hat but some thirty-three years later, as President, he did condescend to wear the traditional topper for Aga Khan day in 1967.
(Irish Press and RDS Archive)

London. Captain Fred Ahern had won the Holland Cup with Ireland's Own and when it came to the prize-giving ceremony the tune 'St Patrick's Day' was played instead of the Irish National Anthem. At some point the Irish were told that there was only one National Anthem, 'God Save the King' — that did not help matters. Neither did the non-appearance of the Irish team members in the Duke of Connaught Cup, which was confined to riders in the British Commonwealth only. Back in 1929, Dan Corry had won the same Cup and not a word had been said about it. However, at this time more hard-line political influences on both sides of the Irish Sea were at work and the team was learning to live with that. It is interesting to note that no British team competed in Dublin between the years 1932 and 1936.

In addition to politics, the international monetary crisis also hit team entries for the 1932 Dublin Horse Show. Against France and Belgium (the only teams to travel to Dublin that year), the home team of Dan Leonard on Miss Ireland, Fred Ahern with Ireland's Own and Ged O'Dwyer on the great Limerick Lace scored the second home Aga Khan Trophy win. It appears that President de Valera was not there to present the Trophy that year and it was not until 1934 that he did arrive to attend the competition. On that occasion he was wearing a soft hat but in following years his attitude appeared to mellow and he consented to wear the traditional topper.

In the winter of 1932 Fred Ahern, James Neylon and Dan Corry made a triumphant Irish return to the USA, winning the Nations' Cup in Boston. Victory was secured only after a dramatic third-round jump-off against France in which just two penalties divided the two sides. They got a prolonged standing ovation for their achievement from an audience in the Boston Garden, which included many Irish. From there they moved on to New York and Toronto. The Nations' Cups eluded them in both venues but at the two shows they took four individual firsts — good news for 'Dev' (de Valera) as such victories helped enhance the image of Ireland in the USA.

With their dreams now focused on winning an Olympic medal in Germany in 1936, Berlin became the Irish team's first target venue of 1933. There the Irish took on the mighty Germans on their home ground and were narrowly beaten by one fence. From that moment Ireland's goal was to beat Germany — preferably in the great Olympic arena in Berlin.

In the meantime, the team struggled through the early part of 1933, being placed fourth in Nice, seventh in Rome, sixth in Brussels and fifth in Lucerne — but matters picked up after that. Ireland came second at the RDS to France and ahead of Switzerland, Holland, Czechoslovakia and Belgium. On the North American tour the team had three firsts in both Chicago and New York before going on to take the Toronto Nations' Cup again. There, Dan Corry, Cyril Harty, and Fred Ahern won ahead of Sweden, the USA and Canada — the sixth team-first since the Army Equitation School's foundation. In all, the Irish had fourteen international wins during 1933, and the Toronto victory capped a year that had sown the seeds of Irish promise for the years ahead.

That promise did not fully blossom on the much curtailed programme of 1934. However, Ireland did have some very memorable moments during that year of European change. In Berlin the team members were introduced to German President Paul Von Hindenburg, who died six months later. His death came at the time of the Dublin Horse Show during which he was honoured with a special ceremony. In Rome they were greeted by Mussolini and there Lieutenant Tom Quinn of Ennis had a good first outing with the team when he came fourth in his inaugural event with Red Hugh.

Germany sent its future Olympic gold medal team to Dublin that year and won the Aga Khan Trophy ahead of France and Ireland. The intense atmosphere on Nations' Cup day was colourfully described in a paper written for the RDS in December 1934 by Hugh Gerard:

> It was a thrilling and memorable moment when in the presence of 20,000 people, with the flags of the seven nations fluttering from their standards, the first nation entered the famous arena. To the music of a stirring martial tune the German team of horsemen came slowly down the ground. Then wheeling they faced the thousands of distinguished people filling tier upon tier, with Lord Powerscourt, the Society's President and President de Valera in the centre. After Germany came Sweden, the Netherlands, Belgium, France, Switzerland, each in turn saluted by the Anthem of their country and each cheered to the echo by people deeply moved by the grandeur of this symbolic pageantry. But the appearance of the Irish team let loose all the pent-up emotion of twenty thousand people as Commandant O'Dwyer and his brother officers came down the Enclosure like conquering heroes. When they wheeled into position the strains of the country's own National Anthem came vibrant and strong, and the other nations honoured the nation of which they were guests by coming to the general salute. On the stands and around the entire Enclosure the people too were paying eloquent and respectful homage to the Anthem of the young State.[7]

However, the most thrilling moment of that 1934 show was still to come on the final day when ninety civilian and visiting military riders competed in the newly instituted Saorstát Éireann Cup presented by the Irish Government. The event ended dramatically in a two-way jump-off over eleven fences between Lieutenant Müller of Switzerland on the Irish-bred Orwell and Ged O'Dwyer on Limerick Lace.

Right: the Irish team of Ged O'Dwyer, Dan Leonard, Fred Ahern and Tom Quinn at Rome in Mussolini's time. Also pictured below are both sides of a medal presented by Il Duce to Dan Leonard and retained by relatives of this early army rider in Limerick. (Mary Quinn and Joan Parker)

Müller had one fence down, but before a hushed crowd, Ged went magnificently clear. What followed may well have been the origin of the term 'the RDS Roar'. The applause echoed around the arena again — the emotion of the moment totally answering any remaining questions regarding the wisdom of founding an Irish showjumping team. There is no record of what was said between President de Valera and Ged when the Irish hero rode forward that afternoon to accept the Irish Free State Cup. These two men, who had vehemently supported opposite sides in the bitter treaty controversy of just twelve years earlier, were now shaking hands in the most dramatic of circumstances; circumstances made possible by the horse and the sport of showjumping. Whatever disagreements they had had in the past, or were to have in the future, were momentarily suppressed as 'The Soldier's Song' that they were both devoted to rang out for an Irish victory of the most stunning kind.

Anyone who has worked with Major Ged O'Dwyer knew him to be a born leader — utterly sensitive, understanding and yet strong. Commandant J.J. O'Neill, who served under him during the war years wrote, 'The O.C. was a colourful figure held in high esteem by all ranks. His favourite dictum, Right or wrong keep going.'[8] At this time, back in 1934, Ged was fully in charge of the Army Equitation School and there can be no doubt that this resounding individual victory at the RDS enhanced his standing with his fellow officers. There were just two years to go before the Berlin Olympics and he had set a gold there as the Irish team's goal. 'We wanted it and none more than me...'[9] he later declared.

An intense period of preparation began at the start of 1935 and, like a great orchestra building to a crescendo, the team results began to grow more and more favourable. In Nice, and then in Amsterdam, Ireland came second to the German A team. In Lucerne, with the team's best score recorded to date, O'Dwyer, Lewis, Corry and Ahern scored no penalties whatsoever to win by twenty-four faults ahead of Switzerland, Belgium, Poland and Italy. From there it was immediately on to the Dublin Horse Show and an even more resounding win by all of forty-four faults over the main opponent, Germany. New York was next and another win was secured there after a tense jump-off with the American home team. Finally, ending that year of true potential realisation on the highest possible note, they won again in Toronto — this time ahead of Holland, Canada, France and Chile.

Then came the fateful year of 1936 which continued with the team's onward and upward progression — first in Nice, leaving Spain, Portugal, Poland, France, Switzerland and Poland in its wake. However, the Dutch Olympic silver medalists beat Ireland in Brussels, and at Olympia, France had three faults to spare over the Irish team. But not so at Lucerne the following week! There the Irish army riders beat France, the USA and Switzerland before returning triumphantly to Dublin.

Instead of a hero's welcome when they arrived at McKee Barracks they received the most devastating blow any team has ever had to absorb in the history of showjumping. Just ten days prior to their planned departure for Berlin, they were bluntly told that the Irish team had been withdrawn from the Olympics. Problems in relation to the athletics team were given as the reason for this damning decision. This was not necessarily believed by all of the team and, to the day he died, Ged O'Dwyer, put the blame on one man. 'We were up against a hostile government and it was de Valera stopped us,'[10] he said. All the exact reasons and motives will probably never be known. It is a simple fact that without any explanation the team was told that it was not going and that was that. 'We were just devastated...,' was Ged's way of putting in words the deep hurt that was felt by the army riders.

Undaunted, they acted like true soldiers, picked themselves up and a few days later came out to win the Aga Khan Trophy, ahead of Britain, France, Belgium and Holland. Nevertheless, the bitter disappointment for O'Dwyer lingered and was increased at the end of the Dublin Horse Show when he received orders that he was to go to Berlin after all — as an emissary. There he was greeted as a great rider by Adolph Hitler himself. Ged walked all the courses in the Olympic arena but he could not do what he had dreamed of and planned for over four hard seasons. Later, he recalled his feelings:

Following the disappointment of not going to the 1936 Olympics, Ged O'Dwyer had further to suffer being sent as Irish emissary. Having seen the competition 'on my two flat feet', he felt that Ireland would definitely have won a showjumping medal if allowed to compete. He met Hitler, who referred to him during the interview as 'the world's greatest rider'. He is pictured here with Vice-Chancellor Hermann Goering. (Noel Hayes)

I sat in my dress uniform unable to jump a fence. In the previous twelve months our team had won eight Nations' Cups. I was looking at the ninth one for sure. But here I was on my two flat feet. I reckoned the most we would have had was sixteen to eighteen faults. The Germans won it with forty-four faults. Holland was second with fifty-one and Portugal third on fifty-six — all teams we had beaten during the season. It was heartbreaking and in the long run, the reason why I left the Army when the war was over.[11]

That was Ireland's best chance ever of winning an equestrian Olympic medal. In all the years of success since then, it is the one achievement that still eludes Irish showjumpers.

Devastated and down-hearted as the Irish team members were after that let-down, they appeared determined to prove over and over again that they would have taken a medal if they had been given the chance. Over the next twelve months they were first or second in every one of the eight Nations' Cups that they jumped in. In New York, they were beaten by Britain only after two jump-offs, and on their first outing of 1937 they were second to Germany in Paris and second again to Belgium in Brussels. Then came one of their truly great triumphs — Olympia in London where they took the Prince of Wales Cup for Ireland's first and only time. Dan Corry on Red Hugh, John Lewis on Tramore Bay and Ged on Limerick Lace put up a total score of twelve, enough to beat the Berlin gold medalists, Germany, by four fences. Surely this was full redemption from the disaster of their first visit there exactly ten years earlier, as well as being supreme proof that they had the ability to beat the Germans.

Further, before the month was out they were to prove this even more convincingly on Germany's home ground. Having come second (only after a jump-off) in Amsterdam and then first in both Lucerne and Dublin, Ged set about driving home the point at Aachen. He did not jump there himself, but on Monday, 16 August, before a throng that included Hitler, Ged's selected team of John Lewis on Limerick Lace, Fred Ahern on Ireland's Own, along with new recruits George Heffernan and John Stack, pulverised the Germans by twenty-four faults to thirty-two. The Irish team's proclamation — 'We are the champions' — hung like sky writing over a continent soon to be plunged into a devastating war. Over the next twelve months they proclaimed it again and again in Nice, New York, Toronto and Lucerne. Even so, these stirring wins, on top of those in London, Dublin and Aachen could not erase the disappointment of not having had the chance of victory at the top level of the world, in the Olympic Games. When war began the Irish Army team was disbanded and was not to be re-formed again until 1945; and then it was to be without the great Major Ged O'Dwyer.

Ged commanded a battalion during the war years. He then retired from the army and returned to his beloved farm and family in Limerick. There he devoted much of his energy to the development of both Irish showjumping and Irish horse breeding. He died at the age of ninety-two in 1995. Between 1926 and 1939 he had scored a total of forty-six international firsts — sixteen of them in Nations' Cup competitions — and most of them on the great Limerick Lace.

A chapter in Irish showjumping history had firmly closed when Ged O'Dwyer retired from the sport.

Footnotes to Chapter Four

[1] Toomey, T., *Forgotten Dreams*, Limerick: O'Brien–Toomey, 1995: p. 167.

[2] Ibid., p. 103.

[3] Author's interview with Major Ged O'Dwyer, 1993.

[4] *An Cosantóir, The Irish Defence Journal*, Dublin: Army Press Office, August 1936: p. 226.

[5] Op. cit., Interview with Major Ged O'Dwyer.

[6] Op. cit., Toomey, p. 114.

[7] Gerard, H., *Souvenir of Dublin Horse Show*, Dublin: Royal Dublin Society, p. 9.

[8] Op. cit., *An Cosantóir*, p. 235.

[9] Op. cit., Interview with Major Ged O'Dwyer.

[10] Ibid.

[11] Ibid.

CHAPTER FIVE

JUMPING THE BORDER

The Irish horse cannot distinguish between the grass north or south of the border.
— BBC TV documentary on the Irish equine sports industry in 1992

International success fed interest in the sport of showjumping at home in Ireland. The number of events, and the amount of riders taking part in them, grew, and so organisation was needed. The drive to have a national showjumping body began in the 1930s but such a body did not become a reality until the early 1950s. In the meantime, there were a number of false starts, unforeseen difficulties, various objections and a host of meetings aimed at the much desired but elusive all-Ireland goal. The essential unity of the sport — on both sides of the border — was the driving force. The political reality of a divided island was the main obstacle that had to be jumped; this leap proved sufficiently difficult to delay for almost ten years the formation of a single representative body.

The first stirrings north and south were mainly brought about through the confused state of judging throughout the island as a whole. A story told of the army jumping team's participation during the early 1930s helps illustrate the state of showjumping judging around Ireland at that time. The riders from McKee Barracks had by then become accustomed to the continental method of adjudication whereby faults alone and not the style of riding determined the score of any given round. However, not so on the national Irish circuit where judging varied from show to show around the country. Thus, when the army team did a tour of the south-west at Kilmallock, Ennis and Newcastle West they scored successive wins against the local opposition; but when they took on a series of events in the north east of the twenty-six counties it was a very different story. At Mullingar, Dundalk and Clones they came up against a certain Mrs Wall, who ran an Equitation School at Clonsilla during the 1930s. The imposing and classy Mrs Wall proved impossible to beat. It appeared that she could have fences down and still be recalled for the second round because of how well she rode or because her horse was of better show quality than those used by the men from McKee Barracks.

There are other stories from the time, like the instance when a rider cleared all the fences in a competition but was not recalled for the second round because she had gone too fast. There were instances where competitors who had won classes would protest that they had fences down and did not deserve to be placed ahead of others who appeared to have gone clear. Their honesty and humility was often rewarded only by the comment 'but you were better mounted', and that was that. While the RDS had, for the most part, made the transition from hunter judging to true showjumping judging, this change in attitude and thinking had not yet filtered across the country. Opinionated judgements based on style and quality of mounts were still the norm at many venues.

A 1928 picture of Hughie McCully, from County Down, jumping the stone wall at the Dublin Horse Show with Cherry. Note the marker at left of the fence recording if any stones were knocked. Hughie's son Billy was a later high-jump champion at the RDS in Ballsbridge. (Northern Whig and Belfast Post)

Right up into the 1940s, at shows in places like Navan, Downpatrick and Warrenpoint, there were jumping classes listed for style and appearance. Also at these shows there was the stone wall class and the judging of this tended to vary very much from place to place. Judge Wylie made reference to this diversity in his 1952 memoir:

> *Personally I think it is wrong to judge a loose stone wall as a timber fence, viz., four faults if the fence is reduced in height. A touch with a hind leg which takes one stone off the wall should not be penalised as severely as when a horse hits it half-way down and takes a barrow load of stones off.*[1]

The first book of rules adopted by the new Irish Shows Association in 1948 outlined the judging of stone walls as follows:

Wall built of stones.

Touching the wall so as to remove one or more stones:

with the hind legs — 2 faults

with the forelegs — 4 faults.[2]

Diversity persisted and several attempts were made at improving matters. For example, at the Dublin Horse Show public address commentary on rounds was used for the first time in 1940 to help explain to the public why a certain competitor had faults. Also in the 1940s at Balmoral an effort at greater communication between judges, the commentator and the public involved the Army Cadet Force sending Morse code messages from the centre of the arena to the jury box.

The art of judging was not the only aspect of showjumping still in its evolutionary stage during the 1930s and 1940s. Grading of horses was another, and attempts were made at creating some sort of handicap system that would give new-comers to the sport a better chance. These early efforts attempted to grade horses into open and novice mounts but where the difficulties lay was with the question of when a horse stopped being a novice and became an open mount. For the most part, it was understood that an open horse was one that had achieved victory in one novice event. However, instances have been recounted of owners wanting good prices for their jumpers on the basis that they had won ten or twelve novice competitions.

Clearly there was need for organisation, but who should do it? Following every latest uproar at over-judging, there would be a cry for unified rules, but then the furore would die down and matters would stay as they were for yet another season.

In 1939, however, a singular event speeded up the urgency to do something about a showjumping organisation — that was the disbandment of the army team at the outbreak of the Second World War. Having come second to France in the Aga Khan Trophy contest in Dublin in August of that year, the riders from McKee Barracks embarked on what was to be their last national tour for six terrible years. They competed at Sligo, where they won a total of £15 prize money, and then, two days after the horrifying outbreak of war in Europe, went on to Ballaghaderreen on 5 September. They were entered to compete at the Great October Fair and Show at Ballinasloe at the beginning of October but they never appeared. In fact, by that time their horses were already being dispersed and the riding officers were assigned to other units as part of Ireland's response to the Emergency. A new unit, known as An Mare Sluagh, was set up, and Commandant Tom Finlay was appointed as its officer in command. His group was in charge of horse transportation within the army and the care of the former jumpers — which had then been turned out to grass.[3] Consequently, at that frightful time in history, the future of equestrian sport in Ireland rested firmly in civilian hands.

What the Ballinasloe show of 1939 lacked in competitive edge, with the non-appearance of the army riders, it gained in historic note. An important meeting of riders and showjumping owners transpired which marked the beginning of efforts to form an organisation devoted to the regulation and growth of the sport in Ireland.

Up to that time, people involved in the sport had for the most part accepted that the army and the RDS would look after matters for them. However, the turmoil of war now threatened both institutions. The Army Equitation School at McKee Barracks was closed, the British Army was already billeted in the show grounds at Balmoral in Belfast and there were rumours that the Irish Free State[*] forces were about to take over the Royal Dublin Society's show grounds in Ballsbridge. There was also fear that both the Spring Show and the Dublin Horse Show there would have to be cancelled. The problems surrounding the judging and organisation of competitions were being compounded by the outbreak of war, the closure of McKee Barracks and the threat to the great national shows. These factors helped nudge showjumping enthusiasts towards taking the necessary steps to gain control of their own sport.

The world-famed Ballinasloe Fair dates back to 1757. The quality of horse available there has varied down through the years, but never the quality of fun and craic that goes with the annual October event. (Ballinasloe Fair Committee)

---

[*] The Irish Free State was formed in 1921 after the Anglo-Irish Treaty was signed. The Treaty provided for the establishment of two states within the island of Ireland: Northern Ireland, which comprised the six counties of modern Northern Ireland; and the Irish Free State which comprised the remaining twenty-six counties of Ireland. Although the Irish Free State was renamed Éire in 1937, its international status did not change from that of self-governing state until 1949, when it became a republic and was renamed the Republic of Ireland.

Coinciding with the Fair is the Ballinasloe show which dates back to the 1840s. The stone wall jump was a feature of that meeting for up to sixty years. Pictured jumping there in the late 1940s are Jimmie Quinn and his brother, former army rider, Tom Quinn of Ennis. Both were at the forefront of efforts to form a showjumping association. (Mary Quinn).

At the Limerick show of 1939, as a result of some very poor judging, some riders held an impromptu meeting under the grand stand. Present were Kerry Kerrison, Mick O'Meara, and Frank and Jimmo Quinn. They decided that a national meeting should be called in Athlone to discuss the matter of judging; there is no record that this meeting ever took place.

However, around this time, at the behest of a Dublin competitor named Sheila Meyers, some preliminary gatherings were held at her home in Rathfarnham. These get-togethers in turn led to a more general meeting being arranged for the first Sunday of October 1939 at Hayden's Hotel right at the heart of the Ballinasloe Fair. There was no better place or time to call such a meeting, since just about everyone interested in the sport of showjumping assembled there from all around the country. Ballinasloe was then even more a Mecca for those involved in the sport than it is today. There was always the chance that among the hundreds of disparate equines and raw country horses on the Fair Green a future star for Ballsbridge or Balmoral could be found.

Buyers like the legendary Jack Bamber from Ballymena made a pilgrimage here each autumn as part of their re-stocking after the August Horse Show. It is recalled that each year Jack Bamber and his brother, Maurice, brought up to forty novice jumpers by special train from the North of Ireland to the RDS and went home with just about all of them sold. More than one of his next year's draft would be found at the heart of fairs like Ballinasloe.

Also drawn there were the likes of the McDowell family from Sutton in County Dublin. Dublin jewellers by trade, they were owners of a top string of jumpers. Jack and Carrie McDowell were prime movers for the formation of a showjumping organisation. They had some of the more prominent competitors of the Second World War years riding their

The Bamber brothers, Maurice and Jack (winner of the 1937 Dublin Grand Prix), seen here during a prize-giving ceremony at Ballsbridge during the war years. Also pictured are young Seamus Hayes and Dan Corry. (Mary Rose Hayes)

horses — Mary Rose Robinson (who later married Seamus Hayes), Sheila Meyers and Eileen Buckley. During the 1940s McDowell horses won the champion stone wall trophy at Ballinasloe three years in a row.

Doreen McDowell

A neighbour and good friend of the Dublin showjumping family, the McDowells, was Doreen Robinson who later married Dr Cecil McDowell. She is daughter to George Hanbury Robinson, who was very much involved in the origins of the Show Jumping Association of Ireland and was largely responsible for the first efforts at formulating a grading system in 1945. Now living by the banks of the Boyne in County Meath, Doreen, who was a good rider in her own right, recalls annual autumn trips to the west organised by Carrie McDowell during the early 1940s:

We would leave Dublin by turf train with about four horses for Eyrecourt in Galway and would take in the shows at Mount Bellew, Loughrea and Ballinasloe from there. On the way out the train would stop in the bog to re-fuel and we would have tea in a little cottage beside the railway. From Eyrecourt we travelled by borrowed pony and trap with the horses in tow. Each year was a new adventure.

The Ballinasloe Group

At that historic meeting in Hayden's Hotel on Sunday, 2 October 1939 many of the McDowell family and their friends were listed among those present — Carrie McDowell, Herbert McDowell, Jack McDowell, Sheila Meyers, Eileen Buckley (rider of Nuggett) and Sheila White of Clonsilla (sister of well known vet Jack White). Also mentioned as being there were army men Commandant Dan Corry and Commandant Fred Ahern. The western section of showjumping was represented by Roscommon's showjumping priest Father M.J. O'Reilly (who rode a bicycle to Ballinasloe with his showjumper Star trotting along behind); Jim Kiernan from Dromod, County Leitrim together with his daughter Maura; and Mick O'Meara of Nenagh who was one of those present at the impromptu meeting in Limerick. In the light of future difficulties in forming a single association for the whole island it is also interesting to note that Mr David McCreedy from Banbridge, County Down, was also there. He had jumped in competitions himself and among the horses he later owned were Kilbeg and Meta which were both on the successful Northern Ireland team of 1948. Sadly David did not see the logical conclusion of the work that was begun in Ballinasloe in 1939. Unfortunately, he died just prior to the eventual inaugural meeting of the Show Jumping Association of Ireland in Dundalk in 1954, which can trace its roots directly back to the first meeting of this so-called Ballinasloe Group, in 1939.

It was inevitable that any organisation of competitors, like that envisaged at Ballinasloe, would eventually have to deal with the controlling body of the sport — up to that time, the RDS. The Ballinasloe Group decided to clear that obstacle sooner rather than later and sought a meeting with Judge Wylie. The pragmatic Judge Wylie agreed to talk to the Ballinasloe Group and a meeting was arranged for early November, at the Shelbourne Hotel in Dublin.

Possibly, unbeknown to this pioneering group, Judge Wylie and the RDS were, at the very same time, also attempting to put some unity and order into the sport by bringing together the various shows from around the country which held jumping events. Judge Wylie wrote of that time, '...whilst on the subject of rules it may be of interest to mention the Irish Shows Association, a body which was brought into being by the Royal Dublin Society at the request of many local shows....'[4] The Society (RDS) felt that if, as far as possible, all shows worked on similar lines, particularly with regard to such matters as entries and rules of judging, it would be a great stimulus to agriculture generally. Consequently, an informal meeting of Show Secretaries was held during the 1940 Spring Show.[5] The previous year (1939) Judge Wylie had written, 'We have achieved a code of rules for judging but their application still leaves something to be desired.'[6] The Irish Shows Association (ISA) itself was established as an off-shoot of the RDS in 1946. It in turn published a rule book for showjumping in 1948.[7]

It is clear then, that when the Ballinasloe Group contacted Wylie after their October 1939 meeting, he was already deeply involved in the problems they were trying to solve. However, it must be borne in mind that Wylie was more interested in having the solutions come through a co-operative effort by the shows themselves than from what might be construed as a sort of competitors' union. Shows at this time were somewhat suspicious of any attempts at forming an organisation that might dictate to them on matters related to showjumping, such as entry fees and prize money. The divergence of view between the Irish Shows Association (ISA) and the Show Jumping Association of Ireland has persisted right down to this day; this is not necessarily a bad thing and it will most probably never change.

Despite his misgivings, Judge Wylie did go ahead and meet the Ballinasloe Group at the Shelbourne Hotel. It may have been a somewhat awkward affair since he had the mind-set of a judge, while the group approached the situation from a competitor's point of view. However, they did agree to hold a more general meeting six months from then during the 1940 Spring Show. On the agenda for that were items such as the creation of an official panel of judges, prize money, entry fees, height of fences, novice and open competitions and inter-hunt events. This latter item must have been very much in need of attention for, according to one competitor of the time, all hell would often break loose after these events in which the judges had to watch the progress of a pair of competitors jumping fences up-sides (when the two riders jumped fences side-by-side — the more together the better). Doreen McDowell can recall an occasion in which she and her sister-in-law, Phyllis McDowell, came fourth in a competition; but over the next week, after the second-placed rider had objected to the winners, and those that had come third had objected to both first and second-placed riders, the fourth-placed McDowells were eventually awarded the first prize!

The Irish Shows Association Logo. (ISA)

The Irish Shows Association

The ISA was not formally established until 1946. At that time, according to Judge Wylie, who was very much a founding father, membership was open to all recognised shows and recognised horse jumping associations in Ireland. He appears to have had the idea that the ISA could be a very powerful organisation, not only in terms of national jumping, but for international affairs and the selection of teams as well.[8]

However, in its early years the ISA, for the most part, was simply a discussion body which aimed at giving moral support to show secretaries. In 1975 the ISA opted to become a totally autonomous body and for the next four years or so it remained somewhat as it had been. Then, under the chairmanships of Corkman Ted Sheehan and Leslie Rothwell of Inistioge, County Kilkenny, it came alive and began to offer some much-needed services to shows. All-Ireland championships, group insurance, a guide book, judges' lists and a professional national secretariat — all funded through a small levy on show prizes. Its budget in 1978 was around £5,000 annually and that grew steadily over the next twenty years. By 1998 it had reached £250,000 — £120,000 of which was sponsored prizes for some fifty all-Ireland championships. Its current secretary, Mary Houlihan, notes that each season she handles results from an astounding 1,000 qualifying rounds in those championships. In equestrianism, its activities are confined to the showing rings and it leaves the organisation of showjumping to the SJAI. The two organisations co-operate where necessary but also maintain a respectful distance within their own spheres.

In addition to Judge Wylie and a group of show presidents, the Spring Show meeting included showjumping representatives from all four provinces — Father O'Reilly from Connaught, Sheila White from Leinster, Mick O'Meara from Munster and David McCreedy from Ulster (who four years later was to be elected chairman of a new Northern Ireland showjumping association). Also there was Sheila Meyers, who, like Judge Wylie, was something of a convenor. Although attending as a private citizen, Commandant Dan Corry did give a presence to Ireland's army heroes, and by some good fortune a very special individual was able to get leave from the British Army and make it to the meeting — Major Joe Hume-Dudgeon.

The main item decided at the RDS meeting on 7 May 1940 was that the national rules should, as much a possible, be brought into line with the international code then in use at the Ballsbridge arena. That certainly suited the RDS but one wonders if it satisfied the Ballinasloe Group and those that they represented. These individuals would have wanted more and must have left the meeting feeling that they would have to work on their own if they were to get what they really desired in terms of a national association. Unfortunately the Second World War ensured that no further progress was made for at least another four years.

Pictured watching Iris Kellett win the 1948 Dublin Grand Prix are her father Harry (right in soft hat) and Colonel Joe Hume-Dudgeon (bowler hat) — both founder members of the SJAI. Looking on behind them is Dick Collen of Portadown and Malahide, whose construction company built many RDS buildings. He was also a founder member of the Northern Ireland Show Jumping and Riding Association. (Iris Kellett)

Joe Hume-Dudgeon

Colonel Joe Hume-Dudgeon (pictured right) is a legend in Irish showjumping. His career spanned two world wars and forty years from the 1920s right through to the 1960s. He was a cavalry officer in the British forces during the First World War and then became a member of the infant British Army showjumping team during the 1920s. This is the same officer who jumped on the English side in the very first Aga Khan Trophy at the RDS in 1926 and who was later been such a help to the Irish team on their maiden visit to Olympia. He was also a founder member of the British Showjumping Association when it was formed in 1925. He had family connections with Ireland and in 1938 he set up a riding school in Stillorgan, County Dublin. This school, together with Harry Kellett's establishment, became a major driving force in the development of the sport in Ireland over the next twenty years. Although recalled to the British Army during the North African and Italian campaigns of the Second World War, Joe still found time to visit and compete in Ireland frequently. He attended the meeting between Judge Wylie and the Ballinasloe Group at the 1940 Spring Show and he was later deeply involved in the formation of the Horse Jumping and Riding Encouragement Association in 1944. Joe trained the British showjumping and three-day-eventing teams for the 1948 London Olympics and did the same for Ireland's competitors in the Helsinki Olympiad of 1952. He became the first chairman of the amalgamated Show Jumping Association of Ireland after it came into being in 1954, and remained in that post for ten years. He was a winner of the Dublin Grand Prix and also took the Balmoral Grand Prix on a number of occasions. He was an immense help in bridging the gulf between Northern Ireland and the Republic during the formative years of the SJAI. His son Ian also became a top-class showjumper and an Olympic rider. Joe died in 1966 and will always be remembered as a founding father of Irish showjumping.

It was not until 1944, in Dublin, that a drive aimed at the organisation of showjumping on the island of Ireland again gathered impetus. Shortly afterwards, efforts in the then Irish Free State (now the Republic of Ireland) were matched in Northern Ireland. One gets the feeling that had the initial moves made by the Ballinasloe Group and Judge Wylie proceeded further, they might well have evolved into an all-Ireland body being formed sooner. Wylie had the respect of some of the most influential people in the North of Ireland, like the Bambers and David McCreedy, and it is conceivable that he could have been able to bring them along with him in the short term. The RDS has always been a home away from home to people from north of the border, and an organisation closely linked to Ballsbridge might well have found common acceptance. However, that was not the way matters worked out. Instead, it was to take almost ten years of negotiations before the two sections of the showjumping community — north and south of the border — were to come together as one within the sport they both loved.

Wartime RDS Shows

The Spring Show of 1940 did go ahead as planned and the RDS, hoping for a Horse Show as well, even printed a Schedule for what became known as the Horse Show that never was. However, on 25 June, at a special meeting of the RDS Council, the decision was reluctantly taken to cancel the 1940 Horse Show. It is recorded in the *RDS Proceedings* of that year that the Department of Defence took over the greater part of the premises in early July. However, the main arena later became available to the Society and a curtailed version of the Spring Show was run in 1941. It was decided:

...that every effort will be made to add to the attraction and utility of the Show by arranging jumping competitions to take place as usual in the Jumping Enclosure.[9]

So successful was that decision that the RDS went ahead with a three-day event comprising jumping, art and flower shows to be held on its traditional Horse Show dates — 9–12 August. That same event was run again in the war years of 1942, 1943, 1944 and 1945 until the full-blown Horse Show, with international jumping, was resumed in 1946. The Spring Show, with its jumping events was run in 1941, 1942 and 1943 but had to be abandoned in 1944, '...owing to the transport crisis.'[10]

The results from those events in Ballsbridge during the Second World War years make interesting reading. Listed as winning a number of events at both the Spring and Horse Shows is Colonel Joe Hume-Dudgeon. Also mentioned as winning is a young rider called Seamus Hayes, and near the end of the Second World War one finds the name of Leslie Fitzpatrick. In gymkhana fun events at the 1941 Spring Show, Iris Kellett is recorded as a winner. She also won a pony and trap driving event that year in which there were twenty-three entries. Other prize winners in 1941 included Jack Bamber, and Ballinasloe Group member Father M.J. O'Reilly of Roscommon.

Organisation in the Republic of Ireland

In 1944, as Allied advances in France began to herald the end of the Second World War, the Horse Jumping and Riding Encouragement Association (HJ&REA) was formed at a meeting in Dublin on 19 May — this time without any apparent reference to the RDS or Judge Wylie. On page two of *The Irish Field* of Saturday 27 May 1944, amongst the racing reports, one finds a small announcement saying that an association had been formed to '...cater for, further and carry out jumping and riding competitions.'[11] This was how the birth of the Horse Jumping and Riding Encouragement Association was proclaimed to the world. Former Officer Commanding of the Army Equitation School, and father of future international star Seamus Hayes, Major General Liam Hayes was named chairman. Major Ged O'Dwyer's brother Nicholas was treasurer and its secretary was the Managing Director of Callaghan's Saddlery shop on Dublin's Dame Street, Tommy Goff.

The first event run under the aegis of the new Horse Jumping and Riding Encouragement Association took place on the lands of Timothy Lloyd at Home Lee, Serpentine Avenue, Ballsbridge. Between then and the Horse Show, in August 1944, ten such affiliated events took place; in addition to five at Home Farm there were others at Blackrock and Rathfarnham, as well as the Defence Forces Show in Malahide and in Finglas, where the open class was won by the young Seamus Hayes.

During the 1944 Horse Show, a few days after that Finglas event, the inaugural open meeting of the HJ&REA was held at Jury's Hotel, Dublin. On the Friday of that week, two stories, which reflected the optimistic mood of the new group, shared headlines on *The Irish Times* front page — 'Allies' New Italian Offensive' and 'R.D.S. Show Still A Big Draw.'

The meeting at Jury's Hotel attracted an attendance of forty-nine interested people from all around the country who were in Dublin for the show. A report in the 19 August issue of *The Irish Field* noted:

> *...the primary object of the Association was to encourage and improve the standards of horse and pony riding in all their branches. The following officers were elected for the coming year, Pres. Maj. Gen. L. Hayes. Vice-Pres. Mr. D. McCreedy, Maj. J.G. O'Dwyer, Lt. Col. J. Hume-Dudgeon, Mr. T.McD. Kelly, Sen. W. Quirke. Hon. Treas. Mr. N. O'Dwyer B.E. Hon. Sec. Mr. T.C. Goff.*[12]

One year later, on 9 August 1945, the first full annual general meeting of the new Association was held at the Molesworth Hall in Dublin. By then membership had grown to 202 and an interesting sentence in secretary Tom Goff's report states that this group was:

One of the few priests ever to jump at the RDS was Father O'Reilly of Roscommon. He is seen here on Star with whom he competed at many local shows. He would finish Mass, get on his bicycle and lead Star behind him to go and jump at shows. He was a founder member of the Show Jumping and Riding Encouragement Association in the 1940s.
(Frank O'Brien)

...representative of the whole country, North, South, East and West. The hope expressed at this meeting last year by our Chairman 'that the Association would extend to the whole country' has materialised and we can safely say we have one member if not more in every county.[13]

As political considerations intervened, the hope expressed at the meeting was not to be realised for another nine years.

Founder members

Founder members of the Horse Jumping and Riding Encouragement Association also included Sheila Meyers from the 1939 Ballinasloe Group; Eddie Gallagher, who ran a riding school at Sandymount; Iris Kellett's father Harry; another former Officer Commanding of the Army Equitation School, Colonel Mike Hogan; hunt Master of the Bray Harriers, Michael O'Brien; Senator Bill Quirke, whose son Michael was an enthusiastic showjumper; Herbert McDowell and George Hanbury Robinson.

Each of these founder members put up a donation of £5 — the equivalent of a good week's wages at the time. This money went toward the purchase of a set of fences that could be borrowed by any show affiliated to the new Association. This move was later copied by the various showjumping branches that came into being in the late 1940s and early 1950s. The Limerick/Clare branch, established in 1949, at the suggestion of its chairman Ged O'Dwyer, voted to spend £40. on fences. Both the Dublin and Limerick/Clare efforts were aimed at getting shows to affiliate, and it worked.

In addition to army officers and the founder members, other contributors to the early stages of the HJ&REA included people like Iris Kellett; Mrs Carrie McDowell; Mrs Nettie Magee (owner of Eileen Buckley's superb jumper Nuggett); Reverend M.J. O'Reilly of the Ballinasloe group; Doreen Robinson; future Taoiseach, Liam Cosgrave T.D.; Professor Martin Byrne, who for years acted as vet at the RDS shows; Professor Ned Mullany; Joe McGrath Junior; J.A. Doyle; former army riders Tom Finlay, Jack Stack and Tom Quinn; along with organisers of the Northern Ireland Show Jumping and Riding Association — Jack Bamber and David McCreedy.

Organisation in Northern Ireland

There is no evidence of meetings similar to the one in Ballinasloe having taken place in Northern Ireland prior to or during the early years of the Second World War. As can easily be understood, showjumping participants within the six counties were either called to the conflict or deeply involved in the defence effort at home. According to Maurice Bamber of Ballymena, the Second World War was almost over before any effort at organisation began to take shape. However, this does not at all mean that the sport slumbered during the early 1940s in the six counties of Northern Ireland. In Dromara, Ballinahinch, Newry, Downpatrick, Bangor, Warrenpoint, Omagh, Ballymena, Banbridge, Lisburn, Augher, and in towns small and large all across the province the showing tradition went on. Just as during the First World War, many gymkhana events were run in aid of the Red Cross and other support charities.

In showjumping terms, contact with the then Irish Free State during the years of 1944 and 1945 was limited to the major shows. For this reason and many others associated with divisions on our island, it is understandable that a separate association was to take root north of the border.

Arising out of preliminary discussions that took place during a one-day show held at Balmoral in August 1944, the founding meeting of the Northern Ireland Showjumping and Riding Association (NISJ&RA) was held at Miss Lilly Hall's Imperial Hotel, Portadown, in May 1945. The first event held under the new association's rules was run one month later at Donacloney.

The individuals involved were Captain Hugh Morrison of Aghadowey, David McCreedy of Banbridge, Herbie Forbes of Belfast, 'Packie' McEntee of Clones, Jim Bryson of Loughbrickland, Jack Bamber of Ballymena, Willie Allen of Moira, Jack Heather of Banbridge, Dick Collen of Portadown and Dublin, Dick Garland of Newry, Johnny Reid of Banbridge and Hill Stewart, father of 1984 Aga Khan Trophy winning team-member George Stewart. (Either as owners or riders, just about all of these people are mentioned in jumping results from the 1944 Balmoral Show.)[14]

With David McCreedy appointed as chairman and Alfie Quinn of Banbridge as secretary, the association had drawn up its own comprehensive set of rules within a year. According to newspaper reports of the time, Alfie Quinn had a very difficult time convincing provincial shows that they should adhere to the new code.[15]

In the course of making a presentation to Alfie Quinn at a dinner dance in Portadown in November 1946, showjumping owner Mrs Richard Garland of Newry noted, 'Without Mr. Quinn's efforts, the Association might not have surmounted the various obstacles and reached its present healthy condition.' In his response Alfie was able to report just what that healthy condition actually meant — 185 members and thirty-five affiliated shows. He also said that the Associations rules were becoming more widely accepted, and he understood that Dublin had requested a copy of them. This latter fact was indeed true and the acceptance of these rules some six years later, by the sister association south of the border, was the beginning of the road towards the unification of the two bodies.

One of the first Northern Ireland teams to compete abroad after the war, shown on its return from winning in Glasgow. In the picture are many of the founder members of the Show Jumping and Riding Association — from left to right: Dick Garland; Billy McCully on Happy; Mrs Garland; Jack Heather; Peggy St John Nolan on Outdoor Girl; Miss Sally Hall; Alfie Quinn NISJ&RA secretary and Barney McGlone on Kilbeg.
(Billy McCully)

In the meantime, though joined in a common love of showjumping, two separate Irish organisations attempted to strengthen their positions. Each sought to have the sport grow in an orderly way within its own sphere of influence on its own side of the border. For the most part, the people who lived through all the to-ing and fro-ing during the post-war years of the 1940s will say that a union between the two associations was inevitable.

Amalgamation

Between the end of the Second World War and the eventual unification meeting of the two associations in 1954, there was, of course, constant contact between members of the two associations, both at home shows and on joint-teams that travelled abroad. It is ironic that this joining-up to form teams created both the catalyst that drew the two sections together and the gulf that kept them apart. Most potential team riders of the time simply wanted to compete at the highest level available to them. Others, however, could not ignore seemingly insoluble questions of flag and anthem which were inextricable from the simple desire to be on a strong Irish team.

In contrast to the pre-war years when team contests were almost exclusively confined to army riders, the late 1940s brought about a revolutionary change which opened up these events to civilian competitors for the first time.

In 1947, a combined thirty-two-county civilian side, made up of Iris Kellett, Joan Uprichard, Jim Bryson and Noel Hayes, competed at team events in Newport and Blackpool against England, Sweden and Italy.

In July 1948, an invitation to attend a show in Scotland was extended to the Irish Free State. However, in a reply to a letter from show organisers, The Scottish Light Horse Association, Judge Wylie gave this brief response: 'We regret to inform you that it has not been possible to form a team to represent Éire at your 1948 show.'[16] It appears that the Judge deemed the army riders to be the official Irish team and had not yet come to terms with the problems of selecting civilians.

However, as early as 1946, the Northern Irish Show Jumping and Riding Association was attempting to put a Northern Irish team together that would compete in Scotland. They did take up Glasgow's 1948 invitation and sent the team of Jim Bryson, Barney McGlone and Noel Hayes which put in a winning performance there in the Nations' Cup-type event, ahead of both England and Scotland. In 1949, Billy McCully and Mrs Peggy St John Nolan joined Barney McGlone in another winning team effort.

From all of this, it was inevitable that the best from both parts of the island of Ireland would seek to make up winning sides that could compete further afield. For most of these riders, considerations of anthems and flags were of minor importance, but this was not necessarily true of others — particularly for someone like John Brooke, who had some excellent horses but who was also the son of Northern Ireland's Prime Minister, Sir Basil Brooke.

The reality of Ireland's divided situation dictated that anthems and flags did matter a great deal and this fact could not be just swept aside by the magic of sporting enthusiasm. It had to be faced by people, on both sides of the border, who had the diplomatic talent and personal credentials required to create ways of rising above the divisions of history. Jumping the border was no easy task, but time has proved that it is possible.

As already indicated, even as early as 1946, initial contacts had been made between the two showjumping bodies in relation to the matter of rules. In the years that followed, strenuous efforts were made by both associations to come to terms with the two problems of jumping rules and horse grading. By 1952, people like Lieutenant Colonel Hume-Dudgeon, and the newly elected Chairman of the HJ&REA, Bernard Fitzpatrick, had held preliminary meetings with their northern counterparts, Jack Bamber, Richard Garland and Tom McNabb, during visits to the Balmoral Show.

These meetings became more formalised in gatherings at the Gresham Hotel in Dublin and the Ballymascanlon Hotel north of Dundalk, during 1953. In a later recollection of these initial contacts Bernard Fitzpatrick said:

> ...these meetings had a dual purpose — to standardise the rules for the whole country and to create one organisation north and south together. They were happy get-togethers. Only once was there an argument and that was over the flag to be used by the team.[17]

Commenting on the same issues, Northern Irish rider Billy McCully notes:

> *There was no such thing as instant agreement and over the next period there were constant and passionate discussions about what flag and anthem the Irish team would use. But gradually good sense prevailed and these potentially contentious matters were considered and in the long run agreement was reached.*[18]

Billy also noted at one time, 'I would have ridden on a bran sack if it meant jumping on an international team.'

Agreement, when it did come, was on the basis of a compromise flag — composed of emblems of the four provinces — and a compromise anthem — the little known 'St Patrick's Day'.

Following months of discussion an important meeting was held at the Hibernian Hotel, Dublin, during the 1953 Horse Show week. The delegates representing the Republic of Ireland's Association included Bernard Fitzpatrick, Lieutenant Colonel Hume-Dudgeon, P.E. Mullaney, Nicholas O'Dwyer and Harry Kellett (whose daughter, Iris, had already jumped on the very first combined thirty-two-county team back in 1947). Speaking for the Northern Irish Association were Richard Garland, Jack Bamber Tom McNabb, James Grey and John McNicholl (whose son Brian became an international jumper on all-Ireland teams during the 1960s). As a direct result of this Dublin gathering and some others that took place during the winter months of that year, an amalgamation proposal was put before a general meeting of both the Northern Ireland and Republic of Ireland bodies.

On 14 February 1954, the annual general meeting of the Horse Jumping and Riding Encouragement Association in Dublin unanimously approved the proposals, and two days later they were also accepted by a somewhat less unanimous Northern Ireland Show Jumping and Riding Association meeting in Portadown.[19] The executive committees of the two showjumping bodies met together at the Ballymascalon Hotel on Wednesday, 14 April 1954, to confirm formation of the Showjumping Association of Ireland (SJAI). Richard Garland proposed that Joe Hume-Dudgeon be appointed chairman and the Dublin riding-school owner took the chair of the first Executive Committee of the SJAI.[20] He was an ideal man for the job, as he commanded great respect both north and south of the border. It is proof of his suitability that he held the post of chairman for over ten years until 1965.

It should not be supposed that everything went smoothly after that. The problems of flag and anthem remained and there are many stories, comical and otherwise, about how the Irish, from both parts of the island, coped with these divisive issues.

Above: Eddie Macken and FAN
Schalkhaar on their way to winning the
1996 Kerrygold Grand Prix at the RDS.
(Fotograf Jan Gyllensten AB)

Right: A few of the hundreds of rosettes,
medals and mementoes accumulated by
army rider Dan Corry during a long career
that lasted from 1926 until 1952.
(Donal Corry)

Above: Barbara Fitzpatrick (née Moore) was on the Irish junior team in the late 1960s. She returned after injury to compete nationally and internationally in the 1980s and 1990s with the Optimist, seen here jumping in Paris. (P.S.V. Jean Morel)

Top right: The Show Jumping Association of Ireland logo combined the symbols of all four Irish Provinces. (SJAI)

Bottom right: Army groom Jimmy Doyle (Doyler) who looked after Rockbarton for both Captain Con Power and Commandant Gerry Mullins. He went on to work for some top stables in the USA. (Army Press Office)

Above: Six-times Irish League champion Francis Connors seen here stretching for a gate with Diamond Explosion which was later ridden by Captain Gerry Flynn for the army team. (Anne Hughes)

Right: Private driving showing event at the RDS during the post-war years. (David Gray/RDS Archive)

Opposite page: Commandant
Gerry Mullins and Rockbarton
jumped their way to fourth place in
the World Championships at the
RDS in 1982. (Bob Angrish)

Above: Post-war jumping
at the RDS.
(David Gray/RDS Archive)

Right: Stephen Smith (son of
international rider Ronnie Smith)
from Fintona, scoring a win at
Balmoral in 1998 on Topaz
Diamond. (Joe Kirkpatrick)

Above: Diana Conolly-Carew jumping at the 1968 Olympic Games with Barrymore. (B. Wilkinson)

Left: One of the growing number of amateur and riding club competitors jumping at the RDS. (Anne Hughes)

Above: Pairs jumping at the RDS.
(David Gray/RDS Archive)

Right: *Jessica Chesney, with Diamond Exchange, was the highest-placed Irish rider at the World Equestrian Games in the Hague, where she came tenth.*
(SJAI/Elizabeth Wolle)

Below: *Francis Connors and Conor Swail taking time out at a local show.* (Tony Parkes)

Above: The victorious Irish team of Peter Charles on La Ina, Captain John Ledingham on Kilbaha, Eddie Macken on FAN Schalkhaar, and Trevor Coyle on Cruising during their lap of honour with the Aga Khan Trophy in 1996. (Sportsfile)

Left: The massed Army Bands have been central to the pageantry of the Dublin Horse Show since the beginning of Nations' Cup competition there in 1926. (Susan Kennedy / Lensmen Photography)

However, one way or another, riders found a solution they could live with. Consequently, since that time, Northern Irish riders like Billy McCully, John Brooke, Brian McNicholl, Jim Bryson, Leonard Cave, Brian Henry, Trevor Monson, John Chambers, Vina Lyons, James Kernan, Trevor Coyle, Harry Marshall, Jessica Chesney, and many more, have been able to represent Ireland at international competition level.

Such were the beginnings of the Show Jumping Association of Ireland — an Association still very much in the making.

Betty Fahy, who was first secretary of the SJAI southern region. She later ran the Greenhill Riding Centre. (Irish Press)

The Anthem and Flag

In representing our divided island, Irish teams have always encountered difficulties in relation to the symbols of anthem and flag. Both the problems presented, and the attempted solutions to them, have on some occasions over the years, given rise to tense moments, while on others resulted in quite comical situations.

The Anthem

Even the all-army team of the early years was not immune to difficulties in regard to the Irish anthem. For example, when Irish winner, Major Ged O'Dwyer, was attending the prize-giving ceremony at the 1928 Grand Prix at Biarritz, the French band did not know 'The Soldiers' Song'; Colonel Michael Hogan tried to have them play 'God Save Ireland' as a substitute but instead they played 'God Save the King'. The incident was taken in good humour but when Eamon de Valera's government took over in the 1930s, it was a bit more sensitive toward such matters. At the 1933 Olympia show in London a refusal by the army band to play 'The Soldies' Song' caused some degree of diplomatic upset.

The problem of the anthem came to the fore once more in the 1950s and early 1960s when Ireland began fielding the first civilian teams composed of riders from both Northern Ireland and the Republic. On one famous occasion, in 1963, Frank McGarry, who was Chef d'Équipe of a team that included John Brooke, was told by the Equestrian Federation of Ireland to bring along a recording of the little known tune 'St Patrick's Day' as a compromise anthem. Either by design or otherwise, some place between Ostend and Rotterdam, somebody sat on the old 78-record of 'St Patrick's Day' and smashed it. Another 78-record with 'The Soldiers' Song' on it appears to have survived and it was eventually played for the team in Rotterdam. McGarry was called to task by the Irish Equestrian Federation on his return. He explained that he had done nothing contrary to international rules; and there the matter has stood since then.

The First SJAI Committee

The first Executive Committee of the SJAI was made up of fourteen elected members, seven from both the northern and southern regions:

Northern Region	Southern Region
Jack Bamber	Joe Hume-Dudgeon
Captain The Hon.	
John Brooke	B.J. Fitzpatrick
Richard Garland	Harry Kellett
James Grey	William McLernon
Alfie Quinn	Professor Ned
	Mullaney
Robert Verner	Major Ged O'Dwyer
Senator W. Wilton	Nicholas O'Dwyer
Honorary Secretary	Honorary Secretary
Geoffrey A. Keatinge	Mrs Betty Fahy[1]
Registrar for SJAI — Geoffrey Keatinge	

The Flag

Once, when a Northern Ireland team travelled to Glasgow, the great Billy McCully was asked to look after the flag. He brought along the green Downpatrick banner but during a happy trip across on the boat Billy mislaid the flag. In desperation the following day, he went to a pool hall near the show, got a piece of green baize and tied it to a pole — it appeared to make a very successful substitute for the team parade. 'Nobody in the crowd was any the wiser,' Billy later recalled. The wearing of the Irish Republic's green, white and orange flag on saddle cloths presented a more difficult problem than that, however. The compromise in this case was the four province symbols that were part of the Showjumping Association of Ireland logo. The issue was argued right into the late 1960s but eventually the tricolour was used for team events while the four province emblems along with the word 'Ireland' was authorised for use at CSI (shows without Nations' Cup contests) competitions. Talk of the problem receded in the 1970s when the tricolour became the universal emblem used for all official international events.

Footnotes for Chapter Five

[1] Wylie, The Hon. W.E., *The Development of Horse Jumping at the Royal Dublin Society's Shows*, 2nd Ed., 1952: p. 13.

[2] *Standard Jumping Rules published by RDS and ISA*, 1948: p. 6.

[3] Ringrose, Col. W.A., *The Equitation School, An Cosantóir, the Army Defence Journal*, Dublin: Irish Army, August 1976: p. 227.

[4] Op. cit., Wylie, p. 13.

[5] *The Irish Horse*, 1944: vol. XII, p. 103.

[6] Wylie, The Hon. W.E., *The Development of Horse Jumping at the Royal Dublin Society's Shows*, 1st Ed., 1939: p. 16.

[7] Op. cit., Wylie, 2nd Ed., p. 13.

[8] Ibid., p. 14.

[9] *Proceedings of Royal Dublin Society*, 1940: p. 7.

[10] Ibid., 1944: p. 33.

[11] *The Irish Field*, Dublin: 27 May 1944: p. 2.

[12] Ibid., 19 August 1944: p. 3.

[13] Printed report on first AGM of the HJ&REA.

[14] McCreary, A., *On With the Show*, Royal Ulster Agricultural Society, 1996: p. 105.

[15] *Belfast Telegraph*, 6 June 1945.

[16] RDS Library Archive.

[17] *The Irish Field*, 20 July 1991: p. 31.

[18] Op. cit., McCreary, p. 105.

[19] *Horse and Hound*, 6 March 1954.

[20] Letter from G.A. Keatinge to John Bamber, 1980.

CHAPTER SIX

A NEW GENERATION

Heretofore, the events of the CHIO (Nations' Cup) were open solely to military officers. To-day that is no longer so and many Federations, for want of officers, are obliged to incorporate Amateurs in the composition of teams — tested civilian riders fit to represent their country in International competitions.
— Fédération Équestre Internationale directive, 7 February 1947[1]

In the late 1940s, the ruling body of world equestrian sport, the Fédération Équestre Internationale, then based in Nice, made a far reaching move by allowing mixed teams of military and civilian riders jump in Nations' Cup competitions for the first time. This opened the top arenas of the world to a new generation of riders and at last their pent-up longing to emulate the military heroes of previous years was allowed full expression. However, it was not to be the case in some top Irish, British and US competitions as official cup jumping for the Aga Khan Trophy in Dublin, the Prince of Wales Cup in Britain and the Madison Square Cup in New York remained confined to army riders only. In fact, it was not until 1963, sixteen years later, that civilian riders were allowed join those from McKee Barracks to compete on the Irish team for the Aga Khan Trophy.

During the intervening period, non-military riders with superb talent had to chip away gradually at a tradition that appeared to be frozen in the pre-war era but was never actually written into the rules. The civilians began by jumping in unofficial and some semi-official team events around Europe in the aftermath of the Second World War. Anxious to imitate the great military contests of the 1920s and 1930s, smaller shows in places like Newport, Blackpool and Glasgow began to run team competitions. Team jumping was initiated at Balmoral in Belfast in 1947, but then as now, Ireland's single official Nations' Cup remained the Aga Khan Trophy in Dublin.

The Army Team Restored

Early in 1945, even before the war ended, there were calls for the restoration of the army team. At a committee meeting of the Horse Jumping and Riding Encouragement Association held on 2 March, the following resolution was passed and subsequently forwarded to the Minister for Defence:

This Association comprised those interested in Showjumping request the Government to proceed with the formation of an Army Jumping Team to succeed the Team which so brilliantly represented this country throughout the world up to 1939.[2]

On 12 May 1945, in the *Irish Independent*, the authoritative equestrian journalist of the time, Stanislaus Lynch, wrote:

Seeing particulars of a draft of surplus horses sold recently by the army makes me wonder if any steps are being taken to ensure that an Army Jumping team will be available when hostilities have finally ceased.[3]

A letter from an interested reader printed soon after that article appeared, reflected the longing of many supporters in the country for a return of the glory days:

Congratulations to Stanislaus Lynch for his timely article on the Army Equitation School. It will bring pride and joy to the hearts of Irish men and women to know that this, one of our greatest national glories is to start again, to raise the flag on far foreign lands and to win applause from admiring crowds of every tongue and clime.[4]

In actual fact, the Government had by that time already acted, and just a few days later, the same paper was able to note, '...a cordial welcome has been given to the announcement that the Army team is to be re-formed.'[5]

Somewhat symbolic of that resurrection, pre-war showjumping rider Commandant Jack Stack played the role of Eoghan Roe O'Neill in the very successful and emotive army tattoo held at the RDS in September 1945. Later, in the autumn of that year, he was one of the team members recalled for training. Although missing some of the great names such as Ged O'Dwyer and Cyril Harty, the new school still had other stalwarts like Dan Corry, Fred Ahern and James Neylon; Colonel John Lewis was put in charge as riding Officer in Command.

Well-loved horses like Limerick Lace, Blarney Castle, Miss Ireland and Red Hugh were also missing, but a few of the veteran mounts did return from grass — Duhallow, Tramore Bay, Lough Neagh and Owen Roe. There were also the new recruits such as Clontibret, Kilkenny, Ardmore, Roscarbery, Enniskerry and his full sister Aherlow, all of which had been quickly gathered to join the veteran jumpers.

After the Second World War, places left vacant by non-returning officers were filled by younger men who had joined the army during the war years — among these were Colm O'Shea, Kevin Barry, Louis Magee and the daring Michael Tubridy, who was soon to rival the great names of the past.

At first, the army team appeared to resume where it had left off before the Second World War. The side of Dan Corry, John Stack and John Lewis won the 1946 Aga Khan Trophy, and Michael Tubridy, who had been named to the side as reserve, won the newly instituted World Championship competition in Kilkenny. (The RDS retained the title of World Championship for its Grand Prix event until the Fédération Équestre Internationale began its own Championship in Paris in 1953.)

The year of 1947 brought a series of second placings for the army side in Nations' Cup events in Nice, Rome, Lucerne, London, Dublin and New York.

A brave attempt to do what the pre-war team was cruelly prevented from doing — win an Olympic medal — ended in disappointment when the army squad of Dan Corry, John Lewis and Fred Ahern suffered elimination at the London Olympiad of 1948. The Irish were performing well and were in the running for a medal but their last rider out, John Lewis on Lough Neagh, had two refusals at the third last fence, then proceeded to finish without trying a third time. He was eliminated and so was the whole Irish team.

Success returned briefly in 1949 when the team of Michael Tubridy on Lough Neagh, Colm O'Shea on Rostrevor, William Mullins on the superb Bruree, and Dan Corry on Clonakilty took the Aga Khan Trophy once again. However, it would be another fourteen very long years before Ireland could repeat this winning performance at the RDS.

The disappointment of the London Olympics, combined with other set-backs, proved that re-creating pre-war form was not going to be easy for the Irish Army team. International courses had become much more technical and difficult; even the tracks on the home ground at the RDS had to be modified to suit the demands of visiting teams. The loss of horse purchases during the five seasons from 1940 to 1945 had also affected the army team and the impact of this lasted well into the 1950s.

Unlike the 1930s, when the Irish Army had had international showjumping all to themselves, the years after the Second World War brought to the fore a whole new generation of riders. These were the civilians who had honed their talents during the early 1940s and were now ready to burst onto the world scene. A veritable phalanx of enthusiastic newcomers — Iris Kellett, Seamus Hayes, Billy McCully, Jim Bryson, Peggy Byrne (later Peggy St John Nolan), Joan Uprichard (later Joan Morrison) Iny de Bromhead and many more — were to help write the Irish showjumping history of the 1950s and 1960s.

Men in waiting — between rounds, civilian riders Billy McCully (Caradore); Monkey McGovern (Clones) and Dick McElligott (Tralee). (Billy McCully)

Wartime Spirit

Typical of the wartime enthusiasm that, against the odds, brought many into the sport during the post-war years, was that exemplified by one young Dublin lady, Elsbeth Gailey. She hailed from Kimmage West, which during the 1940s was still very much farm country. Horses in neighbouring fields became her fascination and trips to the Spring and Horse Shows gave her a great longing to ride them over the jumps which she saw at these events. When she reached her sixteenth birthday she had five shillings saved up and decided to spend it on a riding lesson — but at which school? She had seen an advert in the RDS catalogue for a riding school near Stillorgan and decided to try it. So one day she got on her bicycle and, asking directions along the way, finally found herself at the hall door of Colonel Joe Hume-Dudgeon's home. Sadly the lessons cost seven shillings and six pence — two and six above Elsbeth's budget; she turned away but did not give up.

A few days later, she cycled to a less expensive school near the Phoenix Park; but for her five shillings she was put up on a less-than-animated school cob and then left on her own while the trainer went on with his yard work. She decided to save some more and, with the addition of Christmas money, came up with enough for two lessons at Hume-Dudgeon's school. That was the beginning — she ended up working at the school for ten shillings a week and later competed at the RDS. In the early 1950s she studied with the great Rodzianko and on one occasion after the war she travelled to the Horse of the Year Show in London where she was placed a close second in the Combined Training Championship. During her time at Colonel Joe Hume-Dudgeon's she schooled some top international jumping horses — among them was the great Foxhunter, who starred in eighty wins on the British post-war team for Harry Llewellyn. For many years, Elsbeth has been a judge at the RDS, as well as a committee member and worker for the Showjumping Association of Ireland. She is one of many who grew into the sport during the Second World War and never left it. Her story was duplicated hundreds of times by others all around the country at that time.

The Young Iris Kellett

Among the greatest of the new generation of civilian riders was Iris Kellett, whose story is the stuff of true legend. She was born in 1926 at Mespil Road, Dublin, where by the banks of the Grand Canal her father had set up a riding school after the First World War. In 1951 an *Irish Press* story on her early career was headed: 'She Howled to get on Horseback'. When aged nine she walked her pony, Little Sparklet, to the Dublin Horse Show at the RDS where she was awarded a prize as best girl rider. She was known for being wiser than her years — at the age of twelve she was teaching at her father's riding centre, combining the instruction of up to thirty local students with her studies. On M.D., Little Sparklet's successor, Iris secured second place on their first time out at the RDS in 1941. The winner on this occasion was Seamus Hayes on Snowstorm — another legendary partnership of that time.

By 1945, the same year that she passed her London exam for an Instructor Certificate from the British Institute of the Horse, Iris was dominating both the RDS's Spring Show and the Dublin Horse Show. She had six firsts at the Spring Show and three at the Horse Show on Dusky, Spitfire and General Battle. In 1946 she began her unique union with the miracle horse Rusty; he was twelve years old at the time and had never seen a showjumping arena. During the early part of the Second World War he was used as a plough horse, working six days a week and being hunted on Sunday. At the start of his second season he sustained a cut that became septic and he almost died. Later he was nursed back to health by the then retired Major Ged O'Dwyer. Iris loved Rusty the first time she saw him, being ridden by Ged's brother Nicholas, and within four days of buying him had taken a first and a second with him at the Raheny Show. One week later the new partnership of Iris and Rusty secured two firsts and three seconds at the Dublin Spring Show. That August, she and Rusty were third in the World Championship at the Horse Show behind Michael Tubridy. On that occasion she was quoted in the *London Daily Mail* as saying:

> *I hope to win the competition next year to celebrate my 21st birthday. There is no reason why a woman should not ride as well as a man if she has the courage and strength, for her hands are more sensitive as a rule. I suppose I am as strong as most boys.*[6]

Iris Kellett instructing a group of young riders in the early 1950s — left to right: Peter and Leslie Fitzpatrick; Donal and Paul Mulcahy.
(Irish Times)

That is the Iris who Ireland came to know and love — strong, direct, knowledgeable and charming.

By the end of 1947, total victories in her national career had already reached a phenomenal 150. That was enough to have her named as the youngest member of the first combined north/south civilian team, along with other great performers of the 1940s — Jim Bryson, Joan Uprichard and Noel Hayes.

It was the most important Irish win of the trip when Iris and Rusty took the British Horse Society's Regional Championship in Blackpool. This achievement was headlined in the Irish papers and soon the young star became very well known.

The First all-Ireland Civilian Team

Below: an historic photo taken in Newport in 1947 of the first combined north/south civilian showjumping team. Left to right: Jim Bryson of Loughbrickland near Newry on Robert Garland's Happy, Iris Kellett on her own Rusty, Joan Uprichard from Portadown on William Allen's Martha and Noel Hayes from Banbridge on Miss Lilly Hall's Outdoor Girl. Referred to in the British press as an all-Ireland team, the squad also broke new ground by being the first civilian team to represent Ireland at an official FEI CSIO or Nations' Cup meeting. In Blackpool, they were placed a disappointing fourth behind Sweden, Britain and Italy. However, in Newport they were a close second to the Swedes and ahead of Britain and Italy. All four riders got into the prizes during the tour. Jimmy Bryson won a class on Happy and Iris and Rusty won events at both venues including the British Horse Society Regional Championship in Blackpool. *(Jim Bryson)*

As the bitter memories of war began to fade, Iris came to be seen as a refreshing breath of young Irish life — Ireland's young princess on horseback. At the same time, an equally youthful Royal Princess was about to take the crown in Britain. In fact, that same future queen was soon to help catapult Iris into true stardom when she offered a new trophy to the 1949 Royal International Horse Show at the White City Stadium, London, for a competition confined to lady riders.

In the previous year Iris had already gained further fame when she fulfilled her promise of winning the World Championship in Dublin. She and Rusty jumped three superb rounds to take the coveted Irish Trophy ahead of forty-seven contenders from the USA, Britain, Sweden, Ireland and France — the first woman to win the event and only the second civilian ever to do so.

By the following season Iris had forged such a secure place on the Irish scene that when the invitation came for a woman to join the army team on its trip to the White City Stadium, the young twenty-two-year-old Dublin girl was the obvious selection. Her target was the newly created Princess Elizabeth Cup and she took it beautifully. With Rusty she jumped the only double clear round out of forty competitors from around the world for a win that got extensive media coverage back in Ireland.

The following year Iris and Rusty were beaten in the Princess Elizabeth Cup by the smallest fraction of just one quarter of a time fault behind Jill Palethorpe of Britain. However, in 1951 they were back on top after the most closely fought of the three Cups up to that time. Out of the fifty-nine starters just three went clear in the first round. In the next round, against the clock, all three went clear again — Britain's Pauline Talbott in 80.45 seconds and the great Pat Smyth in a very fast 66.25 seconds; but Iris, the last to go, flew the final fence and crossed the line in 62 seconds for the greatest win of her career up to that time. 'We never went so fast before...,' she later wrote in her diary. For good measure, Iris and Rusty jumped another three perfect clears to win the Selby Cup Grand Prix ahead of Seamus Hayes.

The young lady from Mespil Road was at the pinnacle of her career, but before the next season got under way everything crashed agonisingly down to earth. While schooling a young horse at home she was thrown so heavily that the impact shattered her leg and drove her shin bone right into the ground. 'When I looked down, my leg was at such a crazy angle, I thought my boot had come off,' she recalls.

The onset of tetanus delayed her recovery and nearly cost Iris her life. Although she made a number of determined efforts at a come-back between then and 1960, in reality she was out of action for up to ten years and did not return to full competitive form until the early 1960s.

Iris Kellett being presented with the Queen's Cup trophy by a young Queen Elizabeth. During the presentation Iris's horse, Rusty, became restive and pushed his rider forward with his head, almost making her bump into the Queen. Later, at a reception, one of those present commented, 'What could you expect of a republican horse?' (Associated Newspapers)

Seamus Hayes and the brilliant Snowstorm, which he followed to Britain and a winning career during the late 1940s and the early 1950s. Snowstorm was bought in Limerick for £10 and was sold three years later for £1,000.
(Mary Rose Hayes)

Birth of a Genius

During a career that spanned fifty years, the great Seamus Hayes was hailed as a genius on horseback. He was born in Cork in 1924 but his family moved to Dublin in 1930 when his father Major General Liam Hayes was appointed Officer Commanding of the Army Equitation School at McKee Barracks. His first mount was a donkey won in a raffle by showjumping team member Fred Ahern. The young Seamus would listen outside the door while Colonel Paul Rodzianko instructed the team and would then attempt to fulfil the instructions on Ahern's donkey. In 1932 he got his first pony called Amy (after aviation heroine Amy Johnson), and on his fourth outing with this little mare he won a class — the first red rosette among thousands during a memorable forty-year career.

At Limerick Fair, in 1939, his father bought Seamus a grey pony called Snowstorm for £10. Within ten years the bargain Snowstorm was to become one of the most valuable open showjumpers in the world. First, Seamus and Snowstorm won a host of pony classes at local Dublin shows and went on to take the pony championship at the RDS Spring Show in 1943. Then the following year, they took the RDS open horse title ahead of Iris Kellett on Rusty. Seamus was just beginning to demonstrate his extraordinary ability to get the very best out of any jumper he ever rode and more than one of his opponents over the following thirty years was to declare him utterly unbeatable.

A man completely in love with the horse and the sport of jumping, Seamus would ride for nothing else but to be doing what he did best. 'I jumped for joy and not for the money,' he once wrote.[7]

His career all but ended in 1944 when Snowstorm was sold to Dick Garland of Newry for £300. He quickly proved a failure there until Seamus was brought up to County Down to ride him once more. Soon after that the grey was sold again to a Mr Robinson of Yorkshire. Once more, he was a disappointment at a number of shows until again he was joined by Seamus, who by this time, at the age of twenty-one, had told his parents that all he wanted to do was ride Snowstorm.

He got his chance once more when the Robinsons called him over to jump in Manchester. They won the show championship there — the first of hundreds of victories that Seamus would take against the best that Britain had to offer during the next ten years of his exile.

The day after Manchester, Mr Robinson died and Snowstorm had to be sold once more — this time to a Mr Bennett of Sheffield, who insisted that Seamus come with him. That began a series of twenty-five straight wins in a row for the Hayes/Snowstorm combination. Early in 1948, the Bennett string of horses was sold at the Leeds mart. There Snowstorm made £1,000 when sold to Mr Tommy Makin of Allerton Bywater — a hundredfold increase on the original price paid for him in Limerick.

As was now customary, Seamus went with Snowstorm this time to the Makin yard and stayed there for the next five years during which he won every major championship available in Britain. Snowstorm was joined by Limerick, Sheila, Galway Boy and Prince — a team on which Seamus took a total of £15,000 in prize money, a phenomenal amount for the time. Sadly, so willing was the young Irishman to participate in the sport he loved, he never put a true value on his talent. There were some who appreciated his genius but there were others who were more than willing to take advantage of his selfless approach to the sport. Billy McCully, who was coming onto what might be called the professional scene at that same time earned £1 for every first prize won. He says that at one time Seamus worked for just three pence in every pound won; later he got the princely sum of £2 a week.

However, for Seamus, the art of riding superbly, getting totally in tune with the mind and body of every horse he rode, and winning against the best was his real reward. In that sense, he was very well off indeed during his period at the Makin yard between 1948 and 1953. He won the International Championship of England three times, the North of England Championship three times and the Royal Championship three times. He was Leading Rider of Britain in 1948, 1949 and 1951, took the Golden Spurs at Wembley twice and the Selby Cup at the White City Stadium in 1950 and 1951. Also in 1950 he won a record twelve of the thirteen regional qualifiers for the British Showjumping Association Championship of that year.

He left Makin's in 1953 for a new job with the Powell yard in Cheshire but within a week of arriving there he had broken his leg and was out of action for almost six months. After his recovery, a stint at the Massarella establishment in Yorkshire brought wins worth £5,000, but after just one season there, he took the brave step of setting up his own stables in Lamport, Northamptonshire. Calamity struck once more mid-way through the winter of 1955–1956 when in a fall from one of the many difficult horses which had been sent to him, he shattered his pelvis.

However, he returned to the saddle for another ten months — a period of dedicated effort during which his horse box was his home as he travelled to shows in every corner of Britain during the 1956 season. With less than quality mounts he had little success, and as a dour 1956 ended he was offered the chance of returning to Ireland as trainer of the Irish Army team. He took the chance and arrived at McKee Barracks in January of 1957. The first part of a glorious career had ended in anti-climax, but that was not the end of the Seamus Hayes story.

Years of Growth

When the showjumping associations on either side of the Irish border came into being in the mid-1940s, their combined membership had reached about 200 and was steadily growing. So much so that by 1946 this figure had doubled. When the two bodies combined into the new SJAI in 1954 they could muster about 700 members. The next set of hard figures available for the Association appears in records eleven years after that, when, in 1965, numbers had grown to 1,324.

By the time the Second World War was over, the two Associations in Ireland had a total of seventy-five affiliated shows between them. According to a report from 1955, there were then ninety-eight events affiliated to the new combined organisation for that year, but at that early stage in the battle to get animals registered, they had just 211 horses and 111 ponies on their books.[8] However, in 1956, there were 300 horses and 200 ponies registered. By 1965 there were 201 affiliated shows and a total of 1,583 horses and ponies on the register.[9]

Thus, in the years after the Second World War, the sport of showjumping provided plenty of opportunities for enthusiasts, and there was a growing cohort of contenders from all around the island who were ready to compete. Not only that, but out of this group of riders also came the leaders, the people who would give their time and experience to the committees that brought the new Association through some troublesome seasons and on into the 1960s.

Aiding in that effort were a number of local branches of the SJAI which came into existence in the late 1940s and early 1950s. One of the first of these was initiated by Ged O'Dwyer for counties Limerick and Clare. It held its first meeting at the Glentworth Hotel, Limerick on 15 June 1949 when Ged was named as its first chairman and Mrs D.G. O'Donovan was appointed as its first secretary. One of its later secretaries, Donal Johnston, was to become National Chairman of the SJAI in the 1980s. In Mrs O'Donovan's inaugural annual report she noted that the membership had grown from six at the first meeting to sixty by the end of 1950.

The Tipperary/Waterford Branch of the SJAI also came into being around the same time. Its first secretary was Roberta Malcolmson, herself a championship winner in Cork in 1950. The branch's first chairman was Jeremiah McCormick of the Royal Hotel in Tipperary, and Jack Cranley of Lismore was also an active member.

In the early 1950s, the dedication and efforts of Noel Tanner and Billy McLernan resulted in the formation of the Cork Branch — Billy McLernan also served on the SJAI National Executive until his death in 1965. Commandant John Kearney was the first secretary of this branch and was given credit for boosting the early number on the registry through the diligent inclusion of horses and ponies from his area.

The Kilkenny Branch was organised in 1948, and while still competing with horses like the excellent mare Cherry, Jim Finnegan of Stonyford acted as this branch's first secretary.

Also in the early 1950s Frank McGarry of Sligo was building a strong team of jumpers in the west of Ireland. He was a prime mover in the formation of the Connaught Branch and became the first Connaught chairman. He was soon appointed to the SJAI National

Founder member of the Connaught Branch of the SJAI Frank McGarry of Sligo, who put together a team of international horses ridden by Francie Kerins in the 1960s. He also built one of the first large indoor arenas in the country. (Frank McGarry)

Executive, thus broadening representation on that body during the 1960s to include Connaught. Harry McGowan of Mohill was first Connaught secretary and he was joined on the committee by Joe Martin, Paddy Roe, Pat O'Sullivan, Tommy Hughes, Pappy Connor, Tommy Carney, Jim Coyle and Johnnie Byrne. Their inaugural meeting in 1953 was at the Regional Technical School in Tubbercurry.

Champions of the Northern Region

In the years after the Second World War, horse travel was still restricted and, as a result, local stars emerged in each area of the country. Not all of them can be mentioned here but there were some who shone through in each region and had an impact both nationally and internationally.

In Northern Ireland, there was dashing Jim Bryson of Loughbrickland, Newry, who married another young star of the 1940s and 1950s, Barbara Falloon. Jim was not only a member of the first team from Ireland to win at a Scottish international in 1948, but he also took the individual championship there on David McCreedy's Meta. The previous year he had joined Iris Kellett, Noel Hayes and Joan Uprichard on the first north/south international side at Blackpool and Newport. He served on the National Executive of the SJAI for over twenty years and still judges shows at Balmoral and Ballsbridge.

Joan Uprichard, who was on the Blackpool/Newport side with Jim, helped create something of a showjumping dynasty when she married enthusiastic Aughadue owner and rider, Hugh Morrison. She continued to compete and, on one occasion in the early 1950s, swept the boards at the RDS with three different horses. Before her marriage Joan provided a superb pony for Dublin's Shirley Knowles. Later, from their strong string of horses, the Morrisons also provided mounts for riders such as Drew Reid from Banbridge, whose competitive career spanned the 1930s, 1940s and 1950s.

Billy McCully, of Caradore, jumping 6 feet 3.5 inches at Downpatrick Show in 1946 on Happy. The crowd around the fence give an indication of the public interest in this kind of competition at the time. (Billy McCully)

Jim Bryson, on David McCreedy's Westland, competing at his home show in Newry in 1946. Jim was on the first winning team from Northern Ireland that went to Glasgow in 1948 when he also won the championship on Meta.
(Jim Bryson)

A man named Hughie McCully of Caradore also rode Morrison horses for a time during a long career that lasted from 1921 until 1955. His famous son, Billy, began riding in 1939 at the age of eleven and continued to ride very competitively until the mid-1960s. All but impossible to beat at the high jump, he won hundreds of puissance-type events all around the county, riding for the Garlands of Newry and Dick Collen of Dublin. In 1945 Billy set an Irish high jump record of 6 feet 3.5 inches on a horse called Happy. In 1951, he won the first timed competition at the RDS, and in 1952, he jumped 6 feet 8 inches there to win with Ballyblack.

On another horse called November's Eve, which he bought from Father Mullaney of Roscommon, Billy had the most dramatic of wins at the Horse of the Year Show, in Harringay, in 1956. Live on television he took a very bad fall on the opening night there and was deeply concussed; as he was carried limp from the arena, thousands of people in the hall and in the viewing audience believed the Irishman to be dead. However, he arose on the Friday to win the Daily Telegraph Cup, for which he had qualified in Balmoral, and went on to score wins in Ostend and Rotterdam on Killargue. He became a most effective Northern Region Chairman in the 1960s. His even-handed and calm and generous nature was of great benefit to the SJAI in smoothing some tense moments of controversy over dividing it into four equally representative regions. It was during the 1960s that the Northern Region was redefined to comprise the nine counties of the Province of Ulster — since 1954 it had represented only the six counties of Northern Ireland.

Hugh 'Monkey' McGovern is one of those riders who has left a lasting impression of hard work and good humour on the Irish showjumping scene. He was noted for being the first one up on frosty mornings in Clones as he rode-out jumpers for the McEntees or the

McMahons. He was fast and came into his own in the new timed competitions of the 1950s. One newspaper report about a mishap he had at the RDS noted that he was going so fast, it was felt he might land in the next parish. On another occasion Monkey had a mare that would not go into the ring. A steward approached and suggested that there must be a solution. 'I tell you sir,' said Monkey, 'even if I got down and kissed her backside she still would not go in.' In a memorable high-jump battle with Billy McCully at the 1951 Spring Show he cleared 6 feet 2 inches to win on Packie McEntee's Cappamore.

The Bamber brothers, Jack and Maurice, of Ballymena, are synonymous with this period in Irish showjumping. They put hundreds of Irish horses through their hands and many of them went on to become international stars, such as the Maverick for Alison Dawes and Beethoven for David Broome. Jack won the Grand Prix at the RDS in 1937 on Silver Mist, and went on to win so many novice titles there that the present-day championship cup for Grades D and E is named the Jack Bamber Memorial Trophy.

Frank Kernan Junior of Crossmaglen was another great northern rider He won in both Dublin and Balmoral with Sunbeam and many more. In 1948, with a horse named Miranda, he secured the championship cup in Ballinasloe and then, on another horse bought at the fair, went on to become Northern Champion in 1955. His son James became one of Ireland's top international competitors of the 1970s, 1980s and 1990s. The Kernans have also been leading exporters of showjumpers and supplied horses to David Broome and Graziano Mancinelli among others. One of these mounts, Ambassador, was ridden by Mancinelli when he took the individual gold medal at the Munich Olympics of 1972.

Southern Challengers

In addition to Iris Kellett and Seamus Hayes, talented riders also emerged from Leinster, Munster and Connaught during the years after the Second World War — all eager for a share of the limelight. Among them was the brave Ian Dudgeon (a son of Colonel Joe Hume-Dudgeon) who was a brilliant rider but who was severely wounded in Normandy in the Second World War. He had part of his shin bone blown away and it was said that he would never walk again. However, after a two-year battle back to health, not only did Ian walk again but he returned to full competition riding when the war was over. Alongside Iris Kellett and Tim Hyde he was on the Irish side that won a team-type event at Harringay in 1949. With the superb Go Lightly, he took the Dublin Grand Prix in 1950 and returned to win it again in 1952, a year in which he was also a member of Ireland's three-day-eventing team at the Olympics in Helsinki. During his career with Go Lightly he competed in France, Belgium and Britain, and together they took one championship in Balmoral and ten in Dublin for winnings of £4,500 in total — quite a sum at the time.

Dublin Grand Prix winner Ian Dudgeon (left) walking the course at the RDS in 1949 with Prince Bernhard of Holland, who borrowed a horse from Major Eddie Boylan to ride at the show. (RDS Archive)

Jim and Joan Finnegan of the Kilkenny Branch presented with a service to the sport award by President Hillery. Both showjumped and since retiring have given thousands of hours' service in judging boxes around the country. They were among the first to give 1960s international Tommy Brennan horses to ride.
(Show Jumping Association of Ireland)

Having secured a number of creditable individual wins on Kimono and Kireen, Iny de Bromhead of Waterford took her place on the Irish ladies' team. Alongside Iris Kellett and Roberta Malcolmson, she competed at the RDS Spring Show in 1950 and won two individual classes on that occasion, including the championship. Later, when Iris was injured she took her place as lady invitee on the Irish Army team for the White City show in 1952. She came second that year in the Queen's Cup on J.P. McGarry's Tubbernagat. One of her best performers, Wild Venture, was a thoroughbred on which her future husband Waring Willis of Tara, County Meath, had won the Dublin hunter championship of 1950. Their daughter, Jessica Willis, became both a champion jockey and a leading showjumper in the 1980s.

Looking west at this time, the first name that features prominently is that of Father M.J. O'Reilly of Roscommon. He would finish early Mass on Sunday and then head off for the nearest gymkhana on his bicycle, leading two showjumpers behind him. Also from the west came the Gormley brothers, Jim and Brian, from Granard. Jim competed against riders such as Billy McCully, and his brother Brian became an early teacher and mentor of Eddie Macken, and later SJAI Chairman. Further west were the Daly brothers, John and Pat, of Ballina. They not only competed in places like Ballinrobe but would also travel by trap the thirty-five miles down the old Corrib railway line to Galway with two jumpers in tow. There they tested their skills against local riders such as Tommy O'Brien.

To the south, the debonair Dick McElligott of Tralee created legend with the mare Little Nell, who was not only unbeatable at local level but took her share of prizes in Dublin as well. In County Cork, the big names were Anthony Scannell and the Rohan brothers, Phil and Eamonn. In Tipperary there were Roberta Malcolmson, Tim Hyde and Caroline Walsh. Kilkenny had Jim Finnegan and his wife Joan, along with Pat Hutchinson, whose sons and grandsons have been leading lights in the area ever since. Waterford produced Elsie and Tom Morgan, along with Tony Condon.

Tim Hyde of Cashel made the transition from a brilliant National Hunt career (he won the Aintree Grand National with Workman), to an equally winning one in showjumping. After the war he rode Mrs Mary McDowell's Hack On, to a number of great victories all around the country. In 1951, he asked permission to compete at the Royal International in the White City Stadium in London but was turned down; under the rules of the Fédération Équestre Internationale he was viewed as a professional. Just a few days after this disappointing news, Tim sustained a broken back while competing at a show in Clonakilty and never jumped again. The equestrian tradition has been continued by his son and grandchildren.

There was no shortage of riding talent — male and female, poor and well-to-do — right across the breath of the thirty-two counties of

Ireland. Yet at that time, their efforts were mostly confined to national competition as, for the most part, the door to the big international shows was still closed to civilian riders. It was the view of the sport's ruling powers in Ireland that such events were still the special preserve of the army teams. This, combined with the FEI's strict interpretation of the words 'professional' and 'amateur', was largely responsible for the situation at that time.

Amateur versus Professional

With his legal training, Judge Wylie took the rules laid down by the Fédération Équestre Internationale very seriously. If he could find an interpretation that would help a competitor, he would do so, but if not, he would lay down the law as he saw it and then strictly adhere to it. In July 1951, he published the strict definition by the Fédération Équestre Internationale of the words 'amateur' and 'professional' in relation to world showjumping. This was to have a profound influence on the careers of Irish competitors over the next thirty years, particularly with regard to Olympic participation.

Amateur — *An Amateur is one who rides for the love of it and for his own pleasure, with sport as his only object, and not for profit. He derives no profit from the practice of his sport, either directly or indirectly ... He must not come under the definition of Professional.*

Professional — *Any person who makes his living by the practice of his sport. Thus, anyone who deals in horses, hires, rides, trains, works or uses horses for profit, or accepts payment for lessons, is considered a Professional.*[9]

Footnotes to Chapter Six

[1] Royal Dublin Society Library Archive, Dublin.

[2] *Minutes of First Annual General Meeting of Horse Jumping and Riding Encouragement Association*, 9 August 1945: p. 3.

[3] *Irish Independent*, 12 May 1945.

[4] Ibid., 22 May 1945.

[5] Ibid., 25 May 1945.

[6] *London Daily Mail*, London: 11 August 1946.

[7] Hallam-Gordon, C., (ed.), *International Showjumping Book*, London: Souvenir Press, 1968: p. 39.

[8] Keatinge, G.A., *Registration and Records*, The Light Horse, May 1956: vol. 6, no. 54, p. 18.

[9] *S.J.A.I . Executive Committee Minutes*, 4 September 1965.

[10] Op. cit., Royal Dublin Society Library Archive.

A later picture of Judge Wylie as many would remember him on Aga Khan day at the RDS in the 1950s. He presided over Irish equestrianism for forty years from 1920 until 1960 and did more then anyone else for the development of showjumping here during that time.
(Irish Times)

CHAPTER SEVEN

SUMMONING OF THE CIVILIANS

I arrived with my Pioneer Pin, my Fáinne, my bicycle clips and a dream of
riding for Ireland.
— Tommy Brennan team rider of the 1960s and 1970s.

Looking back over forty years to the 1950s, it is difficult now for us to understand why the rising Irish civilian stars of that time were not jumping alongside our army riders at the world's top Nations' Cup events. Correspondence of the period,[1] newspaper reports and the views of people who lived through those years, would indicate that the most basic answer lay in nothing more sinister than financial worries. Judge Wylie, for one, was convinced that the Ireland of the 1950s just could not afford the cost of supporting a civilian team.

The Judge was still the man making the decisions as head of Irish equestrianism. He had been chairman of the RDS since 1937 and a member of its council since 1921. He was hugely respected as the man in charge and just about everything relating to Irish equestrian sport went across his desk. Essentially, he *was* the Equestrian Federation of Ireland, commanding the Irish Shows Association and controlling a new committee, set up in 1947, to select individual civilian riders for international participation. At the time, he wrote:

> *This is the only way I can see of selecting a team with the consent of*
> *exhibitors and also the only way of preventing illicit teams appointing*
> *themselves and jumping at shows in the national name.*[2]

On that selection committee Judge Wylie was joined by veterinary surgeon, Sean Hyde from Cork, and former British team member Brigadier Edward T. Boylan of Hilltown, Drogheda, who was also the Irish delegate to meetings of the Fédération Équestre Internationale abroad. In the early 1950s, this carefully chosen group was expanded to include Granville Nugent representing Ulster, army rider Dan Corry for Connaught and Nicholas O'Dwyer for Leinster.

That this group shared the financial concerns of Judge Wylie is clearly shown in an article that Brigadier Boylan wrote for *The Irish Field* in 1955:

> *Could a team of civilians do as well as the army for our country? I have*
> *no hesitation in saying that I feel sure they could, so far as ability is*
> *concerned, but where is the money to come from to pay the not*
> *inconsiderable expenses of travel to all these widely separated shows. The*
> *choice, if limited to individuals capable of defraying their own expenses*
> *might well embarrass a selection committee…my opinion is that on the*
> *grounds of expenses alone we could not afford to finance a civilian team*
> *to represent our country as adequately and as widely as the army team*
> *now does.*[3]

There is little doubt that Judge Wylie would have expressed his concerns in the same way as Edward T. Boylan had done. The Judge had negotiated the formation of the army team in the first place and had been a party to the miracle of having it restored after the war. In addition, he knew how civil servants felt about the expenditure involved. He was more aware than anyone of the possibility that the army team could be disbanded if it were not to represent the country and the Irish horse itself — not only in the most important home event at the RDS, the Aga Khan Trophy, but also at the major Nations' Cup shows abroad in places such as London, Rome, Lucerne and New York.

He was privy to the diplomatic representations made to the Irish Government by countries across Europe and in America to have the popular Irish Army team compete at their Nations' Cup events. He was also very conscious that this participation abroad rebounded to the benefit of the Dublin Horse Show in terms of top team participation here.[4]

Almost until the time of his retirement from the RDS in 1959, Judge Wylie adhered to the conviction that there was no other way of having Ireland represented at the top events around the world than through the efforts of the government-supported army team. Particularly during the mid-1950s, when pressure for a mixed team began to build, he did not appear to consider the possibility of fielding combined civilian/army squads. From his point of view the choice was either army or civilian and he could not envisage the sport itself financially supporting a civilian team.

Although it is easier now to interpret Wylie's attitude as being somewhat short-sighted, it is understandable that, in the years prior to the emergence of commercial sponsorship, he could hold that view. However, intelligent man that he was, Judge William Evelyn Wylie gradually shifted with the times and in the end left a very generous legacy when he retired in November 1959 — the establishment of a civilian-team riders' fund, in which the RDS agreed to match private contributions pound for pound. In co-operation with the Show Jumping Association of Ireland, this initiative was instigated in April 1959, and between then and 1979, when the fund was wound up, the RDS contributed a total of £38,867 to it. This was matched by private contributions, from the SJAI itself and also, in the late 1960s, from a controversial 5 per cent levy on prize money awarded at SJAI-affiliated shows. This fund eventually opened the door for a revolutionary change in the life of Irish international showjumping.

Prior to his death in 1964, Judge Wylie was to see a combined army/civilian side win the 1963 Aga Khan Trophy. Also in the autumn of that same year he was to witness a side composed of three army men and one lady rider travel together to compete for Ireland on the prestigious North American circuit.

The Army Under Pressure

Prior to the Second World War, the army riders were seen as heroic underdogs going out to take on the world, but after the team's revival in 1945 these pre-war heroes were somewhat cast in the mould of establishment figures. They now had to stand their ground against new and upcoming civilian stars, who took great delight in beating the men from McKee Barracks at home shows, and appeared ready to fill their boots on the international stage as well. In a way, army riders were then faced with a Catch 22 situation — if they won, it was expected of them, and if they did not, they were told that civilians could have done better.

However, it was not entirely that simple. The army team of that time was up against a whole new situation on the world circuit. As evidenced by Colonel Fred Ahern's annual reports in the *Irish Horse* during the early 1950s, both the courses and the opposition that the Irish riders faced, in Europe and the Americas, were getting more and more daunting. Of a trip to Mexico in 1952 he reported the courses as being, '...so big and difficult that only a great horse well-ridden, could win over them.' In fairness to the men from McKee Barracks, they were by no means buried at the big events during these years of change in the sport. In 1952, for example, they scored thirteen unquestionable international victories including the Nice Grand Prix, the Welcome Stakes in London and the Whitney Stone Trophy at Madison Square Garden which was won by the great Dan Corry, in his final year of competition. That same year there were firsts in Dublin, New York, Toronto, Mexico and Lucerne for Captain Colm O'Shea. Michael Tubridy had taken the Grand Prix in New York in 1950, over a very innovative track, and scored his second championship win in Dublin in 1953. Captain Kevin Barry won the King's Cup in London in 1951, and also the Rotterdam Grand Prix of 1954. The team took Nations' Cup honours in Nice in 1950; Toronto in 1951 and in New York in 1953.

Course Construction [5]

Courses between the two world wars were generally built for army riders by course builders with military backgrounds and comprised rustic fences, banks and ditches — similar to a modern derby course. However, after the Second World War course construction became much more refined. Greater variety was introduced in terms of colour and features; fences got higher and wider, poles got lighter and the cups that held them became more sophisticated. The illustration depicts one of the courses from Madison Square Garden in 1950, the year Michael Tubridy won the Grand Prix there. It demonstrates typical American inventiveness of the time and points the way toward the tracks of today. In Britain, the post-war innovator was Mike Ansell who designed the fourteen-fence course at the White City Stadium, London, for the 1950 King's Cup. It would have been very similar to the one jumped by Captain Kevin Barry when he won the following year on Ballyneety.

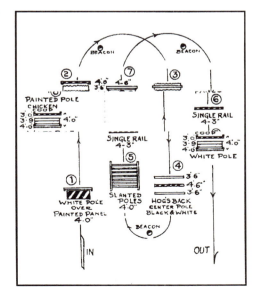

(Showjumping and Horse News)

Great post-war army team performer, Captain Michael Tubridy, seen here winning the 1946 Grand Prix at the RDS on Kilkenny. Sadly very soon after his retirement from the Irish Army in 1954 Michael was killed when riding a young horse at Trimblestown Stud, Trim, which he then managed for Joe McGrath. (Irish Times)

Despite such success by the army riders, it was still not enough to attract the kind of headlines that Iris Kellett received for her Dublin and London successes between 1948 and 1951. For one thing, the army team was not winning at home in the all-important Aga Khan Trophy competition. Changes to the Ballsbridge course, like the removal of approach railings to the fences, the introduction of electric timing and the reduced use of the banks and other natural obstacles, deprived them of some of their previous home ground advantages. They were out on level ground against ever improving foreign sides from Britain, Germany, Italy, France and the USA. Soon *The Irish Field* was bluntly asking, '...should our jumping team be open to civilians?' One article in 1955 declared:

> *...we do not have enough army riders with experience to go into the fray against the champions of other nations. The army, the RDS and the Show Jumping Association of Ireland would do well to probe the possibilities in order that the best use might be made of our unlimited sources of raw material.*[6]

In 1959, frustration boiled over in the same paper following one more Aga Khan Trophy defeat at the hands of Britain, 'One could almost pick blindfolded three civilian teams at the last Dublin Horse Show, which would have been hard to beat in any Prix de Nations competition,' it optimistically declared.[7]

Comments like that must have deeply hurt an army side that was bravely struggling to stay in touch with modern developments in the sport. Just after the Second World War they had installed a whole new schooling ground at McKee Barracks;[8] in 1949 they brought in Major Severyn Kulesya of Poland as trainer and, in an effort to regain the old magic, Colonel Paul Rodzianko was recalled from March 1951 to August 1952.

No Irish jumping team competed in the Olympic Games of 1952 in Helsinki — ostensibly, because of a clash of dates with the Dublin Horse Show. This drew some further bitter criticism in the press. The *Irish Independent* even went so far as to suggest that the RDS and not the Minister for Defence was running the army team. A stinging editorial commented:

> *When an Irishman remembers how Irish soldiers fought in their night shirts at Cremona, it makes his blood boil to think that to-day's Army Jumping Team, with all the facilities placed at its disposal by the indulgent tax-payer's money, will be drawing record crowds to the Dublin Horse Show when it ought to be fighting to raise the Irish Tricolour in Helsinki, in the greatest 'Prix des Nations' event in the world.*[9]

Instead of the stated difficulty of the RDS date clash, the reason for not sending a team might more probably have been based on the assessment of the school's strength by the then Officer Commanding, Colonel Fred Ahern. Some of the horses were off-form and no new world-beating equine stars had yet been discovered. In addition, he may have felt that there was no realistic chance of an Irish team taking a medal in Helsinki, and therefore, he could not justify the cost of going there. (A civilian three-day-event team made up of Ian Dudgeon, Mark Darley and Harry Freeman-Jackson did compete at the Helsinki Olympics and took sixth place in the overall team ranking. It was reported that the bill for their training and travel was £3,000 and that they had only enough money to get themselves to Finland at the time of their departure. Eight years later, in 1960, the estimated cost of sending a team to Rome for the same event was £5,000.)

The mid to late 1950s was a time of change at the Army Equitation School. In 1954 both Colm O'Shea and Michael Tubridy retired and what was called the third generation of officers took over. This included Billy Ringrose of Limerick, who had joined the Army Equitation School in 1952, followed by his brother Des, eighteen months later. They teamed up with Pat Kiernan, Tommy Moroney and Roger Moloney. In 1957 they were joined by Ned Campion, Sean Daly, Pat Griffin, Eamonn O'Donoghue and Larry Kiely. Fresh horses, such as Liffey Vale, Flower Hill, Glencree, Ballynonty, Shannon Grove, and Greenore, replaced some of the older mounts. It was also at this time that Seamus Hayes was brought in as instructor from 1957 to 1959. In 1959, the great eight-year-old gelding, Loch an Easpaig, added an extra touch of world class to the string at McKee Barracks. He was to have five major Grand Prix wins over the following few years with Billy Ringrose.

Colonel Billy Ringrose

A super athlete and naturally talented rider, all of his formal training in the saddle was done in the army. Thus he carried on the classic style that had been the tradition there since Rodzianko's time. His early mounts included Ballynonty, on which he won the Grand Prix of New York in 1956, Flower Hill and Liffey Vale with which he competed at the Equestrian Olympic Games in Stockholm that year. However, it was to be with the brilliant jumper Loch an Easpaig that the name Billy Ringrose would always be associated. This champion horse was bred by the Delahunty family in Mullinavat, County Kilkenny, and sired by Knightly Crusader out of a great Marshal Ney dam, who was twenty-five years old when he was born as her nineteenth foal. He first got the name Crusader and spent his early years as a hunter and farm workhorse. Once, when a prospective purchaser arrived to look at him, he ran off and jumped out of the field then back in again. He was then bought as a jumper for £150 and Vincent Lawlor rode him until 1959, when he was sold to the Irish Army for £1,500.

Colonel Billy Ringrose riding the great Loch an Easpaig. (RDS Archive)

He and Billy Ringrose appeared to be made for each other and their performances together over the next eight years were to prove it. They were highest placed of the Irish at the Rome Olympics of 1960 and they returned to the Eternal City in 1961 when Billy gave one of the greatest performances of his career. Live on pan-European television and in the presence of the Queen of England, he came first and second in the Grand Prix on Loch an Easpaig and Cloyne respectively. He and Loch an Easpaig scored other Grand Prix wins in Nice and Marseilles, and also in Harrisburg in the USA. They took the Daily Mail Cup in London and were on two winning Aga Khan Trophy teams. This brave horse finished his career as dramatically as he had lived it; he jumped a clear round in the 1967 Nations' Cup at Ostend and then fell dead at Billy's feet having suffered a heart attack. Retired from competition riding in 1972, Colonel Ringrose later served as Officer Commanding of the Army Equitation School and is main arena director at the RDS.

In terms of team contests, all this army effort of the 1950s was bound to bear some fruit. This it did in 1954, when the side of Billy Ringrose, Brendan Cullinane, Pat Kiernan and Kevin Barry produced a fine Nations' Cup win in Rotterdam. That same squad (minus Cullinane) took the Harrisburg Nations' Cup in 1955 and went on to win again in Toronto two weeks later. When the equestrian part of the 1956 Olympic Games could not go to Australia that year, because of quarantine restrictions, Judge Wylie and the RDS made a determined effort to bring the showjumping to Ireland; unfortunately lack of funding resulted in failure. The Games went to Stockholm instead and an Irish Army team of Barry on Ballyneety, Ringrose on Liffey Vale and Kiernan on Ballynonty finished a respectable seventh out of twenty nations.

Nonetheless, on the home front, at a growing number of SJAI-affiliated shows and at the RDS itself, the army riders were finding it increasingly difficult to beat the rising civilian tide. More and more the pressure grew to have some of these new faces appear on the Aga Khan Trophy team. As Tommy Wade puts it,

> *...here we were beating the army lads around the country and in the big events at Dublin and yet when it came to Aga Khan day we had to sit in the stand and watch them get beaten. Something had to give.*

The Dublin Shows

Bernard Fitzpatrick, a Dublin businessman and Chairman of the Horse Jumping and Riding Encouragement Association, was intent on upgrading the quality of home events available to the Society's members. He spearheaded a post-war drive to create new specialist shows dedicated to the sport of showjumping in and around the capital city. Along with a close-knit and dedicated band of helpers that included Mattie Harpur, Dan Martin, Tommy Condron, Charlie Wilson, Brian Crowley and Joe Hickey, well-organised fixtures came into being at Mount Merrion, Manresa, Dromcondra, Samacora (Kimmage Manor), Terenure, Finglas and Glenageary. Most of the events were run for charity and also made a small amount of money. However, at the first Manresa show the organisers were left short by £16. However, Bernard's son Leslie had won that amount in prize money and he returned his winnings in order to balance the books. When these events first began some of the fences looked rather dilapidated but improvements were made as time went on.

Civilian Champions

In the late 1950s and early 1960s, while strains remained, the amalgamation of associations north and south of the border developed and the new Show Jumping Association of Ireland grew in strength. Its rule book, published in 1954, was beginning to gain respect at shows around the country, and in 1962, the new SJAI secretary, Fanny Peard, was able to state:

> *This is the second year that the Central Registry has functioned from Dublin and I feel that progress has been made in many ways and that the members are beginning to realise that the Showjumping Association of Ireland is a force to be reckoned with in this sport.*[10]

In the years after the Second World War, there had been constant growth in the number of competitions on offer around the country.

Newly created branches in Connaught, Leinster and Munster helped this development by putting together sets of fences which brought improvements and more diversity to the kind of courses that could be built.

Over a ten-year period, between 1946 and 1956, a new series of Sunday shows had came into being in and around Dublin. By 1957, of the fifty shows affiliated to the Southern Region of the SJAI, one third of these specialised showjumping events were indeed concentrated in and around the capital city. However, agricultural events also came in to being at that time, in seventeen more of the twenty-six counties. By that same year, a further forty shows had been affiliated to the SJAI for the six counties of the Northern Region.

Soon after its formation, in 1954, the Show Jumping Association of Ireland instituted three annual points championship cups — The Pixie Cup for riders of small ponies; the Ferguson Tractor Cup for the larger ponies and, for horses, the Caughoo Cup (named after the McDowell family's Grand National winner). These trophies became the measure of civilian success.

By 1960, although the contacts between them were still being handled gingerly, the SJAI, the RDS and the Equestrian Federation of Ireland were beginning to work more closely together for the development of national showjumping.

With all of this burgeoning jumping activity going on in the 1950s, it is no wonder that some superb new talent emerged — part of it out of the big schools in Dublin but more which came raw and ready from the country — eager to take on not only the army but the graduates of Joe Hume-Dudgeon's and Iris Kellett's as well.

One of those with the benefit of coaching from both Iris Kellett and Colonel Hume-Dudgeon was Leslie Fitzpatrick, or 'The Captain' as he was later called. It was under doctor's orders that Leslie began riding at the age of five. He was born with curvature of the tibias and to correct it both his legs had been surgically broken. As part of his recuperation, riding was recommended and at first he hated it. When it came to learning how to jump he fell off five times at the first fence. Nevertheless, he didn't give in, cleared it on the next attempt, and went on to be one of the most talented and determined competitors that Ireland has ever produced. At his very first attempt, he won the RDS Spring Show Championship on a little pony called Pixie.

As an indication of just how well Leslie rode, he won the Pixie Cup on Brian then the Ferguson Tractor Cup with Dancing Dandy before taking the Caughoo four times in a row, from 1955 to 1958, on Hi Society. When he was seventeen, his father bought Hi Society for him at Ballinasloe Fair from John Hassett of Spancil Hill, County Clare for £170 and £10 back for luck. His name derived from that of the street where the deal was done. Within a year he won his price back in prizes and was soon to bring Leslie onto the first ever Irish civilian team in 1960. He and Hi Society were to help score early civilian team wins in

DALKEY GYMKHANA

Horse Jumping, Riding, and Driving Competitions

Sunday, June 10th, 1945

at

CASTLE PARK, DALKEY

(By kind permission of D. S. Pringle, Esq.)

Commencing at 2.30 p.m.

GYMKHANA COMMITTEE:
Chairman : Charles L. O'Reilly, Esq.
Hon. Secretaries : Arthur K. O'Duffy, Esq., Queen's Hotel, Dalkey.
Thos. C. Goff, Esq., P.C., 35 Grey Gates, Mount Merrion, Blackrock.
Hon. Veterinary Surgeon : Miss B. D. Taylor, M.R.C.V.S.
Judges : Col. M. Hogan and Mr. N. O'Dwyer.
Chief Steward : Mr. J. Walsh.

PROGRAMME - - - - 6d. each

This happened 100 years ago

"Dalkey Boat Races this Day.—Mr. Hornick, Proprietor of Queen's Hotel, respectfully apprises those Ladies and Gentlemen who intend visiting Dalkey to-day, that, as usual, he has made every preparation for their creature comforts and accommodation. Wines of Finest Quality."

Extract from "Freeman's Journal" of Saturday, September 17th, 1845.

Visit the QUEEN'S LUXURY LOUNGES
IN THE HOUSE WITH A TRADITION.
GOOD 100 YEARS AGO—VERY GOOD TO-DAY.

SAMACORA GYMKHANA

(Under the auspices of the S.J.A.I.)

in aid of St. Mary's College, New Church and Building Extension Fund

KENILWORTH SQUARE
RATHGAR

Sunday, 23rd May, 1954

at 2.30 p.m. Sharp

Patron :
Very Rev. J. J. Gilmore, C.S.Sp.
Chairman :
C. M. Wilson, Esq.
Judges of Jumping :
N. O'Dwyer, Esq., M.R., Prof. P. K. Mullaney, M.R.C.V.S.;
G. H. Robinson, Esq., B. J. Fitzpatrick, Esq.
Chief Steward :
J. J. C. Bermingham, Esq.
Hon. Referees :
Lt.-Col. J. Home Dudgeon, O.B.E., M.C.,
F. R. Doherty, Esq.
Hon. Treasurer :
James A. Kavanagh, Esq., F.B.I.
Hon. Veterinary Surgeon :
Prof. Martin Byrne, M.R.C.V.S.
Ambulance Service :
Knights of Malta
Hon. Secretary :
Frank Reddy, Esq.
Hon. Call Stewards :
Matt Harper, Esq., D. Martin, Esq., John Doherty, Esq.
NOTE—Every care will be taken, but no responsibility or liability can be accepted for Accidents to Horses, Riders or Members of the Public.

PROGRAMME - - - SIXPENCE

PRINTED BY ABBOTT, THE PROGRAMME PRINTER, DUBLIN.

ENTRY FORM

GYMKHANA

(Under the Rules of the Horse Jumping and Riding Encouragement Association)

WILL BE HELD AT

DONABATE, CO. DUBLIN

IN AID OF PAROCHIAL FUNDS

ON

SUNDAY, 10th JULY, 1949

Events No. 1 will commence punctually at 2.30 p.m.

Every precaution will be taken, but the Organising Committee accept no responsibility for any accident to any Horse, Rider or Individual.

Completed Entry Forms, together with Fees, to be forwarded to reach SEAN MORAN, JUNR., *Hon. Secretary*, Somerton, Donabate, Co. Dublin, not later than MONDAY, 4TH JULY, 1949.

BUTLIN'S MOSNEY HOLIDAY VILLAGE
(Nr. LAYTOWN, CO. MEATH)

HORSE JUMPING COMPETITION

(Under the Auspices of the Littlegrange Harriers Hunt Committee and The Horse Jumping and Riding Encouragement Association)

ON

SUNDAY, AUGUST 14th, 1949

2 p.m.–6 p.m.

OVER £100 IN PRIZES

INCLUDING

THE BUTLIN CHALLENGE CUP

For full details of Events see Entry Form.

ALL JUMPING EVENTS TO BE JUDGED UNDER THE RULES OF THE IRISH SHOWS ASSOCIATION.

ADMISSION - - - - 2/6
(Children under 10 years) 1/-

See Entry Form for special G. N. R. Rates for transportation of Horses to Mosney.

THE TEMPLE PRESS LTD., DUBLIN.

IS IT A SUCCESS?

WE THINK SO, BUT COME AND SEE FOR YOURSELF

"MARLAY"

HORSE SHOW & JUMPING COMPETITIONS

1943 Entries Totalled 79
1944 ... 111
1945 ... 140
1946 ... 164
1947 ... 254
1948 ... 260

HUNDREDS OF SPECTATORS

LAST YEAR SAW THE CREAM OF IRELAND'S JUMPERS COMPETING FOR THE "MARLAY" PERPETUAL CHALLENGE CUP, AND IN MANY OTHER EVENTS.

THOUSANDS OF SPECTATORS

ARE WANTED AT THIS YEAR'S EVENT, WHICH TAKES PLACE ON

SATURDAY, 23rd JULY

Commencing at 1.30 p.m. prompt.

AT

"Marlay," Grange Road, Rathfarnham

Hon. Secretary :—
P. A. LOVE,
MARLEY, RATHFARNHAM.
Telephone 96276.

TEAS. ICES. MINERALS.

Admission: Adults 1/6; Children 6d.; Cars 2/6.

D.P.S., 30 Lr. Baggot St., Dublin. Phone 65533.

MACRA NA FEIRME

KILTERNAN & NORTH EAST WICKLOW YOUNG FARMERS' CLUBS

GYMKHANA

AT

MONASTERY, ENNISKERRY

(by kind permission of Mr. Fenelon)

ON

SUNDAY 14th AUGUST, 1949

COMMENCING AT 1.30 O'CLOCK

Entries close on Saturday 6th August, 1949

With :—H. M. FITZPATRICK, Kendalstown, Delgany; F. KELLETT, Ballyogan Road, Carrickmines; J. LITTON, Kilternan.

FEES MUST ACCOMPANY ALL ENTRIES

TOBIN, PRINTERS, BRAY.

NAAS HARRIERS

Jumping Competitions

..... and .....

GYMKHANA

•

JOCKEY HALL

The Curragh Co. Kildare

(By courtesy of Jockey Hall Ltd.,)

•

SUNDAY, 3rd JULY

Commencing 2.30 p.m. Prompt

Horse Jumping and Riding Encouragement Association

British Legion

GYMKHANA

at

Kilruddery, Bray,

(By kind permission of The Right Hon. The Earl of Meath)

on

Saturday, 9th July,

JUMPING STARTS AT 3 O'CLOCK, SHARP

PROGRAMME - - 1s.

HIBERNIA PRINTING WORKS, ADELAIDE ROAD, BRAY.

Aachen, Ostend, Wiesbaden and London against Olympic champions. It was during this time that Leslie became known as 'The Captain' because he was put in charge of seeing that the agreed SJAI 'St Patrick's Day' anthem and Four Provinces flag were used. However, he admits, with a mischievous wink, that he did not make a very good job of it.

Another young rider coming onto the Dublin circuit during the 1950s was Diana Conolly-Carew of Castletown, Celbridge, County Kildare. It was one of her ancestors who bought the first RDS Horse Show champion on Leinster Lawn back in 1868. Thus, right from the beginning, her family had been deeply involved in the new sport. Castletown was used as training ground for Ireland's Olympic three-day-eventing teams in 1952 and 1956 and it was also the home of annual Horse Trials. Diana's early training was with the Pony Club and, in 1958, she became one of the youngest masters of hounds in Ireland at the age of eighteen. Prior to that time, Diana had excelled in pony jumping events with Mick be Nimble, Donny and Copper Top on which she won championships in Edinburgh, Belfast and Dublin. In junior competition Diana and Donny jumped seven clear rounds to win the Balmoral championship in 1954 and 1955. Her first top-class horse was Tubbernagat, which her grandmother leased for her from J.P. McGarry of Sligo and which had previously been ridden by Iny de Bromhead. With this mare she went clear in the preliminary round of the Junior European Championship at the White City Stadium in 1957 and was well on her way to winning it when, in her enthusiasm, she went before the bell and was eliminated.

> My name was called and just then the Queen Mother arrived. I waited while she was seated. My name was called again and off I went [the bell had not yet sounded]. Next thing I heard the elimination buzzer and I was out.

She made up for that mistake later in her career when acting as Chef d'Équipe to Ireland's first Junior European medal winners.

It was said of Diana, at the time, that she had a magnificent and kindly way with her horses and, as a result, they all performed very well for her. That could certainly be said of her next star — the superb grey, Barrymore. This little 15.3-hands-high thoroughbred was bought for £240 and trained by Diana herself. He won a hack class at the RDS in 1959, was then brought slowly up through the showjumping grades and was ready when Diana Conolly-Carew's name was called for the Aga Khan Trophy team in 1963.

Also ready for that call-up was the indomitable Tommy Wade of Tipperary, who had to fight every stride of the way to the big time. Above all else Tommy was the quintessential competitor; he thought, schemed, and dreamed of being first. It was not just for the money involved — he had a strong amateur side to him as well. For him, winning was everything as was the proof of such winning — cups, medals and trophies were what he also set his mind on. In 1961, he heard that during the coming season, there would be a gold watch on offer for a competition in Belgium, a golden tankard for another in the south of England and a gold medal for the SJAI Championship in Belfast. With the same type of confidence that the great American baseball hero Babe Ruth exhibited when he pointed his bat at a spot in the stand and planted a winning home-run hit in the exact spot, Tommy set out to win all three 1962 gold awards and did so. He still has these trophies as proud family possessions at his home in Dundrum.

Riders in the west competing at a show under Cnoc na Rea, Strandhill, Sligo in the 1950s — left to right to right: Jimmy Gormley, Jimmy Kilfeather, Francis Kerins and Pat Ann Prinz.
(Champion Art Studios)

Tommy won a lot more than that though. In fact, over a ten-year period from 1957 to 1967, he was to become the greatest folk hero the sport has ever had in Ireland. His avowed mission was to take on the Dublin and Irish Army establishments and beat them. He did that so superbly, crowds would flock to shows just to see him and the great Dundrum jump. He was a determined character and was willing to argue showjumping rules with judges, stewards, show organisers, the SJAI and EFI, and anyone else, in order to make his point if he felt he was not being fairly treated. To people all around the country, who might otherwise know nothing about showjumping, the names Tommy Wade and Dundrum soon became very familiar.

From a smallholding in the townland of Boherlahan near the town of Dundrum, the Wade family ran a farming and agricultural contract business. His father, James Wade, encouraged all of his three sons Tommy, Eddie and Jimmy, in their enthusiasm for jumping. With ponies called Croughmore, Pinto and Little Chip, Tommy gained his first Dublin successes by winning three Horse Show competitions when he was fifteen and sixteen in 1953 and 1954. His introduction to horse classes began with Ballingaddy on which he beat the Olympic rider, Harry Freeman-Jackson, at the Charleville show on their first outing together in 1956. This gelding was later to win classes for Tommy in Dublin, Balmoral, Cork and Clonmel. For Lady Dorothy Mack of Dublin he also scored on Brown Trout and Grasshopper. During those early years between 1955 and 1958, he and his brothers brought on a host of young jumpers for their father — Golden Sovereign, Sallypark Rover and Setanta, to name but a few.

The name Tommy Wade will always be synonymous with the name of his champion horse, Dundrum. Fate brought them together in 1955 and the magic partnership won the hearts of the public from whom they enjoyed a massive following all around the country. Part Connemara pony, part thoroughbred (by Little Heaven), Dundrum was just as tough and single-minded as his future rider. He was first used as a cart pony by his breeder, Mrs Croagh, for bringing packages up from the railway station to Tierney's shop in his namesake village of Dundrum. However, one day he decided that he was having none of that and ran away, smashing the cart into little bits. With what was

Early riders on the civilian teams of the 1960s — Tommy Brennan, Seamus Hayes, Brian McNicholl and Leslie Fitzpatrick in Lausanne. (Jean Bidel)

left of the shafts dangling by his side, he was found some three miles away enjoying his freedom in a field which he had somehow managed to jump into. James Wade bought him for £15 plus a replacement pony in the hope that the runaway would make a good jumper. In fact, it turned out that jumping was in the little rebel's blood — his dam, later bought by the Wades, won two competitions at Cork show before going on to a successful career in England; his father, Little Heaven, created a dynasty of jumping sires from his crosses in the Connemara line.

Dundrum was little more than 15 hands high and in early competitions at local shows Tommy would first win with him in a pony class and then go on to take the open and whatever else was on offer in the horse section. However, while local shows were fun, Tommy's sights were set on a wider world. He had the feeling that Dublin-based organisers and riders were creating a monopoly in the sport and once declared, '...we from the country are being ignored....' From the moment he sat up on Dundrum and found just what this wonder horse could do, he was intent on shifting the balance of showjumping power in Ireland.

Tommy's first big opportunity came in 1957 when he took on Leslie Fitzpatrick and Diana Conolly-Carew, among others, to win the Dublin Horse Show's civilian championship. The following year he travelled to Belfast to beat riders from the six counties in four competitions — including the championship itself. For Tommy, 1958 continued in a similar vein as he and Dundrum scored at shows all around the country and had a treble of wins at the RDS. One of these was the high wall, and during his later career the little horse was to endear himself to television audiences for his performance in this particular competition. When performing at events such as Wembley, he would first disappear out of sight behind the wall, and then, as if by magic, rise over it to win against all apparent odds. On one occasion, during a power failure in Ostend, he won the Puissance in the dark over a wall of 7 feet 2 inches and was depicted the following day in the Belgian papers as having sprouted wings. After one victory in London that had been intently watched on television in his home county, he was paraded into Dundrum town on his return like an All-Ireland winning Tipperary hurling team, complete with marching bands. Tommy and Dundrum were indeed ready to justify fully the arguments for a combined army/civilian team.

Seamus Hayes was another rider who provided fuel to that argument. After just twenty-seven months in the post, he retired as trainer of the army team, and returned to the jumping ring in April 1959. Unable to compete while at McKee Barracks, he had developed itchy feet and was delighted to take the opportunity of riding for Dublin-based millionaire Omar van Landeghem. This Belgian enthusiast had built up an excellent team of Irish horses and brought a whole new spirit of competitiveness into showjumping in Ireland.

Soon Seamus was back to his old form, and within three months he had won the Dublin Grand Prix on Kilrush. However, not everyone was pleased with the outcome; there were complaints from the visitors that Seamus was a professional, as had been said when Jack Bamber took the title back in 1937. It took five months and some twenty letters between Seamus, Omar, Judge Wylie and the Fédération Équestre Internationale before the matter was sorted out. Finally, in January 1960, Seamus was accepted as an amateur, who could ride in Nations' Cup events. However, he was told that he could not compete at Olympic Games. Thus began part two of the Seamus Hayes story. During 1960 he became all but unbeatable on the national circuit — even Tommy Wade admitted as much. After two seasons, Seamus left Van Landeghem's Skidoo Stud, near Swords, and went to Joe McGrath's stables in Sandyford, County Dublin, where he was to strike up exciting partnerships with great horses like Goodbye, Doneraile and Ardmore. This combination of human genius and equine power responded brilliantly to selection on the 1963 Aga Khan Trophy team.

Omar Van Landeghem

The only rosette is a red rosette was this ebullient Belgian businessman and sportsman's motto. He did things in a big way and demanded the best from the riders who competed on his string of showjumpers in the 1950s and 1960s — Seamus Hayes, Tommy Brennan, Leslie Fitzpatrick, Sue Sinclair, Jimmy Quinn, Peter Fitzpatrick, Sylvia Craigie, Brian McNicholl, Michael Hickey and Johnny Kyle. After the Second World War he built up a huge live-beef export business and on one occasion he created a record for the most cattle bought at the Dublin mart in one day — 1,568. He shipped from every port on the east coast and flew special lots out by air. This last enterprise was of great help to the new civilian team of the 1960s since he was able to get special rates for flying out teams of horses to continental shows. Over 800 first-prize rosettes won by Tommy Brennan during a three-year stint at his Skidoo Stud, gives some idea of his showjumping involvement. At his training centre he had created replicas of the major fences encountered at that time in shows across Europe. Nothing was left to chance and while he was a hard task master he has to be given credit for bringing the sport to a new competitive level here in Ireland. Asked what he was like to work for, most of his riders will say 'impossible', but they all admit that their time at Skidoo was like a university education. When his yard was in top operation during the 1960s two lorry loads of horses from there would travel to shows all around the country. He sold thousands of Irish horses abroad for top prices, and on one occasion the Queen of England even took a fancy to one of his good young jumpers. When she showed some signs of reluctance to finish the deal, she was told by the curt Omar, 'Ma'am you do not have enough money to buy him.'

Show Jumping and Riding Encouragement Association Cup winners of the Pixie, Ferguson and Caughoo Cups in 1956 — left to right: Juliet Jobling-Purser, Leslie Fitzpatrick and Susan Lanigan-O'Keefe. (Leslie Fitzpatrick)

Following Seamus Hayes at Omar Van Landeghem's was a young twenty-one-year-old — Tommy Brennan. 'I arrived with my Pioneer Pin, Fáinne and bicycle clips,' the tall, good-humoured and verbally expressive man from Kilkenny recalls of those early days of innocence. He had first wanted to be a jockey and rode point-to-point winners for Paddy Murphy in his home county before concentrating on showjumping. He even beat Seamus Hayes and Kilrush in the 1960 Dublin Spring Show Championship on Jim Finnegan's Cherry Blossom. (It may well have been this victory that had him accepted by Van Landeghem when, the following year, he applied for the job of farm manager at Skidoo Stud.) He was to win that same title again for the next two years running. Tommy was and is one of the best international horse judges and dealers in the world. In a career that spanned twelve years, he not only rode the great Kilkenny that went on to win Olympic and pan-American medals, but also a series of other horses which progressed to further success: Westcourt, which was sold to Frank McGarry and which was later a winner for Mary Rose Hayes and for the Italian team; Ambassador, which went on to win Olympic Gold for Graziano Mancinelli of Italy; Abbeyville, who created a world record in winning 173 Puissance competitions for Nelson Pessoa of Brazil; and Marcella, on which James Kernan later won junior European gold. Even with these mounts sold on, there were still enough left for him to be a powerful jumping force in his own right during he 1960s — powerful enough to have Stanislaus Lynch declare at the time, '...it would be unrepresentative to send a team abroad without Tommy Brennan.' In addition to Dublin and Belfast, he had a total of over 1,000 first prizes to his credit, including over fifty international wins in places like Amsterdam, Enschede, Ostend, Turin, London, Brussels, Rotterdam, Wiesbaden and Aachen.

Through a combination of bad luck and circumstances not of his making, Tommy's much-desired goal of Olympic showjumping honours eluded him. Just a few days prior to departure for the Mexico Games, his horse Tubbermac broke a leg at Dublin and had to be put down. He had two great mounts ready for Munich but the Equestrian Federation of Ireland barred his participation by branding him a professional. Despite such setbacks, from the time he brilliantly burst on the Irish scene in the late 1950s, Tommy Brennan's name became synonymous with what is best in Irish showjumping — superb natural talent, unstoppable determination and a sense of humour that not only helped him overcome some almost insurmountable obstacles, but also encouraged others to do the same.

Many of the horses used by civilian riders who were to reach prominence during the 1960s came from Frank McGarry's centre in Sligo. First ridden for Frank by Francis Kerins, they went on to be winners for other international riders from at home and abroad — Westcourt (Mary Rose Hayes), Feltrim (Eimear Haughey), Baronscourt

Previous page: *Queen's Cup and Athens Grand Prix winners Marion Hughes and Flo Jo.* (Irish Horse Board/Kit Haughton)

Above left: *Captain John Ledingham and his double Hickstead Derby Winner Kilbaha.* (Anne Hughes)

Above right: *1985 Irish Champion Vina Lyons.* (Belfast Telegraph)

Left: *Peter Charles on his 1995 European Champion Traxdata La Ina.* (Sportsfile)

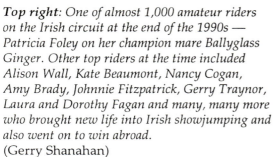

Top right: *One of almost 1,000 amateur riders on the Irish circuit at the end of the 1990s — Patricia Foley on her champion mare Ballyglass Ginger. Other top riders at the time included Alison Wall, Kate Beaumont, Nancy Cogan, Amy Brady, Johnnie Fitzpatrick, Gerry Traynor, Laura and Dorothy Fagan and many, many more who brought new life into Irish showjumping and also went on to win abroad.*
(Gerry Shanahan)

Bottom right: *The Devil's Dyke at Hickstead, which Paul Darragh had to jump when winning the 1975 Derby on Pele. Paul is pictured **above** competing in the Hamburg Derby with Heather Honey.* (Michael Slavin/Melita Huck)

Opposite page: Trevor Coyle on the great Irish-bred stallion Cruising — winners of the Millstreet World Cup and Grand Prix events in Lucerne and Pavarotti International. (Sportsfile)

Above: The 1994 British Grand Prix winner at Hickstead, Commandant Gerry Mullins on Pallas Green, chatting with runner-up Michael Whitaker of Britain on the great Irish-bred Monsanta. (Gerry Mullins)

Right: One of the many Irish grooms who have distinguished themselves in the care of team horses over the years, Jan Kennedy brings Trevor Coyle's horse Cruising to the ring at Pavarotti International where he won the Grand Prix in 1995. (Trevor Coyle)

Left: Star of the Land Rover League circuit during the late 1990s Clement McMahon of Clones. (Siobhán English)

Below: Eddie Macken and Boomerang dominated the 1970s — Eddie remained the backbone of the Irish team up to the end of the 1990s. (Ruth Rogers)

Opposite Page:
Top: The RDS Show Grounds in Ballsbridge — it has hosted the Dublin Horse Show since 1881 and is one of the very few remaining jumping arenas at the heart of a major European capital. (RDS Archive)

Right: The 1998 British Grand Prix winner at Hickstead and new member of the Irish team Eric Holstein. (Siobhán English)

Above: Staff in the computerised SJAI office of 1998 — Maeve Dowdall, Elsbeth Gailey, Denise Halford and Jason Patterson. (Tony Parkes)

Above: Team parade at the RDS during the post-war years. (David Gray/RDS Archive)

Below: Winner of the individual gold medal at the 1995 European Pony Championships, Emma Wilson of Belfast. The same event was won the previous year by Patrick Hanlon of Longford on Shalom Outlaw. (Tony Parkes/SJAI)

(Iris Kellett), Oatfield Hills (Eddie Macken) and Sensation (Raimondo D'Inzeo).

Frank, who ran a successful cattle business, was in love with the horse. When he was only six he told his father, '...one day I will be on the Aga Khan team.' Later, he confided '...just the smell of leather was enough for me....' During the 1950s he battled to build up showjumping in the west of Ireland and was a founder member of the Connaught Branch of the SJAI which was finally given the status of a Region in 1964. He served on the SJAI National Executive for sixteen years, was many times chairman of his region and spent fifteen seasons on the international selection committee. He was also the first person from his area to be named a member of Bord na gCapall.

With Francis Kerins in the saddle, Frank McGarry's horses were part of civilian teams of the early 1960s which travelled abroad to Rotterdam, Ostend, Aachen, Lisbon, Barcelona and Madrid. Frank (McGarry) himself served as Chef d'Équipe on many of these trips and, true to form, always brought both the tricolour and the official SJAI flag with him. A good singer, Frank made up some very comical songs about the exploits of that time and was reputedly the best story-teller ever to enter a judges' box.

During their time together as owner and rider, Frank McGarry and Francis Kerins won thousands of rosettes. Their best jumper was Go Sly Up (up Sligo backwards), a nimble little grey that began his career pulling logs until the workers discovered he would jump a wall. They first saw him at Enniscrone show where he had been entered with no saddle and just a rope for reins. Two days later Frank bought him for £72.10s.00d at Ballina Fair and the following Thursday, Francie won double his price on him at Ballinrobe. Over a ten-year period Go Sly Up won 513 firsts and a total of £8,000 in prize money. He was retired at Ballinasloe having won the Championship there and two other classes in 1967. In 1972, Frank built one of the most modern indoor jumping arenas in Ireland at the time. It is still being run by his son Declan, while Francis Kerins' son Darragh is now one of Ireland's young international riders.

Leslie Fitzpatrick, Diana Conolly-Carew, Tommy Wade, Tommy Brennan, Francie Kerins, along with Seamus Hayes, Iris Kellett, Billy McCully, John Brooke, Brian McNicholl, Ada Matheson, Marion McDowell and others were the riders who made up the civilian teams of the 1960s. Together with army men, Billy Ringrose, Ned Campion, Sean Daly and Larry Kiely, they helped keep Ireland in the forefront of international showjumping at a time when the sport was again going through massive changes world-wide.

James Wade of Tipperary bought the best of ponies for his young sons Tommy and Eddie his reward was to see Tommy and Dundrum become the most popular Irish showjumping combination of all time. (Felicity Wade)

Footnotes to Chapter Seven

[1]   Royal Dublin Society Archive, 1945–1959.

[2]   Ibid., 13 February 1947.

[3]   *The Irish Field*, 26 November 1955: p. 4.

[4]   Op. cit., Royal Dublin Society Archive, January 1953.

[5]   *Showjumping and Horse News*, London: January 1951: vol 1, no. 9, p. 295

[6]   *The Irish Field*, 26 November 1955: p. 4.

[7]   Ibid., 22 August 22 1959: p. 6.

[8]   *Irish Independent*, 5 August 1957.

[9]   Ibid., 27 April 1952.

[10] SJAI Archive, January, 1963.

CHAPTER EIGHT

TEAMS OF THE 1960S

People power put us on the Aga Khan team.
— Tommy Wade on the breakthrough of civilians
into the top selection of Irish Showjumping

Until the RDS and SJAI created the Travel Fund in 1959, there had been no international outlet for the ever-growing number of talented young Irish civilian riders. The new initiative quickly became the civilian team's passport to the world of top competition, in which they had long been waiting to perform. In its first year, private contributions and grants from the SJAI amounted to £1,653 in total. This was matched pound for pound by the RDS, and over £3,000 became available to the civilian riders during the 1960 season. By then the Showjumping Association of Ireland had formed its own Selection Committee which included its first director general and future chairman, Colonel J.J. Lewis. Joining him were Billy McLernan, of Cork, along with Dermot Buchanan (another future chairman) and James Bryson, both from the Northern Region. The first team officially selected by the committee travelled to the Continent in the spring of 1960, competing in Wiesbaden and Ludwigsburg, in Germany, and at a Nations' Cup meeting in Enschede, Holland.

For this first civilian team — Leslie Fitzpatrick and Seamus Hayes (of the Southern Region) and Captain John Brooke (of the Northern Region) — this was a journey into the unknown. It attracted extensive press coverage at home; Tony Power in the *Irish Press*, Brian McSweeney in the *Irish Independent* and Stanislaus Lynch in *The Irish Field* kept readers up to date on the team's progress at all three shows. It was the kind of press coverage we now associate only with the exploits of stars such as Jack Charlton's heroes in the 1990s. This first trip by Hayes, Fitzpatrick and Brooke, was seen as a test of whether or not the civilians could deliver what they had promised when representing Ireland abroad.

Rivalry between the civilians and the army team was played up at this time as press comment continued to snipe away at the ban on civilian riders from the Aga Khan Trophy team. There had also been a degree of negative editorialising on the army team's seeming reluctance to engage the civilians on the national circuit during the latter part of the 1950s.

For reasons best known to the leaders in McKee Barracks, they did not register their horses under the new SJAI rules and thus were ineligible to compete at SJAI-affiliated shows, particularly those on the very competitive Leinster circuit. Finally, in 1959, that log-jam was broken and some brilliant contests took place between the army men and the civilians during the 1960 season. The change brought this rather caustic comment from *The Irish Field*:

*The stultifying hibernation behind the walls of McKee has
ended and the army jumping team will in future come out
and take its wins and its defeats in public at local jumping
competitions.*[1]

Thus the early years of the 1960s became something of a test of
strength and will between the emerging civilian teams and the
traditional wearers of the green. Each vied for as much coverage as
possible for any success achieved either at home or abroad.

On its first trip abroad in 1960 the first official Irish civilian side
certainly lived up to the expectations of both press and public.
Undaunted by the opposition or the newness of the challenge, they
took on the best in Europe and won. Seamus Hayes had two wins in
Wiesbaden on Kilrush (owned by the team's Chef d'Équipe, Omar van
Landeghem), while Leslie Fitzpatrick took the Puissance on Hi Society
ahead of John Brooke. Seamus was Leading Rider in Ludwigsburg
and, despite the fact that John Brooke was part of the tour, it was said
that the Irish tricolour flew over the Germany show and that it also
decorated many of the trade stands. (For this first tour the team
performed in red jackets, trimmed with green collars, while the horses'
saddlecloths displayed the four provinces flag with the word 'Ireland'
emblazoned on them.)

In Enschede Seamus won a jump-off class on opening day, and
both he and Leslie joined forces to take the pairs competition on the
second day. In the Nations' Cup, the Irish accumulated a mere total
of four faults — enough to secure first place ahead of Britain,
Holland, Germany and France. Seamus Hayes and Leslie Fitzpatrick
were the only two riders with double clears and had to jump-off for
the individual championship. Leslie and Hi Society won, while,
based on his performance over the entire three days, Seamus was
declared Leading Rider. It was a great start to a new era in Irish
showjumping. Later that year, Seamus and Leslie were Ireland's first
participants in a World Championship when they travelled to
Venice to compete in this new tournament which was being run for
only the fifth time.

In the World Championship there were prizes in each of the three
individual legs of the competition and it was imperative to be
successful in all of them to qualify for a chance of a medal. Although
the Irish did not make it through to the final, the team finished
strongly in one of the legs and this in itself was an achievement
considering that it was Ireland's first performance in this competition.

Four riders competed in the final — Raimondo d'Inzeo of Italy
took gold on the Irish-bred mare, Gowran Girl, while silver went to
Carlos Delia, of Argentina, and bronze to the young David Broome on
Sunsalve. Within a month, Delia was to help his country win the Aga
Khan Trophy at the RDS, while Broome took his first Dublin Grand
Prix. Later that year, Fitzpatrick and Hayes scored two more wins at the

new Amsterdam Indoor Championships — Seamus was first and third in the Grand Prix of Holland, while Leslie took the Puissance.

The civilian side had certainly put up the challenge to the army riders during its first official season. An attempt at response by the men from McKee Barracks, in the Dublin Horse Show, failed as British riders Pat Smyth and David Broome dominated the individual events. In the Nations' Cup, over one of the stiffest courses yet built at the RDS grounds, Argentina took the Aga Khan Trophy ahead of Britain and Ireland. Only a double of wins, in a jump-off and a speed class, from Tommy Wade on Dundrum kept the Irish flag flying. Not surprisingly it was not long before there were more demands that civilians be put on the Aga Khan Trophy team.

Matters did not improve at the Rome Olympics for the three members of the Irish Army team — Captain Billy Ringrose was the highest-placed Irish rider on Loch an Easpaig, finishing seventeenth. The next Irish performer behind him was Sean Daly, finishing thirty-first, and when Lieutenant Eamonn O'Donoghue was eliminated, the entire Irish team went with him.

However, the army men were not going to take a back seat that easily. Later, in the autumn of that year, they bounced back to produce some very promising results on the North American circuit as they picked up forty-six rosettes between Harrisburg, Washington, New York and Toronto, where they were second to a very strong USA team in the Nations' Cup. There were better things to come from them in 1961; strengthened by the first inclusion of Lieutenant Ned Campion, they made a blazing start to the new season by winning a tough Nations' Cup in Nice. The squad of Billy Ringrose with Loch an Easpaig, Eamonn O'Donoghue on Cillan Fhail, Sean Daly on Loch Gorman and Ned on Cluain Meala, won ahead of Spain and the Italian side which included Olympic gold and silver medalists Raimondo and Piero d'Inzeo. It is interesting to note that three of the officers on that team — Sean Daly, Billy Ringrose and Ned Campion — were to become Commanding Officers of the Army Equitation School over the next thirty years.

Rome was next, and there Billy Ringrose gave a performance that *The Irish Field* termed 'sparkling brilliance' as he dominated the main individual events. Live on pan-European television, Billy and Loch an Easpaig scored Ireland's first Grand Prix win in Piazza di Siena since John Lewis from Crecora, County Limerick, took it on Limerick Lace in 1938; and for good measure, Billy was also second on Cloyne. Billy triumphed again in Sunday's main jump-off with another one-two as he took first on Cloyne and second on Ceannanas Mor. As the year went on, Ringrose kept up the pace on Loch an Easpaig with a win in the Manifestation Stakes at the White City Stadium, London, ahead of David Broome on Sunsalve. He took another first on the opening day of the Dublin Horse Show in 1961, and also in New York on an autumn tour during which the army had four firsts and nine seconds.

Billy Ringrose on Loch an Easpaig, winning the 1961 Grand Prix in Rome. (O. Cornaz)

In the meantime, the civilian attack for 1961 was strengthened by the arrival of Tommy Brennan. He had taken over at Omar van Landeghem's while Seamus Hayes had moved to Joe McGrath's yard to compete on the very strong string of jumpers there. In what has to be a unique rise to glory in the history of Irish showjumping, Brennan powered his way onto the national circuit in 1961. He had certainly tasted success with Westcourt and Cherry Blossom over the previous two years, but once he got command of the Skidoo team all the longing of this charismatic Kilkenny man burst into winning form. He soon proved himself well able to take on Tommy Wade, Seamus Hayes and Leslie Fitzpatrick, and his classic touch made him an obvious choice with the SJAI selectors when choosing a team for the German tour scheduled for the spring of that year.

Selected for the side to jump in Hamburg, Cologne, Aachen and Enschede were John Brooke with Tyrenny, Leslie Fitzpatrick on Hi Society and Plutocrat, Brian McNicholl with Kilcurry, and Tommy on Kilbrack and his Spring Show champion, Briarly. Omar van Landeghem was again appointed Chef d'Équipe.

Sadly, fortune was not on the side of the young civilian squad. Tommy Brennan had broken his arm at the Balmoral show and was just struggling back to form when the team left for Germany. They had little luck on their first visit to the great Hamburg Derby meeting and, in fact, John Brooke decided not to continue with the tour afterwards. There was hopeful improvement in Cologne where Leslie and Hi Society hit form to win two classes — one of them with the only two clears out of 120 starters. That form was maintained in Aachen where, on opening day, the twenty-three-year-old Dubliner took the Puissance ahead of European Champion Fritz Thiedermann and 1956 Olympic gold medalist Hans Gunther Winkler. Leslie also shared first in the opening round of the European Championships and qualified for the final.

With his arm re-set, Tommy Brennan led the team to a brilliant finale in Enschede where they won six of the seven competitions on offer; Tommy himself took both the Puissance and Grand Prix with Kilbrack. Then on the final day, McNicholl, Fitzpatrick and Brennan ended on a superb zero score in the Nations' Cup to beat Germany, Italy and South Africa. Just like the army riders after Nice and Rome back in May, the trio got a hero's welcome home at Dublin airport.

They were not the only jumping heroes of 1961 as more civilian drama unfolded. On Westcourt, Mary Rose Robinson (at that time engaged to marry Seamus Hayes) was narrowly beaten by Pat Smyth for the Queen's Cup at the White City Stadium. Then, in Dublin, came one of the shining moments in the careers of Tommy Wade and Dundrum as they won an incredible total of five major competitions — the Boylan Trophy, the Wylie Trophy, the National Open Jumping, the Ballsbridge Trophy as Leading Rider; and finally the Grand Prix of Ireland ahead of Raimondo d'Inzeo, Hans Gunther Winkler and Pat Smyth.

Leslie Fitzpatrick on one of his first trips abroad with the civilian team, heading for a win at Aachen in 1961. (Leslie Fitzpatrick)

The first Hickstead Derby of 1961 — Seamus Hayes said, 'I came over to show you how to jump that bloody bank.' He is shown doing so on Goodbye. (Jean Bridel)

In September of that great year, the Hickstead Derby was run for the first time, and Douglas Bunn was putting up £1,275 in prizes — the largest ever in the history of showjumping. Seamus Hayes decided to take it on with Lady Stanhope's superb gelding, Goodbye. '...I came over to show you how to jump that bloody bank,' he said on the night before the event. That he did as he delivered the only clear round and won the inaugural event.

Douglas Bunn

What Judge Wylie or Noel C. Duggan have been to Irish showjumping, Douglas Bunn has been to the sport in Britain. Born in 1928, his schooling led to his qualification as a barrister, but always there were the ponies, the horses and his passion for showjumping. Following graduation from Cambridge he trained with Colonel Joe Hume–Dudgeon and went on to jump internationally. He was responsible for both David Broome's Beethoven and Marion Coates' the Maverick being bought from Jack Bamber, and he rode both of these horses before they went on to these riders.

The successful 1961 civilian team welcomed home at Dublin Airport — left to right: Omar Van Landeghem, Brian McNicholl, Leslie Fitzpatrick, Tommy Brennan, Colonel John Lewis (SJAI selection committee) and SJAI founder member Bernard Fitzpatrick. (Irish Press)

Douglas Bunn's dream was to create a permanent showjumping course in Britain. Soon after he bought Hickstead Place, in Sussex, during the winter of 1959, he set about realising his dream — initially by visiting the course in Hamburg and, during a blinding snowstorm, measuring its derby bank. Hickstead first opened in 1960 on the same weekend that Princess Margaret married Lord Snowden. There were few on hand to attend that year but Hickstead survived to run its first Derby in 1961, when it was won by Seamus Hayes. Douglas Bunn has never forgotten the support he received from Irish riders during the early years of struggle and on many occasions the Irish team has stayed at his own house beside the course itself. Douglas is now a legend in world showjumping as is his famed Hickstead.

Soon afterwards, Seamus and Mary Rose Robinson were married and, for their honeymoon, they went on a showjumping tour of Geneva, Brussels and Amsterdam. Seamus won the Puissance in Brussels and Mary Rose was Leading Rider in Amsterdam.

Finishing his brilliant year, Tommy Wade won the Horse of the Year Show Championship, at Wembley, beating David Broome on Sunsalve and Nelson Pessoa on the great Beau Geste. On his return, Tommy was the first Irish showjumping rider to receive a Sports Star of the Year award — the then Caltex Trophy.

Not surprisingly, Tommy Wade's fame had spread to the USA, and early in 1962, he received a special invitation to jump in the autumn of that year at Madison Square Garden. The man from Dundrum turned it down because he had other plans, for this was the year in which he had set his sights on scoring his unique treble of golden trophies (See Chapter Seven). Since one of these prizes was offered at an event which happened at the same time as the New York Horse Show, Tommy had no option but to turn down the attractive invitation.

Those who did not know about Wade's secret plan expressed surprise at the time when his application came in for the Newcastle-on-Tyne show. However, the selectors were glad to have him on the Irish side, which included Diana Conolly-Carew, Heather Moore, Seamus Hayes and Brian McNicholl.

With precise accuracy, from a starting field of sixty, he took the first trophy on his list — the Vaux Gold Tankard. On the way to victory he had the chance to turn the tables on Pat Smyth and the great Flanagan, who had beaten him and Dundrum that same year in a two-way jump-off at the Hickstead Derby. In addition to the Vaux Tankard, this Newcastle win also netted the Tipperary man a first prize of £525.

Tommy Brennan was not idle at this time either. He jumped in Wiesbaden and Ludwigsburg that year and brought home eighteen prizes. Also in action was Billy Ringrose who won two events in Barcelona, including the Championship, on Cloyne. He also jumped two superb clears at the Dublin Horse Show, although Ireland only came a disappointing fourth in the Aga Khan Trophy behind Italy, the USA and Britain. Piero d'Inzeo won the Grand Prix that year on Irish-bred, the Rock.

Tommy Wade and Dundrum again upheld home honour by winning two international events in Dublin that year. Immediately afterwards, he travelled north for the second leg of his golden tour. Three clears in the SJAI Championship, at Balmoral in Belfast, secured the win, and Tommy took the first-place medal, the second of his golden goals, plus £200 in prize money. His next stop was the Horse of the Year Show, at Wembley, where he took another double. The Puissance there came down to a two-way jump-off between him and Seamus Hayes on Goodbye. Seamus faulted and it was all down to Tommy. *The Irish Field* takes up the story:

> *Excitement was at fever pitch when Wade and Dundrum approached the huge 6' 11" wall — beside which both horse and rider seemed apparently insignificant — but when they cleared it they received the loudest applause of the entire week.*[2]

From Wembley it was on to the final part of Tommy's triple crown — the gold watch on offer in Brussels. There, he and Dundrum had two clears to win ahead of Pat Smyth and Hans Gunther Winkler. Thus with one more dream realised, Tommy had had hit his home run. He still has the three golden prizes to recall those glory days — however, the £1,440 total winnings in the three events is long since spent.

Following Brussels, Tommy and Seamus joined up with Tommy Brennan for the Amsterdam show where they won a total of eleven prizes, including the car, which Brennan took on Kilbrack.

During the first three years in which the civilian fund was in operation, riders had been assisted to attend twenty-eight shows at a cost of £7,000. As if to justify this expenditure, they had accumulated 200 prizes to their credit, including eighteen firsts. In the meantime, the army had four wins on the 1962 American tour, two of them from Billy Ringrose and two from Ned Campion, who scored the first individual international victory of his career in New York.

Despite the good individual performances of both the army and civilian riders during 1962, the season was still a total failure in terms of major Nations' Cup participation. Out of eight starts by the army their best result was a second in Harrisburg. They were sixth in London, third in Lucerne, fourth in Barcelona, Rotterdam, New York, Toronto and, sadly, also in Dublin. It was now obvious that in the modern competitive world of international showjumping, neither the army nor the civilian team was separately strong enough to hold their own in the big Nations' Cup competitions. The logic of combined efforts became undeniably obvious.

At the start of 1963, press clamour for change grew louder; but unknown to the pundits, the much-desired decision had already been taken by the army and the Equestrian Federation of Ireland. Although not officially announced until July, agreement was actually reached in the spring of that year, according to then Officer Commanding of McKee Barracks, Colonel James Neylon. Writing in the army magazine, *An Cosantóir*, some thirteen years later, he recalled:

> *During this time civilian jumping under the SJAI, and in particular its chairman, Col. Jack Lewis was making considerable progress, as was the BSJA in Great Britain. Horses had considerably decreased in European armies and mixed army–civilian teams were now the order of the day. In the Spring of 1963 the Dept. of Defence approached the Equestrian Federation of Ireland with the proposition that mixed army–civilians should be the National Team in future. The Chairman, Judge Wylie, readily acquiesced. The Officer Commanding Army Equitation School was appointed Chef d'Équipe.[3]*

Thus, in its own time, the army had done the right thing and, contrary to Judge Wylie's previous worries, it had brought the Government along with it on matters relating to the Army Equitation School. Funding of this unique institution was continued and is still provided to this day for Irish competitors travelling throughout the world. Except for a bit of unfinished business in relation to the appointment of Chef d'Équipe, the controversy over army exclusivity was over. It was now up to both the army and the civilians to make the best possible job of a combined team.

However, the changed situation did open up one other can of worms, which, in the interest of the sport, also had to be resolved — that of the anthem and flag. From the time that the Team Travel Fund had been established in 1959, discussion of this matter had increased at SJAI National Executive meetings. By 1962 the members appeared to agree on the following items for civilian teams going abroad:

1. The word 'Ireland' emblazoned on both sides of saddle cloths
2. Green jackets with a badge that included the crests of the four provinces inside a horse shoe
3. An official flag featuring the four provinces crest
4. 'St Patrick's Day' as the anthem

However, this whole array of compromise, while good on paper, just did not work in practice. Above all else, there was no way that it was acceptable for a combined army–civilian team. Even for the civilian sides of the early 1960s it caused problems — new stars like Tommy Wade and Tommy Brennan had been no part of the difficult negotiations that brought about the compromise in 1954. They were now being asked to ride under a flag that meant nothing to them.

There was also confusion at shows abroad. Organisers at foreign venues, which had been used to the army team before the war, were now unsure which tune to play for the Irish team anthem. On one occasion, Irish riders refused to doff their hats when 'St Patrick's Day' was played as the anthem. At other times, Irish people travelling abroad with the team did not stand for the tune, either because they did not recognise it or as an objection to it. In the end, official Irish Diplomatic contacts were made with shows requesting that they use 'The Soldiers' Song'. On the home front, the matter began getting a good deal of press comment. One article in the *Irish Press* was headlined, 'Riders Revolt', and hinted that some were refusing to compete under the Four Provinces Flag. In March 1963, the SJAI had to take the unusual step of issuing a lengthy statement on the matter. It explained the need for a compromise anthem and flag and stated that no anti-national sentiment was intended.

However, this statement solved nothing. The problem remained and finally at an October 1963 Executive Committee meeting, the following realistic solution was agreed:

> Teams selected to compete at CHIO Shows should wear the saddle cloths bearing the National Emblem, and the flag and a national anthem should be used (The tri-colour and 'The Soldiers' Song').

> Teams selected to compete at CHI Shows should wear the saddle cloths of the Showjumping Association of Ireland and the flag and the anthem of the Association should be used (The Four Provinces Flag and 'St Patrick's Day').[4]

Time has shown that both of these major decisions taken in 1963 — the opening up of the Aga Khan Trophy team to civilians and the

Although John Brooke, son of Northern Ireland's Prime Minister, Sir Basil Brooke, had disagreements with the Irish team over the use of flag and anthem he also had some wonderful light moments with the likes of Iris Kellett, Leslie Fitzpatrick and Seamus Hayes.
(Belfast Telegraph)

settling of the flag and anthem controversy — were necessary. They demonstrated a maturity in the organisation of the sport here that was soon to bear fruit.

However, the main order of business in that year, as in any year of Irish showjumping, was the winning of the Aga Khan Trophy. The new-look team for that competition was announced in July — four civilians and two army riders.

It included Tommy Brennan, who earlier that year was Leading Rider at Enschede and winner of the Grand Prix at Wiesbaden; Diana Conolly-Carew, who had been fourth in the European Championships at Hickstead, Leading Lady rider at Aachen and winner of the Grand Prix at Enschede; Seamus Hayes, who performed well with both Ardmore and Goodbye at the Dublin Spring Show, and Tommy Wade on Dundrum, along with Ned Campion and Billy Ringrose from the army.

In the months building up to the Dublin Horse Show that year, all of these riders prepared for the Aga Khan Trophy contest in winning style. However, there was also a real scare in store for Tommy Wade at the Dublin Spring Show. At the conclusion of a tense battle with Tommy Brennan for the Championship, Dundrum burst a blood vessel and emerged from the arena with blood pouring from his nose. From then on, this was to be a problem for the game little horse but it did not stop him giving superb performances over the next five years.

He had certainly fully recovered by July, when he and Tommy took the King's Cup at the Royal International in London — Ireland's first win in this event since Kevin Barry had taken it twelve years earlier, in 1951. Joining Tommy in the three-way jump-off for the coveted King's Cup were George Hobbs of Britain and Graziano Mancinelli of Italy. Hobbs, on Brandy Soda, went clear in 34.9 seconds, and Mancinelli, on Rockette, was two seconds faster but had three fences down. Wade and Dundrum, however, went clear and shaved almost three seconds off Hobbs' time to take first place. Another boost to Irish morale for the task ahead in Dublin, came from Seamus Hayes and Ardmore, when they won the Imperial Cup, presented by none other than Colonel Rodzianko. For good measure, the combined Irish team was second to Britain in the Nations' Cup.

The tension and expectation of Dublin was already building when the team returned from London. Crowds for Horse Show week at the RDS swelled to 124,000 — up by 10,000 from 1962.

Fully living up to their reputation, Tommy and Dundrum won both the Top Score and the Boylan Trophy, while Graziano Mancinelli starred in early competitions for the visitors. However, the moment of truth came before jammed stands, on the Friday afternoon, in the fight for the Aga Khan Trophy. Neither Tommy Brennan's nor Ned Campion's mounts had been on form, and thus the team selected by Colonel Bill Rea was Seamus Hayes on Goodbye, Diana Conolly-Carew on Barrymore, Billy Ringrose on Loch an Easpaig, and Tommy

Wade on Dundrum. They were up against crack teams from Switzerland, Germany, Italy and Britain. Ireland were drawn first to jump and Seamus Hayes brought the crowd to its feet with a superb opening clear round. The Germans responded in kind, and Diana on the lovely grey, Barrymore, had just the corral fence down for four faults, while the Swiss accrued only a quarter of a time fault. Ireland's attack was weakened somewhat when Billy Ringrose returned with two fences down, for a total of eight faults. Nevertheless, they were soon back in the running when Tommy and Dundrum gave one more of their electrifying performances to go clear and boost the Irish into second place. At the half-way stage of the competition, Ireland stood at four faults to Switzerland's quarter of a time fault. The script could not have been more excitingly written.

On the return, there was a groan from the stands when Goodbye had one foot in the water, but then, fully recovering from first-round faults, both Diana and Billy delivered pressure clear rounds. It could go any way between Ireland, Switzerland and Germany. In the end, it all came down to Tommy Wade's final round on Dundrum. The grand old arena at Ballsbridge is familiar with this kind of tension but the suspense has never been greater than in this round jumped by the cool Tipperary man. Tommy and Dundrum were at their best — not even tipping or tapping a pole — and flew around as if Cashel angels were lifting them over the twelve fences. At last they were safely home and bathing in the loving applause of the appreciative crowd. Ireland had won the Aga Khan Trophy for the first time in fourteen long years.

However, this proved to be a hard, hard act to follow. Incredibly, as matters turned out, those four horses and riders were never to jump together on the same team again.

Hard to follow or not, this 1963 win was a true high point in the history of Irish showjumping. And it bore fruit — the heroes of that moment were like pop stars when they visited local shows around the country.

Eddie Macken still recalls a very special day from that time when his idol Seamus Hayes came to Ballinamore show and he was allowed sit up on Goodbye. It was a bonus of that era that all of the stars were still home-based as this meant that they were very active performers on the national circuit. Crowds at local shows could expect to see their favourite stars battle it out for Grand Prix honours with newer contenders such as Ada Matheson of Joe Hume-Dudgeon's School, Marion McDowell who was carrying on her family's great equestrian tradition, Leonard Cave (who later married Marion McDowell), together with Michael Hickey and Ned Cash both of whom made it onto the Aga Khan Trophy team in the early 1970s.

The enthusiasm of the time led to the birth of more jumping events and the number of affiliated SJAI shows leaped from 171, in 1963, to 231 in 1965. This growth encouraged the SJAI to make a move it had only dared dream of until then. It legislated that, for the 1964 season,

The victorious 1963 Irish team of Billy Ringrose, Diana Conolly-Carew, Tommy Wade and Seamus Hayes; during the parade, not all were riding the horses they rode in the cup. For many reasons, this same side never jumped together again. (Reiter Revue)

its members could jump only at fully affiliated shows and, except for confined local competitions, non-members could not compete at such events. However, it took some years before the Association could claim 100 per cent compliance with this rule. Nevertheless, irrespective of such compliance, it had certainly taken its stand as a strong overall governing body of the sport.

Other far-reaching decisions followed quickly, and in October 1964, the SJAI began moving towards a fully fledged, four-province organisation. On 6 March 1965, a proposal was passed that the SJAI henceforth be composed of four regions — the Northern Region, (now comprising all nine counties of Ulster), Munster, Connaught and Leinster. In this re-organisation, Ulster would have twelve members on the National Executive, Leinster would have eight, Munster three and Connaught one.

When the amalgamation of the two associations happened back in 1954 it did so on the basis that there would be two distinct, equal and, to some degree, autonomous regions — Northern and Southern — each with twelve members on the SJAI Executive Committee. During the early 1960s, Muriel Neill was the Secretary of the Northern Region and retained that post long after re-organisation happened. Oliver Walsh was Southern Region Secretary. As membership increased and local branches in Connaught and Munster grew in strength the arrangement began to look somewhat undemocratic. When the re-organisation did come in 1965, it was only half-baked. What really happened was that the Northern Region retained its twelve members on the Executive, while the South simply divided up its twelve among its three Regions.

That was fine until Munster and Connaught called for stronger representation in order to reflect their share of membership more accurately. Much more detailed negotiations began in 1968 and, during these talks, the strong personality and brilliant legal mind of Justice Robert Lowry (future Chief Justice for Northern Ireland), played an absolutely crucial role. Several times during those two critical years, the Northern Region and the Southern Region came close to going their separate ways once more. Fortunately, every time the members of the executive looked over the brink they saw what that would mean to the sport here and each time they pulled back and asked Judge Lowry to talk with both sides once more. In the end, on a night in November 1969, a set of detailed proposals put forward by the Judge was unanimously approved. In an executive expanded to twenty-seven, the Northern Region and Leinster would each have nine members, Munster would have six and Connaught three. In our divided island, it was inevitable that the creation of a fully democratic and representative Association was never going to be quick or easy. A final equal alignment of five members per Region came into being only in 1994; it had taken fifty years of sensitive discussion to reach this eventual resolution which has undoubtedly worked towards the betterment of the sport.

As the 1960s faded, SJAI membership and registrations were each nearing 2,000, and this growth brought its own problems in terms of management. Fanny Peard had taken over as registrar from Geoffrey Keatinge in 1960 and remained in that post until 1967. Her office was initially at the Phoenix Park race course, where her husband was manager, then it moved to premises provided by Iris Kellett on Grafton Street, and finally, from 1962 onward, it settled at small rented quarters on Dawson Street. Fanny Peard's work was voluntary with the assistance of one paid secretary. A small Management Committee was created in 1965 to help with the day-to-day running of the organisation and, in August of 1967, it was decided that a professional secretary General was needed. Colonel Jack Lewis, who had followed Dermot Buchanan in the chairmanship in 1966, applied for the job and was accepted at a salary of £1,000 a year. Dr Tom McNabb took the chair from March 1968 until Billy McLernan, of Munster, was elected to the post in February 1969.

Silent stands wait to erupt as Tommy Wade and Dundrum dramatically clear the last fence to bring Ireland victory in the 1963 Aga Khan Trophy — the first by a combined army/civilian team.
(Irish Press)

Through a very difficult two-year period of re-adjustment, Colonel Jack Lewis vigorously grappled with a job that was still very much in the making. He and the office staff of Mrs Marion Callaghan and Elsbeth Gailey, faced an ever-increasing workload which would eventually demand the installation of a high-tech computer. Unfortunately, Colonel Jack was injured in a freak car accident late in 1969 and had to resign from the post. He was replaced by Gordon Hickson of Carbery, County Kildare, who served a two-year term until April 1972, when Ned Campion (not the army Ned Campion) took over.

While the increased organisation of the administrative end of the sport was being tackled, international participation during the 1960s continued to rise. Following that stirring 1963 Aga Khan Trophy win by Ireland, a logical sequel was the selection of the first combined army/civilian team for the North American autumn tour. Billy Ringrose and Ned Campion were joined by Diana Conolly-Carew, who proved herself by jumping clear and taking fourth place in the New York Grand Prix. The team came third in both Harrisburg and Toronto, while dropping to fourth at Madison Square Garden.

At the very same time, a full civilian side, composed of Tommy Wade, Tommy Brennan, Seamus Hayes and the young Ada Matheson, who was getting her first cap, was to travel on a Continental tour to Amsterdam, Brussels and the Nations' Cup in Geneva. Sadly, this was to be an ill-fated tour; just days before the team's departure, Tommy Brennan broke an ankle and could not travel, then, Leslie Fitzpatrick, who went out on short notice, had to withdraw as his horses had not had time to prepare fully for the international circuit. Although Wade, Matheson and Hayes put in a good performance in Amsterdam, it did not prevent another disaster which struck when Tommy Wade's mare, Pearl, became ill and the Tipperary star returned home. This left just Ada and Seamus who travelled on to Geneva, but obviously they could not compete in the Nations' Cup there.

This disappointing outing can be viewed as a flavour of things to come. Pundits who had claimed a great new revival of Irish fortunes abroad with the combined force of army and civilian riders were soon to be proven terribly wrong — here was no quick fix for Irish showjumping at this time. During those very years the good brood mares of Ireland were being sold off to the farms of Holland and France. In fact, between the end of the Second World War and 1970 there was to be a drop of 300,000 in the Irish horse population. With a dwindling national stock it was becoming all the more difficult to keep the army and civilian riders on winning form. In fact, except for a repeat Aga Khan Trophy win in 1967 and one in Ostend in 1971, Ireland was to be starved of Nations' Cup success in twelve of the fourteen years between the resounding 1963 triumph and the return of euphoria in the late 1970s.

However, the Irish battled on, and during the rest of the 1960s there were to be some superb individual wins scored by both the army riders and the civilians. In 1964, Frank McGarry led a civilian group — Francie Kerins, Diana Conolly-Carew, Heather Moore and Patricia McKee — on an eventful three-month Iberian tour to Valencia, Madrid, Lisbon and Barcelona. On one occasion they even lost their horses for a whole day when the Spanish railway shunted their freight car up a siding and forgot about it. Nevertheless, there were great times too as the group scored six wins and took away fifty-two prizes from the four events.

At the Dublin Horse Show, in 1964, Ned Campion, on Inis Teag, and Tommy Brennan, on Kilkenny and Donegal, scored two speed wins together with one in a jump-off. Also, at the end of the season, Seamus Hayes took his second Hickstead Derby, on Goodbye, and then went on to win the Grand Prix in Rotterdam.

Billy Ringrose opened the scoring for Ireland in 1965 by winning the Nice Grand Prix on Loch and Easpaig, and he, Seamus Hayes, Ada Matheson and Diana Conolly-Carew came second to a mighty British side in a five-way Aga Khan Trophy contest. Ireland's best result came from Marion McDowell, who took first and second in the Sandymount Stakes on Blue Heaven and Sweet Control.

An outbreak of Swamp Fever on the Continent caused cancellation of the 1966 Aga Khan Trophy competition. However, this made way for the first head-to-head between the Irish Army riders and the civilians. McKee Barracks fielded Billy Ringrose, Ned Campion, Larry Kiely and the young Ronnie MacMahon, while the civilians selected Tommy Brennan, Tommy Wade, Diana Conolly-Carew and Seamus Hayes. Britain sent its B team and it was this side that won. There was little between the two Irish sides, but, for the record, the civilians finished ahead of the army team. Diana Conolly-Carew put the icing on the cake for the civilians by winning the Grand Prix on Barrymore.

Diana Conolly-Carew on the brilliant grey Barrymore, winners of the 1966 Dublin Grand Prix. The partnership also won the Enschede Grand Prix and went on to jump in the Mexico Olympics. (Independent Newspapers)

At the beginning of 1967, Seamus Hayes and Doneraile won the first indoor Grand Prix in s'Hertogenbosch, Holland, and that was Ireland's last major international Grand Prix for some ten years.

In 1967, Seamus's continued success put him onto the Aga Khan Trophy team once more, alongside Ned Campion, Billy Ringrose and Tommy Wade. Again Tommy was to be the centre of attention and drama during the run-up to the show. Right up until opening day, doubts lingered as to whether he and Dundrum would jump for Ireland as, at the time, he and the SJAI were in conflict over an incident at a show in Dungarvan. The conflict had arisen when Tommy, his brother Eddie and Gerry Costello had wished to divide the prizes after they had already jumped four rounds in the main competition and were still tied for first place. The judges insisted that they jump, so, one by one, the three of them came into the ring and

A star of the 1960s — Tommy Brennan, seen here in winning form with Kilkenny — who went on to be an Olympic and pan-American medal winner. (Tommy Brennan)

retired. Thus the judges were forced into a position where they had to declare the three riders as dividers of the prizes anyway. The competitors were called before a Munster disciplinary committee and suspended. However, the suspension applied only to national competitions and so Tommy was still eligible to be selected for the Dublin Internationals — as it turned out, this was just as well.

Nevertheless, it was neither a clear nor easy victory for the Irish. In the first round Seamus and Goodbye went clear on their first crack at the course but had eight faults on their second; Ned Campion, on Liathdruim, had just a quarter of a fault on their first attempt, followed by a round of eight faults; while Billy Ringrose and Loch an Easpaig kept the Irish in touch, with a total of four faults for the entire first round. Then disaster struck as Dundrum flung Tommy Wade out over the fence after the water jump. He re-mounted but returned with the discard score of twenty-two faults. However, the British and the Italians also faulted and, at the break after the first round, it was Ireland: 12.25 faults, Britain: 16 faults, and Italy: 33 faults. The British put up just eight and a quarter faults in the second round, which meant that, again, it was all down to Tommy Wade. Making a full recovery, he came out this time and jumped the perfect clear round which Ireland needed to win.

Sadly, however, that home victory was only a temporary reprieve on Ireland's downward spiral into near oblivion in Nations' Cup competition. The first major blow came just weeks after the victory in Dublin when, after jumping a clear round in the Ostend Cup, the great Loch an Easpaig suffered a heart attack and fell dead at Billy Ringrose's feet. There could have been no greater loss to the Irish team. At the time this great jumper was still young enough to give at least two more years of service, but in one agonising second he was gone. With the Olympics coming up in just twelve months' time, his death meant an even greater loss to Billy and the Irish team.

Debate soon began as to whether Ireland should now send a showjumping team to the 1968 Mexico Olympiad at all.

For the most part, the SJAI remained cool to the idea of taking on such a mission. One of its most prominent members, Omar van Landeghem is quoted as saying at the time:

> *...in my opinion we have neither enough riders or horses of Olympic standard to make up a showjumping team for Mexico and to send one would only discredit Irish riders and horses.*

The final decision was left until after the London and Dublin Nations' Cup competitions of 1968. London was a disaster as the team came last out of five while Harvey Smith and David Broome dominated at the first commercially sponsored Dublin Horse Show. In the Nations' Cup for the Aga Khan Trophy, the home side of Diana

Conolly-Carew, Iris Kellett, Ned Campion and Tommy Brennan finished third. Unfortunately that was not the worst of it. In the first round Tommy took a crashing fall after the water jump that resulted in his short-listed Olympic mount Tubbermac breaking both his leg and his back. The hush of the stands was broken only by a vet's pistol shot tragically signalling the demise of this great son of Tubbernagat. As this echo of death faded away, so too did one more part of Ireland's hopes for the Mexico Olympics.

Within hours, an emergency meeting with the EFI was called by the Show Jumping Association's selectors who argued for a withdrawal from the Games. They were overruled by the Federation which was intent on sending a team and whose word was final. The eventual selection of three riders and horses consisted of Diana Conolly–Carew and Barrymore, Ned Campion and Liathdruim, and Ada Matheson with Sir John Nugent's San Pedro. The outcome in Mexico could almost be interpreted as justification of the SJAI's misgivings.

The Mexican Disaster

The Irish showjumping team for the 1968 Olympics went early to Mexico for an acclimatisation period. The team's first crisis arose in a violent thunderstorm, when the transport lorry got stuck in the mud. As it was being dug out, Ada Matheson's horse, San Pedro, tried to lie down inside the back of the lorry and, in the process, cut part of his hoof away on the partition. With good veterinary care over the next few weeks he was declared fit, and only then could the team start training. When it finally came to perform in the competition, Diana and Barrymore went first for Ireland. However, luck was not on their side as he burst a blood vessel during his round, had three refusals and was then eliminated. Immediately it was announced that the whole Irish team was eliminated — actually an incorrect decision as, under the rules, Diana should have been given the worst score of the round plus twenty as her penalty. The Irish Chef d'Équipe, Colonel Bill Rea, protested and was initially turned down but, eventually, he was told that his other two riders could jump. However, by this time, Ada Matheson had left the main arena warm-up pocket and was in the preliminary practice ring fifteen minutes away. Bill's request for a delay was refused and Ada did not jump in the first round. Ned Campion did jump in turn but Liathdruim had several fences down. When the round ended, it was announced that Ireland had been eliminated because one of its riders did not jump. Bill protested again unsuccessfully and, in a final irony, while he was talking to the appeal jury, Diana and Barrymore went in and jumped their second round. They finished this time with a reasonably good score of sixteen but it was to no avail. Ireland were disqualified.[5]

Ireland won its first European showjumping medals in 1969. Iris Kellett took individual ladies' gold at the RDS and Paul Darragh individual junior silver at Dinard. The full junior team included Paul, Ann Lowry, Sandra Duffy, Pat Tobin and Barbara Fitzpatrick. Diana Conolly-Carew was Chef d'Équipe.
(Leslie Fitzpatrick)

One positive result did come from the Mexican debacle — the SJAI demanded, and got, a greater voice in the decision making process of the Equestrian Federation of Ireland. Within the year, they had their representation doubled to two members — National Chairman Robert Lowry joining Philip O'Connor on the seven-member body which, since 1931, had been totally controlled by the RDS.

Despite this demoralising low in its history, Irish showjumping, as always, picked itself up, re-mounted and tried again. Before the decade was out it received a superb moral boost through the winning of its first international medals in 1969 — one from the ever reliable Iris Kellett in the Ladies' European Championship, and the other from a very young Paul Darragh in the Junior Europeans.

With Diana Conolly-Carew as Chef d'Équipe, Ireland made its fifth attempt (out of the eighteen events so far) at the Junior European Championship, fielding the side of Paul Darragh, Sandra Duffy, Pat Tobin, Barbara Moore (later married to Leslie Fitzpatrick) and Ann Lowry (daughter of Robert Lowry). The team finished eighth out of fourteen but Paul Darragh, on Diana's Errigal, took the individual silver medal — beaten by two tenths of a second by Bertrand Dufour of France.

In 1969, the eleventh Ladies' European Championship was held at the RDS in conjunction with the Dublin Horse Show. Iris Kellett helped Irish showjumping forget the disappointments of the recent past as she stormed to a convincing win on Morning Light. Since her recovery from two bouts of tetanus and a broken shoulder, Iris had scored 400 first prizes at home and abroad — forty-four of them on Morning Light. In this, her final championship contest, she took second in the opening speed phase to Anneli Drummond-Hay of Britain on Zanthos. She then turned the tables with a double clear in the Grand Prix second phase. In the two-round final, the Irish heroine was first again — this time ahead of Alison Westwood on the great Maverick.

Iris was the undisputed champion and soon after her victory she retired from international showjumping. She passed the great Morning Light on to her star pupil Eddie Macken, who the following year, was selected for the Irish team for the first time.

Eddie was soon joined by James Kernan, Paul Darragh and Con Power in an exciting revival of Irish showjumping .

Footnotes to Chapter Eight

[1] *The Irish Field*, 11 June 1960: p. 8.

[2] Ibid., 30 October 1962: .p 10.

[3] *An Cosantóir, the Irish Defence Journal*, Dublin: Army Press Office, August 1976: vol. xxxvi, no. 8: p. 231.

[4] Show Jumping Association of Ireland Archive, 1963.

[5] *Official Report on Ireland's Participation in XIXth Olympiad*, Dublin: Irish Olympic Council, 1969.

CHAPTER NINE

THE BOOMING 1970S

We have come to beat the world.
— Eddie Macken and Ned Campion the night before
the 1974 World Championships at Hickstead

The 1970s were completely dominated by Eddie Macken and Boomerang — a mighty combination of giant riding talent and massive horse power that rose above all others just at a time when Ireland was in search of new heroes. Eddie rose to prominence on the national scene in the early part of the decade and it was only a matter of time before his imprisoned energy exploded onto the continental circuit. Once at large in the European arena, he went straight to the top of the World Computer Ratings. Moreover, he was the dependable captain of a new squad that put Ireland back into the mainstream of Nations' Cup competition. With Eddie as leader, Con Power, Paul Darragh and James Kernan made up a side that became as feared and respected as the Irish Army team had been in the 1930s.

As the 1970s began, Irish showjumping was in transition. The winners who had kept Ireland on the map over the previous twenty years were retiring; Iris Kellett had ended her career in glory with the 1969 European Championship, and in 1971 Colonel Billy Ringrose passed the sword of light to Ned Campion and Larry Kiely as he took over the Officer Commanding post at McKee Barracks. The champion Dundrum was injured late in 1967 and never jumped internationally again, and Tommy Wade himself, having gone through a period of suspension over the Dungarvan show incident, proudly said his time was over in 1972. Seamus Hayes was injured in a fall at the Spring Show and jumped for the last time in 1973. Leslie Fitzpatrick continued to campaign and took wins on Carnaby Street until 1974, while Tommy Brennan on horses from Frank Kernan and Charles Haughey remained a force until 1976. In January 1974, Charles James (Tony Power) prophetically wrote in *The Irish Field*: 'Ireland is between eras, one fading, one not yet arrived....'[1]

In the meantime, a new group of jumpers came onto the national scene. Riders such as Michael Hickey, Ned Cash Junior, Margie Lowry, Con McElroy, Tom Vance, Leonard Cave and George Stewart were to see international competition and achieve a degree of success in speed wins and jump-off placings. However, speed wins alone are not enough in the dynamic world of modern showjumping competition; its vital marrow derives from Grand Prix, Derby and Nations' Cup wins.

In speed competitions fences are not as high, wide or numerous as they are in the big Grand Prix events when the heights can go to about five feet, whereas in Derby-type events, fences are more varied, complex and rustic, and few clear rounds are realised. Courses for Nations' Cup-type events are much like those for Grand Prix classes but the added pressure of team jumping is great.

Army riders of the 1960s and 1970s Ned Campion (above) and Larry Kiely (opposite) — with a low budget for buying horses they were starved of good replacement mounts for much of the time but nonetheless they scored many international wins and jumped on winning Nations' Cup teams at Dublin, Ostend Nice and Rotterdam.
(Irish Times)

As Ged O'Dwyer realised back in the 1930s, an individual or a team must go for the most important events — the classics — if they are to be truly counted in world terms. Between 1967 and 1975 Irish riders were starved of such morale-boosting successes at the great contests in London, Rome, Aachen, Brussels, New York, and also at the new indoor shows. At that time, events at such venues were being dominated by names such as Hartwig Steenken, Gerd Wiltfang, Alwin and Paul Schockemohle of Germany, Nelson Pessoa of Brazil, and Raimondo d'Inzeo of Italy along with Britain's David Broome and Harvey Smith.

It was ironic that the latter four riders — Smith, Broome, Pessoa and d'Inzeo, were generally mounted on exported Irish horses. In 1970, there were over seventy Irish-bred horses competing for countries like Switzerland, Brazil, Britain, Italy and the USA. That same year, more than 5,000 horses and ponies were exported from Ireland — many of them at prices that Irish riders, and even the army jumping team, could not afford. In the early 1970s the Irish Army's annual purchasing budget for horses was little more than £10,000, and even with that, there was a limit on what they could pay for any one remount. 'How can we hope to retain the good jumpers when other countries are offering £40,000 and up for them...?' Tommy Brennan commented at the time. By 1973, the Army Equitation School had come very close to being closed altogether as the Government concentrated funding on the newly created Bord na gCapall. However, in the end, the Army Equitation School's hallowed tradition won out.

Bord na gCapall

It was in an effort to cope with the decline of the Irish sport horse that Bord na gCapall was set up in 1971 with an annual budget of £200,000. As far back as the mid-1960s this idea had been mooted by the then Minister for Agriculture, Charles J. Haughey TD. From then until the bill for its establishment was published in 1970, great hopes were raised within the SJAI. It was very optimistic as to what this new input of Government money could do for the sport of showjumping in terms of paying for team training and travel, among other matters. That hope never materialised — even when the Bord's annual grant reached £1 million, at the end of the decade, the SJAI, which was then in debt, was allocated just £8,000 (less than 1 per cent of the total grant).

Although Noel Tanner, a showjumping representative to the new Board, became its first chairman, it was made clear from the start that no money would be paid out directly to an organisation like the SJAI. It had to be channelled through one overall equestrian body, the Equestrian Federation of Ireland. It was soon realised, that the Federation would have to become a wider, more representative organisation if it was to cope with the scramble for funding from all of the equestrian bodies.

Thus, in 1973, its membership was changed to include two representatives each from the SJAI, the Horse Trials Society (the three-day-eventing organisation) and the RDS. In addition, a new National Equestrian Committee (NEC) was established to oversee both the dispersal of funding and the development of Irish equestrian sport. Its membership included four representatives from the SJAI, three from the Horse Trials and two from the RDS. Although it did some good work in the training of young riders, the NEC never really got grass roots support and it survived for only four years. In 1979, the EFI was again reconstituted and remains much the same to the present day: SJAI — five members; Horse Trials — three members; RDS — three members; Pony Society, Department of Defence and Irish Driving Society — one member each. Bord na gCapall lasted for sixteen years until it finally closed down in 1988. During that time, it spent £10 million trying to grapple with all of the problems besetting the Irish equestrian industry but, for the most part, it was unsuccessful. In the end, its greatest contribution was the learning process it afforded as to what mistakes to avoid in the future. The new Horse Board of the 1990s did indeed learn these lessons, and so far has sustained support in its efforts at coming to grips with the inherent problems of Irish sport horse breeding.

The weakness of Irish showjumping was graphically underlined in 1971, a year in which £15,000 worth of prizes were on offer in Ireland between a new international at Balmoral and at the Dublin Horse Show. However, only £1,000 of this money was kept at home. No Irish showjumpers competed at the Munich Olympic Games in 1972, as it was not possible to send a strong enough team.

However, behind these dark clouds the bright stars were gathering that were to illumine the second half of the 1970s — not only in terms of riders, but also owners who were willing to forego big rewards in order to put good horses at the disposal of the Irish team.

One such owner was Iris Kellett, who placed Morning Light, Linnett and Maxwell at Eddie Macken's disposal after her retirement from international showjumping; this was just what the incredibly lucky young man from Granard needed. From his earliest days, all Eddie wanted to do was ride horses. His father Jimmy once recalled:

> ...the stools in my butcher shop, the chairs at home, walls, whatever became horses and even then he rode them with style.

On one occasion he was given a cowboy set for Christmas and people in the town still recall him galloping up and down Main Street on an old farm pony while firing the toy six-shooter into the air. He once tried the same trick with the local hunt and was sent home. His great friends and mentors, Ann and Brian Gormley, say they could set their watch by young Macken's arrival at their equestrian centre after school to ride their ponies. School itself was not for Eddie and the months at St Mel's College, away from the horses, were torture for him. 'Take me out or I'll take myself out,' he pleaded with his father. So Eddie came home to work in the butcher shop and ride when ever he could — 'I think I learned my sense of balance carrying sides of beef,' he once noted.

Eddie Macken's first great piece of luck came in 1969 when the Gormleys recommended him to Iris Kellett. Having seen him ride a pony named Granard Boy in Dublin a few years previously, she was willing to take him on as a working student. Later she recalled:

> He came to me as a rough country boy but when he sat on a horse it was magic — he had an excellent build, was supple, had the temperament and natural sensitivity. Above everything else he had a feel for the horse.

Macken's progress was fast, Iris never letting him away with anything. She would run down the school after him to make sure he was following instructions. He listened like he had never listened to a teacher before and he learned — he learned enough to be on the Aga Khan Trophy team within eighteen months, in August 1970, and for the next ten years, he was never off the side. In 1971 he had his first continental trip to Ostend where, on Oatfield Hills, he joined Ned Campion on Garrai Eoin, and Larry Kiely on Inis Cara in Ireland's first victory in the Nations' Cup there. That trip induced a longing in Eddie, for a wider exercise of his talent, which was to draw him back to the Continent to stay some four years later.

In that same year of 1971 another mighty talent was beginning to emerge — that of Dublin-born Paul Darragh. In all the history of Irish showjumping there has never been a rider to match Paul in his single-minded effort to succeed. Showjumping was not the chosen family path for this young student of the 1960s. It was thought that he would follow his father Austin into the medical profession, but a hole in the hedge of their home in Killiney was to determine otherwise. When he was just five years old he found his way from their garden into the small riding school next-door and from then on his heart and mind lived in the world of horses. It is to the credit of his parents that they did not come between him and his obvious love of things equine. With a little pony named Peggy Sue, he was introduced to jumping competition at the age of nine. When he was ten he went to Iris Kellett's school where he developed the polished winning style that was to become the hallmark of his career. It was while on Ireland's junior team, back in 1971, that his riding first began drawing attention. For three years running he had taken European Championship medals; in 1969 he won silver with Errigal, and in 1970 they also took the bronze. The following year, at Hickstead, on Diana Conolly-Carew's Woodpecker II, he joined Charlie Curtis, Marilyn Dawson and Kevin Barry in winning team gold. He took individual silver once again that year, missing gold by only a tenth of a second in a jump-off. He was to return to Hickstead four years later to attain further glory in the Derby on the great Pele.

In the meantime, Eddie Macken, the man Paul Darragh would spend a lifetime having to beat, was blazing a winning trail to every corner of Ireland on Iris Kellett's team of horses. Where Eddie went, he won; not only that, he also often took both first and second in the show's main events. New championships were being inaugurated all over the country in the early 1970s — the Strokestown Chrysler Challenge, the televised Benson and Hedges TV Championship and the Bord na gCapall League. In their first years of running (1972 and 1973) Eddie Macken, Ned Cash and Tom Vance all dominated the qualifiers, but it was the man from Granard who won the finals. The name Eddie Macken was soon known to everyone associated with horses right across the land — and this was just the beginning.

However, on a quiet Sunday afternoon in 1973 near Iris Kellett's newly built centre at Kill, County Kildare, Macken's marauding march was unceremoniously halted by a tall, slim, smiling twenty-year-old army officer by the name of Con Power. As he crossed the line ahead of Eddie to win the Grand Prix there on Cluain Aodha, he could almost be heard declaring in his own enthusiastic way: 'That will teach ya.' Con knew Eddie well. In fact, his father had bought the winning pony, Granard Boy, from the Mackens when Eddie had outgrown him, and Con enjoyed wins on him as well. Born onto a thriving horse-breeding farm in Folksmills, County Wexford, it was always a certainty that he would ride professionally. During his school years racing was his first choice, but as his frame rose to six foot three, showjumping became a more plausible option — but where could he practise his art? 'There were few outlets for a lad like me, so I took a shot at the army,' Con recalls. He was commissioned in 1973 and first scored horse trial wins. However, he was soon given some reasonably good showjumpers with which to compete. With the trebling of the McKee Barracks' buying budget the year he arrived there, new mounts like Coolronan, Castlepark and Rockbarton were soon on the way. Con was to make the best of them with Grand Prix wins in Wiesbaden and Deauville plus Leading Rider awards in Dublin, Ostend, New York and Toronto.

There was a prophetic line-up in the 1974 Irish Field Awards with Eddie Macken as best over-twenty-one rider, Con Power as best under-twenty-one rider and one James Kernan as best under-sixteen rider.

James Kernan was the son of former international rider, Frank Kernan of Crossmaglen. He had been the youngest ever winner of the SJAI Pixie Cup at the age of ten and, just like his father, while still

Ned Cash Junior, son of legendary horse judge and dealer Ned Cash, was one of the young riders who joined the Irish Army during the early 1970s. (Irish Times)

riding ponies, he took the Balmoral Championship. When it was time for him to graduate onto horses, he was lucky to have both Tommy Brennan's instruction and a number of his trained string available to him, including the superb mare Marcella. With her, he joined Justin Carthy, Margie Lowry and Eimear Haughey on the Irish team which took the bronze medal in 1972 at the European Championships in Cork. On that occasion gold went to a Belgian side that included Eva van Paesschen, Ferdi Tyteca, Patrick Ronge and future business partner of Paul Darragh at Tara, Alain Storme. James had a superb 1973 national season on Marcella, and then, in 1974 in Lucerne, he won Ireland's first Junior European Championship gold medal. Brian McMahon of Limerick was to follow suit in 1976 when taking Ireland's only other individual gold in the event on a legendary mare kept for Ireland by Jimmy Flynn of Ennis — the great Heather Honey. In the meantime, James Kernan honed his talent further during a six-month training stint in Italy with Munich Olympic gold medalist, Graziano Mancinelli, to whom the Kernans had sold the Irish-bred winner, Ambassador.

Paul Darragh spent sixteen months during 1972 and 1973 riding horses that Bord na gCapall had bought and stabled at McKee Barracks. His only pay was the opportunity of studying under the renowned Polish teacher, Colonel Wladislaw Zgorelski, who had been employed by the Bord as National Trainer. Paul's career suddenly reached a crossroads though, when his contract was terminated at the end of 1973. However, his inner compulsion to ride once again manifested itself when, instead of taking up another career, he enlisted for a tough eighteen-month training tour with Harvey Smith and Trevor Banks in Yorkshire.

Another important occurrence in the latter half of 1973, which was later to bear fruit, was the purchase of Fiona Kinnear's champion hunter Pele, by Iris Kellett. Iris had seen her star pupil Eddie Macken and this magnificently athletic gelding win the national championship in Dublin a few weeks previously and had decided that the two should remain together. The true wisdom of that decision was to show itself in 1974 when Eddie got the opportunity to test his talent fully against the best in the world. This was the challenge he longed for and he grasped the opportunity majestically. Having scored five wins at the Spring Show that year, he and Pele had an initial away outing at Hickstead's Spring meeting and were then selected for the World Championships at the same venue in August. There, before a crowd of 32,000, the young twenty-four-year-old was to emerge as a truly world-class rider who fully lived up to Ned Campion's half-jesting, half-serious prediction on the eve of the event — 'We have come to beat the world.'

From a starting field of twenty-nine riders from sixteen countries, Eddie and Pele took three cool clear rounds over the initial speed and jump-off phases. They then went into the semi-final rounds with a two-point lead ahead of Hartwig Steenken of Germany, Britain's European Champion Paddy McMahon, and every top rider in the sport at that time. 'I had never seen fences so big but the rest were better at knocking them than me,' he later quipped in *Horses of Ireland*. After the semi-final phase he was through to the final along with Steenken on Simona, Frank Chapot on Main Spring, and Hugo Simon on Lavendal. At the conclusion of this challenge, in which they had to ride each other's horses over one round each, Eddie emerged in a four-fault tie with the German.

The Championship had to be decided in a timed jump-off. For some reason that was never explained; the judges decided that the Irishman should go first, against the clock. Pele had stepped in the water with both Chapot and Simon during the four-way contest and there was no way that he would jump it after that — no matter who was riding him. 'I knew I was on four faults before I started and drawn first I had no option but to go fast'. That he certainly did, finishing in 45.60 seconds; but in addition to the water he had the sixth fence down as well. The German ace took full advantage of being last to go and, although also faulting at the water, he stayed clear after that to return the winner on four faults in a slow 65.40 seconds. Eddie Macken was runner-up, but Avril Douglas, in her report from Hickstead for *The Irish Field* declared, '...this brilliant young man has single-handedly put Ireland back in World Class showjumping.'[2] Later, Eddie gave his own reaction to those dramatic moments:

> I lived with that defeat for the next four years and vowed it would be different next time.[3]

His first step in that direction was a move into the heartland of continental competition when he went to the Schockemohle brothers in Mühlen, Germany in the Spring of 1975. Impressed by Eddie's riding in the World Championships, rich German owner Dr Herbert Schnapka eased the young Irishman's way into exile by providing horses for him to ride in the Schockemohle yard. There, he was shortly re-united with an Irish-bred gelding, now named Boomerang, that he had previously ridden and found difficult at Iris Kellett's. Easter Parade, his best horse at the time, had broken his back in a freak accident on the way back from the cancelled spring meeting at Hickstead in 1975. By way of an interim replacement, Paul Schockemohle said to him: '...take my speed horse Boomerang for the time being until you get something better.'[4]

Better! Soon there was to be no better than Eddie Macken and Boomerang in the whole world. Over the period between 1975 and 1979, they were to win, or take second, in a record-breaking thirty-two major Grand Prix or Derby events across Europe and in the USA. Ireland's thirst for showjumping glory was quenched as all of the big classics that had eluded her for years, suddenly fell to the green. Eddie triumphed in

British team at the Dublin Horse Show in the early 1970s — left to right: Harvey Smith, Graham Fletcher, Paddy McMahon and David Broome all had success on Irish horses.
(Ruth Roger)

London, Rome, New York, Brussels, Aachen, Nice, La Baule, Calgary, St Gallen and Gothenburg. He was Leading Rider at Wembley, Washington, Rome, Dublin, Olympia, Aachen and Calgary. He topped the World Computer Ratings in 1976, 1977 and 1978, while he and Boomerang amassed £250,000 in prize money — record winnings at the time. British journalist Judith Dreaper, in her book, *The Stars of Show Jumping*, writes:

> *Eddie Macken, the supreme stylist, will go down in sporting history, not just as one of the greatest riders to come out of Ireland but as one of the greatest riders of all time in the world.*[5]

Objective commentator and head of RTÉ Radio Sport, Ian Corr, referred to him as:

> *...one of the very few Irish internationals of his time who had such a cool and detached lack of awe for the opposition he faced. In that respect I place him in the same category as the great cyclist Seán Kelly.*

Of all Eddie's triumphs, those that impressed his home fans most were the ones that came across so vividly on the BBC television coverage of competitions at Hickstead, at Olympia, at Wembley and at the Professional Championship in Cardiff. His record of four wins in a row on Boomerang in the Hickstead Derby still holds and still endears the memory of this partnership to lovers of the sport here.

The year 1975 not only initiated the magic union of Eddie and Boomerang, it also brought a number of other far-reaching developments within the sport at home in Ireland. Perhaps as a direct result of the increased interest that Macken's exploits engendered, the new season began with a record 3,900 horses and ponies being registered with the SJAI. The membership of the Association topped 3,000 and a total of 416 shows became affiliated to the organisation. To help keep track of this activity, Secretary General Ned Campion introduced official pony measuring for the first time, and the rule that all horses must wear plastic registration numbers was enforced. A total of seventy riding establishments were listed with Bord na gCapall, whose annual budget had by then been boosted to over £500,000 for that year. However, the number employed at the Bord's headquarters was by then thirty-five and some 70 per cent of the grant money was going into administration. The National Equestrian Committee, which had been established the previous year, had £10,000 available to it for 1975 (this was increased to £25,000 in 1976). Also in 1975 an era ended at the RDS, as its course builder, Eddie Taylor, oversaw the removal of its famous banks which had been installed some ninety years previously.

There were other developments within the sport itself that year. Con Power, a Lieutenant at that time, began riding Coolronan and jumped in his first Nations' Cup in Rome. In June, Sean Daly took over as Officer Commanding at McKee Barracks and was to be an inspiring leader of the young Irish team over the next two years as Chef d'Équipe. That same month, Paul Darragh, who had returned from Harvey Smith's, took up the reins on Iris Kellett's Pele. He was selected for the official team for the first time to compete at the Dublin Horse Show along with Ned Campion, Larry Kiely, Tom Vance, Michael Hickey and Eddie Macken. Eddie had just won the championship at Wembley on Boomerang and was to jump clear as Ireland came second to Britain in the Dublin Nations' Cup. Individually he came a close second to Raimondo d'Inzeo on Bellvue in the Grand Prix. In addition, Ned Cash and Kevin Barry boosted Ireland's performance further by winning the pairs relay.

Soon there were to be even more heartening results from Hickstead. Eddie Macken, wearing the red jacket of Germany,[*] won the Derby Trial ahead of thirty other competitors, on Boomerang, but the first part of the Devil's Dyke[**] denied them in the Derby itself. However, it was Paul Darragh and Pele who took up the running as they went through to a two-way jump-off with Britain's Tony Newbury. In the end Paul had one fence to spare over Tony and took the £2,500 first prize. He was welcomed with bands and a victory parade when he returned to his new Dublin base at Marlay Grange that evening. As the year ended, Eddie Macken, confirmed his new supremacy with Boomerang when he won the Grand Prix both in St Gallen, Switzerland, and at Wembley in London.

With the start of the new 1976 season came the promise of a return to Irish glory in both team and individual performances. Ned Campion and Eddie Macken scored wins in Rome, and the Irish side was second in the Nations' Cup in Lucerne; Eddie and Boomerang also came second in the Grand Prix before travelling to Cardiff and winning the first ever Professional Championship held there.

Ned, Eddie and Con Power were joined by the eighteen-year-old James Kernan for his first performance on the Aga Khan Trophy team in 1976, when Britain beat the Irish by just one fence. Con had a superb Ballsbridge show on Coolronan and was the first Irish competitor to take the Leading Rider award there. Con, James Kernan, Larry Kiely and Ned Campion were then beaten in the Nations' Cup in Rotterdam, only after a jump-off, before going on to win in Ostend, where Con was again declared Leading Rider.

---

[*] As Eddie was employed by a German owner at the time he was free to wear that country's colours if he chose — this he did for one season only.

[**] The Devil's Dyke is one of the most difficult obstacles in showjumping. It comprises three very flimsy fences made of light poles. The middle one is at the bottom of a hollow with room for only one stride before. The space between it and the last element demands one long stride. These difficulties are compounded by the proximity of the obstacle to the crowd, which may distract the horse.

The famous Dublin banks provided exciting jumping in the RDS arena for ninety years before they were removed in 1975. Everything could go right or very wrong — as it did for superb Meath rider Fidelma McGiven on one occasion when her mare decided to stop and send Fidelma into a dramatic somersault across the bank.
(Irish Times and Jean Bridel)

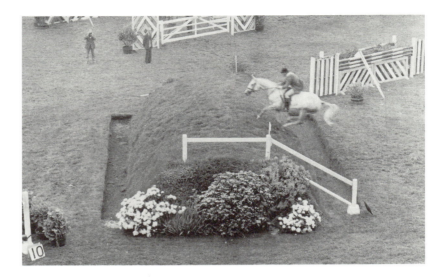

In the meantime, Eddie was busy at Hickstead where he and Boomerang jumped the only clear to win his first of four Derbies. From there he travelled to Hamburg and took the Derby there as well before heading for the Horse of the Year Show, at Wembley, where he won the Grand Prix and was also Leading Rider.

In the autumn of 1976, Con Power won a Chrysler Car which was the main prize at the show in Strokestown and was awarded to the winner of the Grand Prix event there. To get around the strict amateur/professional stance of the Irish Equestrian Federation, show organiser Ado Kenny gave the trophy vehicle as a wedding present to Con and his wife Margaret. Soon after this, the army team got one of its best boosts in years when it acquired the great horse, Rockbarton. Then known as Buccaneer, he was bought by Tommy Wade as a young horse in 1974 and then went to David Mitchell of Comber, County Down —a rider on the national circuit and a very talented trainer of young showjumpers. Colonel Sean Daly first saw Rockbarton (Buccaneer), at Ballivor Show, in County Meath in 1975. Con had won the Grand Prix there, while Ned Campion took second, fourth and fifth; sandwiched in between them, in third, was David Mitchell on Buccaneer. After negotiations at the Dublin Horse Show, the army paid £40,000 for him — the highest price paid for any horse by McKee Barracks up to that point. He proved to be worth that, and more, during the years ahead. With Ned Campion in the saddle, the renamed Rockbarton made his first trip to New York at the end of the 1976 season. Con Power then took up the reins and, when he returned to the American circuit again in 1978, he helped Con to the title of Leading Rider of the entire winter tour of Washington, New York and Toronto.

However, in the winter of 1976, it was Eddie Macken who took the honours. He was Leading Rider in Washington where he scored two wins and went on to take the Grand Prix in New York; more wins in Toronto gave him the overall award for the three shows. The forces were gathering for what proved to be the true resurrection of the Irish team.

The year 1977 witnessed the advent of rider sponsorship to Irish showjumping for the first time. Making the initial move in that direction was the Irish Dairy Board, who ensured retention of Pele in the country through a leasing deal with Iris Kellett. Following his superb performance, in the World Championships with Eddie Macken, and in the Hickstead Derby with Paul Darragh, offers poured in from abroad for this great gelding and he could have been sold for a record price. Fortunately, Iris wanted to hold on, and early in 1977 Eddie, who was preparing for a return to Ireland, teamed-up with Pele once again. Then, with encouragement from equestrian journalist Jim Norton, the Irish Dairy Board agreed to sponsor Pele and he was re-christened after their brand-name 'Kerrygold'. The Irish Dairy Board, through this product name, later expanded its backing of the sport of Irish showjumping, and the name 'Kerrygold' is now very much associated with it.

Also at the start of 1977, P.J. Carroll and Company gave their name to Paul Darragh's brilliant little horse Nuxer, and he was re-named P.J. Carroll. Under his new title he was to become the champion speed horse of the world with close on 100 wins to his credit. At the same time, Paul began his famous partnership with Jimmy Flynn's horse, Heather Honey, when Brian McMahon moved from his Ennis stables to work for Noel C. Duggan in Millstreet. The Dublin rider was then in command of a sufficiently strong string to take his full place on the Irish team.

The Carroll tobacco company soon extended their sponsorship to include Paul and Eddie's complete stables of horses. Carroll's also financed an extremely useful public address and timing unit, which was available free of charge to the major shows throughout the country. Their input was huge at this time and it lasted right through the 1970s and 1980s. Carroll's, Kerrygold, the Ministry of Defence and other sponsors who were to follow suit provided the kind of funding

The Irish dream team of the late 1970s which won the Aga Khan Trophy Competition in 1977, 1978 and 1979 — top left: Eddie Macken on Boomerang; top right: James Kernan on Condy; above: Con Power, who had the distinction of riding three different horses on the 'three-in-a-row' side — Coolronan, Castlepark and Rockbarton; bottom right: Paul Darragh on Heather Honey; middle right: Chef d'Équipe Colonel Sean Daly sharing the Aga Khan Trophy with Eddie Macken in 1977.
(Mames Ansell, Horseman Photography, Irish Press, and Irish Times)

needed to ensure that the Irish riders of the time could remain competitive while still being based in Ireland.

Just how competitive they were was soon to be very evident as the 1977 season got under way. Eddie opened with a Grand Prix win on Kerrygold, at the Hickstead Spring meeting, and followed that with three wins in Rome, where he was also declared Leading Rider and took runner-up position in the Grand Prix. 'I think I am doomed to be second by fractions,' he once commented laconically. This was to prove true at his next major outing in the European Championships in Vienna. There, he and Kerrygold battled their way into a two-way tie on eight faults with Holland's Johan Heinz on Seven Valleys. Eddie was first to go in the jump-off and he returned with four faults in 51.50 seconds. Johan also had four faults but was a tenth of a second faster, finishing in 51.40 seconds to take first place. Again, Eddie had missed gold by fractions but, undeterred, he pressed on and began preparing for a Horse Show in Dublin which he will never forget.

Also building for the big home show was James Kernan, who now had a massively talented team horse by the name of Condy. James's dedicated sister, Shirley, has to be given credit for keeping this horse at home in Ireland. He was within minutes of being shipped to Italy along with a lorry load of young jumpers from the Kernans' Crossmaglen yard, when she intervened, 'That one has to stay for James to ride,' she insisted, and so he was returned to his stable. Her judgement proved sound as Condy went on to win the Boylan Trophy in Ballsbridge in 1976 and also took first place at the Royal Windsor Horse Show and in Ostend. He had a good outing along with Paul Darragh on P.J. Carroll and Heather Honey at Hickstead in 1977, and was also ready for the big Dublin Show that year. In the meantime, Con Power and Eddie Macken performed well in La Baule, France, where Ireland were second to Germany in the Nations' Cup and Boomerang won the Grand Prix.

In what proved to be a controversial decision, the only rider from McKee Barracks to make the Aga Khan Trophy team that year was Con Power. Veteran stalwarts Ned Campion and Larry Kiely lost out as Paul Darragh, Eddie Macken and James Kernan (who was still just nineteen years old) made up the foursome finally chosen by Sean Daly. His confidence in this, the youngest side ever fielded by Ireland, was not misplaced. Over the first three days of the show, Eddie Macken gave the young team members the best possible encouragement, as he won four of the six events on offer with Kerrygold and Boomerang. In the Nations' Cup the team was up against the European silver and bronze medal sides from Vienna — Britain and Germany — along with the Italian and Belgian teams. After two tense and close-fought rounds, Ireland and Germany were tied on eight faults apiece and, for only the second time in the history of the event, they went into a jump-off.

After Eddie Macken and Boomerang won the Hickstead Derby three times in a row a trophy was struck depicting the famous pair coming down the bank. It has been presented to the winner of the event ever since.
(Bunn Family)

Paul Darragh on Heather Honey, Con Power on Coolronan and James Kernan on Condy delivered three speed rounds that will forever be etched in the memories of Irish showjumping fans and competitors. Germany could not match that and when Paul Schockemohle knocked the first part of the double it was all over. 'I will never forget looking through the pocket gate and seeing that pole hit the ground,' the ever-enthusiastic Con Power recalled. It was Con who took the shining Aga Khan Trophy and carried it in an exuberant and mould-breaking circuit of the arena, 'It almost broke my arm but by God it was worth it,' he said afterwards.

That was not the end of the glory by any means — there was a win by the team of Larry Kiely, Con Power, James Kernan and Paul Darragh in the Nations' Cup in Rotterdam and, at the Derby meeting in Sussex, Con had two wins while James and Eddie took one apiece. Then to crown it all, Eddie took a unique first and second in the Hickstead Derby with Boomerang and Kerrygold respectively. No man will ever dominate this testing challenge of cool courage and skill with such consistent brilliance as this Irishman. In testament to his talent, the image of Eddie coming down the Hickstead bank is now the event's appropriate perpetual trophy. The classic year of 1977 gave him his second victory in that event.

Also to come that year were two more Grand Prix wins for Macken and Boomerang, as once again they conquered the Horse of the Year Show at Wembley and followed this by taking the Brussels classic event as well. Eddie was Leading Rider at Olympia on Dutch and German-bred horses while, for the second year in a row, he went top of the World Computer Ratings. However, none of these victories could be topped by Eddie Macken's very best reward of 1977 — the outright gift of Boomerang to him from Dr Schnapka. Then, as he returned to make his home in Kells, County Meath, P.J. Carroll & Company extended their sponsorship to include Boomerang — the future looked bright indeed.

Unfortunately, despite the Irish master's good fortune, clouds were gathering on the horizon — Boomerang took temporarily ill and Virginia, a good young horse in Eddie's string, had to be put down. Furthermore, the Equestrian Federation of Ireland, against the best of advice, reaffirmed its outdated decision to ban all Irish riders from jumping with anything but Irish-bred horses in international competition. Disagreement on this decision and issues surrounding the professional/amateur status of riders were to result in court battles both in Ireland and Europe.

However, the jumping continued in 1978, and with Boomerang returned to health, Eddie had one of the most eventful seasons of his career up to that time. During that year, he won the indoor Grand Prix in Gothenburg, and the outdoor Grand Prix events in Nice, Hamburg, Rome, and Aachen. He also triumphed at the show championships of Rome and Aachen, as did Paul Darragh who won four classes. Eddie also took the Hamburg Derby, but only after obtaining a High Court Injunction which allowed him to ride the German-bred horse, Boy. He again had to go into the High Court to be allowed ride foreign-breds at the Royal International at Wembley and in a symbolic win took the two-horse challenge there with Boomerang and Boy.

The Equestrian Federation of Ireland in Court

Twice during the 1970s the Equestrian Federation of Ireland was brought to court — once by Tommy Brennan in 1974, for having declared him a professional because he was director of a blood stock company, and again four years later, by Eddie Macken over its ban on him riding anything other than Irish-bred horses. In the Brennan case, Judge Kenny ruled in the international rider's favour. Eddie Macken also won in the High Court but this time the EFI would not let it stand at that and appealed to the Supreme Court. There the EFI won on a judges' decision that was split three to two. Left with the option of either retiring at the end of Boomerang's career or fighting on for rider freedom, Macken took the matter to the European Court. He was on his way to winning there when the Federation offered to settle — it would removed its ban if Eddie agreed not to pursue the matter further. In a generous gesture, Eddie agreed to the settlement. It was a very sad episode in which the Equestrian Federation of Ireland and Bord na gCapall, which between them put up some £40,000 a year in funding, appeared to close their eyes on the realities of Irish horse breeding and professional showjumping. The SJAI itself held fairly liberal views in relation to both the amateur/professional controversy and the 'Irish-bred only' ban but it failed to make its opinions influence the EFI. The amateur/professional issue also surfaced over the car offered as a prize by Ado Kenny at the Strokestown Show. Army rider, Captain Larry Kiely, won it in 1973, but was unable to accept for fear of losing his amateur status. The same thing happened to Captain Con Power but, as mentioned previously, Ado Kenny found a way around the problem.

As the year progressed there was also news from McKee Barracks — Colonel Billy Ringrose replaced Sean Daly as Officer Commanding, and the Army Equitation School's budget for horse purchasing, was increased to £100,000. Con Power was injured and out of action for May and June, and both Ned Campion and Larry Kiely retired from jumping altogether. They were replaced by John Roche and Gerry Mullins who were selected for the international squad that year.

As the Dublin Horse Show loomed ahead Ireland looked set for victory. James Kernan had won the silver tankard in Hickstead, on Condy, and Paul Darragh had been the winning force on the home circuit with P.J. Carroll and Heather Honey. With Con Power returned to fitness, there was no controversy over the selection of Ireland's team this time and it went in as second favourite to win the Aga Khan Trophy. The Irish team proved better than the odds by winning again, after a spine-tingling jump-off in which Eddie Macken's final crunch clear on Boomerang sealed the victory over France. This star partnership also came second to Mike Sewell, on the great Irish-bred Chainbridge, in the Grand Prix. While their performance on home ground was an encouraging one, this final result can now be seen as an omen of what was to come in the World Championships at Aachen.

Eddie had longed for this event and the chance to exorcise the narrow defeat of 1974. Sadly, the Irish team of himself, Robert Splaine, Paul Darragh and Gerry Mullins had a disappointing outing, but Eddie and Boomerang were in the fight all the way for individual gold. They came a respectable fourth in the opening speed round, were joint-third in the second leg, runner-up in the big third round and thus made it through to the final four along with Gerd Wiltfang on Roman, Michael Matz of the USA on Jet Run, and European champion Johan Heinz on Pandur Z. Although neither Eddie nor Boomerang ever knocked a fence during the horse-swapping decider, Eddie's hopes were dashed in his round on Pandur Z. He later explained what happened:

> When I went to get up on Pandur, he just seemed to get in a panic — so during the first part of the round I concentrated on just getting him to accept me, to work with me. But in getting him into that rhythm, I was out in my calculations by one eighth of a second that gave me quarter of a time fault. I blame myself — will always blame myself for letting Boomerang down — he deserved to be champion.[6]

Just like Boomerang, Eddie had everything accomplished but the winning itself. He too deserved to be champion — runner-up by fractions in three major championships is a record of excellence in itself — but it seems he will never see it as such. Not weeping in his misery over Aachen, he bounced back just a few weeks later to win the Hickstead Derby on Boomerang for the third year in a row. They followed this up with more victory, taking the Health Trophy at the first ever Dublin Indoor International.

Con Power and Paul Darragh also ended the 1978 season in winning form. At a very rainy inaugural Millstreet International, Paul was the first Irish Derby champion with Heather Honey, and this same partnership also took wins at Olympia in London. Con forewent the Dublin indoor events and took in the North American circuit of which he became Leading Rider of the season. He won in Washington and Toronto, and was Leading Rider at Madison Square Garden, from where he and Rockbarton made the front page of the *New York Times*.

The year 1978 was one of innovation and change in Irish equestrian circles. In addition to rider sponsorship and the opening of the Dublin Indoor and Millstreet Internationals, it also saw the announcement by the SJAI of a new horse-grading system, the retirement of Frank O'Reilly as Chairman of the Equestrian Federation of Ireland, and Bord na gCapall's introduction of a new horse registration passport.

Change continued into 1979 as the National Equestrian Committee was disbanded and a new Equestrian Federation of Ireland was formed under the chairmanship of Patrick Conolly-Carew. It had annual support of £40,000 from Bord na gCapall and established offices along with the SJAI on Upper Leeson Street.

The beginning of 1979 was marked by Eddie Macken being declared Supreme Irish Sports Star of the previous year. He had no easy time of it living up to that accolade and, along with some notable successes, he had some disappointments as well. He was second in the Grand Prix in Geneva, and having qualified for the first ever Volvo World Cup in Gothenburg, Eddie finished joint third on Carrolls of Dundalk behind Hugo Simon. Con Power who had also qualified for that event finished joint eleventh on Loughcrew.

However, as the season progressed the Irish winnings began to accumulate once again. Con Power and Loughcrew took first in the Grand Prix in Wiesbaden just before joining Paul Darragh, John Roche and Eddie for a historic Nations' Cup win in Aachen. Not since 1937 had Ireland won this particular classic cup. This time the team triumphed ahead of eleven others and proved that the Irish were right back to world-class standard. Con Power delivered a first-round clear that left Ireland equal with the home team on eight faults. There was again nothing in it in the second round and Eddie Macken, last to go, had to come up with yet another pressure clear round. Pressure or not, he went clear to beat the Germans by three-quarters of a fault. In addition, Con Power won two classes and Paul Darragh continued his string of speed successes there with P. J. Carroll.

Eddie and Boomerang followed on with a quality win in the Grand Prix at Hickstead that made up for a disappointing performance in the Nations' Cup there. In an eleven-horse jump-off he was drawn to go fourth and he put up a devastating time which none of the others could match. Power took up the torch at Dublin where he and Rockbarton had a stirring win in the Puissance. The elation at Con's win lasted through the following day when he joined James Kernan on Condy, Paul Darragh on Heather Honey, and Eddie Macken on Boomerang to win the Aga Khan Trophy for the third consecutive year. Not since 1937 had Ireland won three in a row and taken an Aga Khan Trophy outright. (Con will always remind people that he was the only rider of the four to do it on three different horses — Coolronan, Castlepark and Rockbarton.)

Austin Woulfe who was involved in all the major developments of the 1970s including Dublin Indoor International and the Millstreet show. (Show Jumping Association of Ireland)

The European Championships, in Rotterdam that year again proved a bitter disappointment for Eddie Macken. He and Boomerang did not knock a single fence in the first three rounds and helped Con on Rockbarton, Gerry Mullins on Ballinderry and John Roche on Maigh Cuillin to a bronze medal behind Britain and Germany. He himself was in the individual lead and heading for gold when a judge made a late decision that he had hit the tape at the water jump, Eddie rode back to protest but all to no avail and he finished in fourth place.

Once again he picked himself up and made the Hickstead Derby meeting his own. He took his revenge on all the stars of the European Championships: first in the Derby Trial, with a one–two on Boomerang and Kerrygold; then in a very wet Derby he had the only four-fault round to score his record fourth consecutive win on Boomerang. 'We are very lucky to have seen this horse jump — we may never see his like again,' he said afterwards.

In the fading weeks of that year and, as it turned out, the fading moments of his magnificent career, Boomerang proved how great he was again and again. In September, he and Eddie made their first trip to Calgary, won the main class every day and took the du Maurier Classic Grand Prix. From there, in October, it was on to Wembley and their fourth win in the Horse of the Year Grand Prix. Then, at the second Dublin Indoor International in November, they won the main events on the Thursday and Friday, followed by third place in the Grand Prix. With a double clear, they were fourth in the Grand Prix at Olympia just before Christmas, and that was to be Boomerang's last major individual outing with Eddie.

He was retired early in 1980 and on a May day three years later he died. His grave in Kells has four evergreens planted on it. They are symbols of four Hickstead Derby wins, four Championships at Wembley, four clear rounds in the final of the 1978 World Championships, and four years in a row without a fence down in the Aga Khan Trophy competition in Dublin. *Ní bheidh a leithéid arís ann.*

Boomerang's grave at Kells, County Meath.
(Suzanne Macken)

Eddie Macken's Five-Year Blitz

1975
First place — Grand Prix, Wiesbaden
Second place — Grand Prix, Cologne
First place — Mini-Grand Prix, Aachen
First place — Grand Prix, Royal International, Wembley
Second place — Grand Prix, Dublin
First place — Derby Trial, Hickstead
First place — Grand Prix, St Gallen
Second place — Grand Prix, Salzburg
First place — Grand Prix, Horse of the Year, Wembley

1976
First place — Mini-Grand Prix, Aachen
Second place — Grand Prix, Lucerne
First place — Professional Championship, Cardiff
First place — Grand Prix, Hickstead
Second place — King George Cup, Wembley
First place — Grand Prix, Wembley
First place — The Derby, Hickstead
First place — Grand Prix, Westphalia
First place — Grand Prix, New York
Leading Rider — Washington
Leading Rider — American Circuit
Leading Rider — Wembley

1977
First place — Grand Prix, Brussels
First place — Grand Prix, La Baule
Second place — Grand Prix, Rome
First place — Grand Prix, Hickstead
First place — The Derby, Hickstead
First place — Grand Prix, Horse of the Year, Wembley
First place — World Computer Ratings
Second place — European Championships
Winning Team-member — Aga Khan Trophy, Dublin
Leading Rider — Rome
Leading Rider — Dublin
Leading Rider — Olympia, London

1978
Second place — Grand Prix, Geneva
First place — Grand Prix, Gothenburg
First place — Grand Prix, Nice
First place — Grand Prix, Rome
First place — Grand Prix, Aachen
First place — Championship, Aachen
First place — The Derby, Hamburg
Second place — Grand Prix, Dublin
First place — The Derby, Hickstead
Second place — World Championship, Aachen
Irish Supreme Sports Star of the Year
First place — World Computer Ratings
Winning Team-member — Aga Khan Trophy, Dublin

1979
Second place — Grand Prix, Geneva
First place — Grand Prix, Royal International, Wembley
Winning Team-member — Nations' Cup, Aachen
Winning Team-member — Aga Khan Trophy, Dublin
First place — Derby Trial, Hickstead
First place — The Derby, Hickstead
First place — Grand Prix, Calgary
Leading Rider — Calgary
First place— Championship, Wembley
Third place — Grand Prix, Dublin Indoor International

Footnotes for Chapter Nine

[1] *The Irish Field*, 12 January 1974.

[2] Ibid., 24 August 1974.

[3] Doran-O'Reilly, Q. (ed.), *Horses of Ireland*, Dublin: Agri Books, 1982: p. 15.

[4] *Horse and Hound*, London: 11 February 1988: p. 36.

[5] Dreaper, J., *The Stars of Showjumping*, London: Stanley Paul, 1990: p. 98.

[6] Op. cit., *Horses of Ireland*, p. 18.

CHAPTER TEN

SURVIVAL IN CHANGING TIMES

1980 has seen the end of the Boomerang era and our major successes are declining at an alarming rate.
— SJAI Chairman, Brian Gormley, on the plight
of Irish showjumping in the early 1980s

As if falling from the injured Boomerang, Irish showjumping suddenly plummeted from elation into depression at the turn of the new decade. Spurred on by the successes of the 1970s, and the promises of funding from Bord na gCapall, the sport had, in many ways, leaped too high too fast — at the start of the 1980s, there was but one way to go and that was down.

In 1980, Bord na gCapall ran into serious trouble when it suffered its first budget cut of £200,000. Naturally, this reduction had to have a knock-on effect on the equestrian organisations it had previously helped to fund. The loss of backing, in tandem with rising operating costs, resulted in the SJAI being suddenly burdened with a deficit of £36,000. In order for the Association to survive, new chairman, John Moore, had to sanction the imposition of a £10 members' levy. Adding to the bad news, the RDS announced a loss of £111,000 in 1980, while the independently run Dublin Indoor International was down some £25,000 by the end of 1981. It was taken over by an equally ailing Equestrian Federation of Ireland (already £30,000 in debt) and eventually abandoned in 1982.

These financial headaches did not impinge quite as much on the operation of showjumping at local level. An increasing number of shows were being run each year, prize money was on the increase, and several new initiatives, such as the Jumper of the Year and Irish Championships, were to come into being by the mid-1980s. However, it was not so for the international showjumping team itself, which was certainly encountering problems. As if blown apart by a bomb, the great three-in-a-row Aga Khan Trophy winners suddenly seemed to disintegrate.

Having taken a strong stand on the manner in which army-rider winnings were distributed, Con Power resigned from McKee Barracks in the autumn of 1979 and began building his own team of jumpers. He had success at national level and was league champion four years running from 1984 to 1987. As though mirroring the great shortage of top horses at the time, he never again achieved major international prominence. His efforts were first hindered when he broke his leg in 1980, then sadly in 1988, Con was mown down by a run-away horse while coaching at a show near Dundalk. Although he recovered well enough to enjoy a family life, his injuries were so severe that he was told never to ride again.

Eddie Macken lost four top horses between 1979 and 1980 — Boomerang, with a broken pedal bone; Kerrygold, who died; Silver Pin and Boy, who both physically broke down that year and never returned to competition. With the EFI ban on foreign-breds still in place, he found it almost impossible to find replacements. It was not until the ban was finally lifted in 1984 that Eddie gradually climbed the World Computer Ratings once more with a variety of home- and continental-bred horses.

Although, by an odd coincidence, both James Kernan's Condy and Paul Darragh's Heather Honey sustained injury early in 1980, they did return to competitive form by the time of the Dublin Horse Show that autumn. However, as these horses ended their international careers over the next few years, both riders had difficulties finding replacements. Paul concentrated on buying Irish-breds back from abroad, and Young Diamond, which had been ridden by Royne Zetterman of Sweden, made a most promising start on his return in 1980. They took Grand Prix prizes in Bordeaux and at Olympia, but then the gelding hurt his back in a practice-ring fall at Gothenburg and after that was confined to Puissance competition only. James Kernan did not find a suitable international horse until the start of the 1990s.

"A horse! A horse! My Kingdom for a horse!"

Reflecting the decline of the early 1980s are Caroline Lee's pensive picture of Eddie Macken (opposite page) and Bob Fannin's cartoon for The Irish Field *of 8 August, 1981 (above). Like all Showjumpers, Irish riders, no matter how great their talent, have always been totally dependent on their supply of horses.*
(Caroline Lee and Irish Field)

Dublin Indoor International

Ireland's first attempt at running a major indoor international event began in 1978 and ended in 1982. In large measure, the event grew out of the Champions of the Year Show — a great end-of-season bash that was Ireland's answer to Britain's Horse of the Year. Strongly supported by Tommy Brennan, it began at the Grand Hotel, Malahide, in 1964 and was incorporated into the first Dublin Indoor International three-day programme in 1978. Tommy Brennan was on the committee of the new £200,000 event that offered £36,000 in prize money. Joining him were other leaders of the sport at that time: Eddie Taylor, who was the prime mover behind the venture; Ned Campion of the SJAI; Noel C. Duggan, who thirteen years later gave Ireland its permanent indoor international; Harold Lusk, who at that time had built a huge indoor arena of his own in County Antrim; Peter Bolt, Patrick Conolly–Carew, George Dagg and Eddie Macken. The show directors were Captain Austin Woulfe, Captain Tommy Ryan, Seamus O'Reilly and Major Eddie Boylan. Show Secretaries included Michele Knapp, Leslie Wrafter and Maria Woulfe. John Bland was Chairman, and the Vice-chairmen were Stan Diffley of Bord na gCapall, SJAI Chairman George Monson and NEC Chairman, Captain Simon Walford. From an entertainment and organisational point of view the show was a success, becoming a World Cup qualifier in 1979. The top international riders all took part, and at the last show in 1982, Maxie Scully set an Irish bareback jump record of 6 feet 8 inches.

In the end, finance killed off the event since the seating and the floor had to be installed each year at the Simmonscourt arena at the RDS — the pre-show costs amounted to close on £100,000. The overall projected costs for 1983 show were put at £245,000 — two thirds of which would have to be covered by sponsorship. It was not possible to continue at such expense. Noel C. Duggan vowed he would bring the event to Millstreet, County Cork, and he eventually achieved the move in 1991. The show was a great success and there it has lasted ever since. The Champions of the Year has also survived, going to Frank McGarry's arena in Sligo for 1983, and then to Navan, where the International Riders Association ran it for nine years under the direction of Frank Greaney. It then moved to Kill, County Meath, where the Flannelly family gave it its present home.

The early 1980s were indeed *anni horribili* for the Irish team. Between 1978 and 1981, Ireland had fallen from third place on the Nations' Cup table to a dismal twelfth. There was no participation by an Irish equestrian team in the 1980 Olympics, and a sixth placing in the 1981 European Championships did nothing to improve morale. From 1980 to 1989, the Irish had just one away Nations' Cup win, and between 1980 and 1985, they took only five international Grand Prix wins, compared with over twenty-five in the previous five years.

However, the curve of depression was to swing upwards again and matters so improved from the mid-1980s onward, that Ireland went to number one in *L'Année Hippique* ratings for 1995, when they were termed 'The hottest team in the world.'

A graph of international wins during the intervening years looks like a depiction of the hills of Donegal, with peaks and hollows alternating every few years. There were no such things as the sustained plateaux of the 1930s, early 1960s or late 1970s. Ireland was in a new situation where her top riders were often buying older horses that only jumped for one or two seasons before having to be retired. Thus these short bursts of glory, rather than the prolonged periods of success of the past, became the new norm for Irish showjumping competitors.

From a high of fifty-eight international wins in 1978, Ireland's total dipped to twenty-five in 1981, rose again to sixty in 1984 , plunged to seventeen in 1987, and then, after a slight jump to twenty-four in 1993, powered back up to over fifty again in 1995. As horses became available again, there were enough Irish riders with the talent and experience to get the very best out of them. Finding these new mounts was one problem, affording them was another. Back in 1980, for example, the British team's great stallion, Tigre, was officially valued at £160,000 — and prices kept on climbing after that. Today, in the late 1990s, a top international jumper can cost up to £2 million; it is, therefore, something of a miracle that Ireland has stayed in the business at all over these past ten years of incredible inflation in horse prices. It was a miracle brought about by incomparable rider talent and the oftentimes inexplicable dedication of owners who forewent big profits in order to provide the animals for Irish competitors. In addition, there has been the survival of the Army Equitation School, which every year has had at least one Irish-bred mount available for the national team.

As the dream team of 1977, 1978 and 1979 searched for new mounts, and sought to gain a second breath, newer team members emerged on the Irish showjumping scene: the Doyle brothers Jack and Edward from Blessington; the indomitable Harry Marshall from Antrim; Trevor Coyle from Derry, plus a host of lady riders such as Margaret Tolerton; Heather Gahan (later to become Mrs Trevor Coyle); Christine Ledingham; Jessica Willis (daughter of 1950s international, Iny de Bromhead); and the very talented Mandy Lyons, who was sadly killed in an accident while on the way from a show in Claremorris to another in Ennis. In addition to these new civilian stars, powerful fresh talent was also emerging from McKee Barracks — John Roche, the 1979 Aachen Nations' Cup team member; John Ledingham, soon to be a Hickstead Derby star; and Gerry Mullins, now united with Rockbarton.

Rider of the 1950s and 1960s Colonel Billy Ringrose headed the Army Equitation School during the 1980s. Each year there was an effort to recruit a group of young Irish horses. Along with their grooms, he is shown with one draft from that period. (Irish Field)

Gerry Mullins, from Limerick, had joined the Army Equitation School at a time when severe cut-backs were being put in place there back in 1973. He first competed successfully in three-day-eventing but in the late 1970s turned his full attention to showjumping. Gerry had a pure gutsy competitive spirit and his heart was set on winning. He got that soul satisfying opportunity in 1979, when he was given the demanding mission of taking up the reins on Rockbarton after Con Power resigned. They gelled well enough to have Mullins emerge as Leading International Rider at that year's Dublin Indoor Show, but it was soon decided, at McKee Barracks, that the two should start from the ground up during 1980. With the 1982 World Championships at the RDS as his main target, Rockbarton was given a full year off. Then, starting with quiet rides in the Phoenix Park, he and Gerry got fully acquainted with each other ever so slowly. By 1981, they were ready to compete again and proved their training period worthwhile by winning events in Reims and La Baule, while taking second in the Vienna Grand Prix. Gerry and Rockbarton won the Leading International Rider title in Dublin in 1981, and his next major outing was back in that same arena, the following July, for a shot at the world title.

On the strength of Eddie Macken's two great performances in 1974 and 1978, the World Showjumping Championships were assigned to Dublin for 1982 — at that time it was a relatively affordable event to host, costing about one £1 million to run. Sadly, Eddie was to play only a minor role this time around due to lack of horse power. Early in 1980 though, he discovered the skills of a horse called Royal Lion, which his mother-in-law, Patricia Nicholson, had given to his wife Suzanne, as a twenty-first birthday present. After a few initial international outings, including a Puissance win at Dublin, Eddie named this gelding, which had been sired by King of Diamonds, as his Championships mount. Sadly, the bad luck that weighed the master down at this time struck again early in 1982, when Royal Lion went lame. Eddie replaced him with his 1981 Hamburg Derby winner, Spotlight, and together they jumped for Ireland on the World Championship team in 1982. Joining them on the squad were: Captain John Roche, on Loughcrew (another horse previously ridden by Con Power); Jack Doyle, on his good Hickstead performer, Hardly (then sponsored by Kerrygold), and Gerry Mullins, on Rockbarton.

Olympic course builder Olaf Petersen of Germany (left) with Ireland's Steve Hickey, who built the 1982 World Championships course at Dublin. (RDS Archive)

Coming in to strengthen the Irish attack of the 1980s were the Doyle brothers, Jack and Edward, from near Blessington. They have not only contributed to the team but also to the organisation of the sport in committee work and the running of Blessington Show.
(Michael Slavin)

The team finished a disappointing eighth behind medal winners France, Germany and Britain. However, Gerry Mullins and Rockbarton saved the Irish Championship from being a total failure in terms of home interest, with a brilliant individual performance which saw them through to the final four on Sunday. They had a double clear in Saturday's big two-round third-leg competition which boosted them from overnight seventh into fourth overall. This was the author's first effort at live commentary for RTÉ Radio, and he well remembers watching names of the riders, who stood between the army man and the final group of four, gradually disappear from the computer screen, until there were just Gerry Mullins, Britain's Malcolm Pyrah, Germany's Norbert Koof and Michel Robert of France left for Sunday's horse-swapping decider.

The RDS stands filled for the first time that week, as the crowds gathered for the final; but hopes of an Irish victory faded as two fences fell for Gerry and he ended fourth behind Koof, Pyrah and Robert, in that order. Later that year, Rockbarton scored Ireland's first Grand Prix win since 1979, when taking the La Baule feature in France. He followed that in December with Ireland's first win of a Volvo World Cup round since the series began, in the winter of 1978.

Sponsorships for James Kernan and Con Power gave some hope for the 1983 season, as did the addition to Paul Darragh's team of Sprout and Emerald Isle. Eddie Macken also had a boost when he purchased El Paso, from Paul Schockemohle, and became the rider of Eddie McGinn's mare, Wendy. There were some successes as the year got under way and Macken was declared Leading Rider in Dortmund and London; Jack Doyle won at the Kerrygold-sponsored Hickstead Easter meeting with Kerrygold Flight. Reluctantly, the Irish sent a team back to the Sussex venue for that year's European Championships, and the reticence proved well justified when the side of Doyle, Macken, Mullins and Ledingham finished a disappointing sixth. However, they returned to Dublin the following week to give new European champions, Switzerland, a real battle for the Aga Khan Trophy — Ireland were beaten by only a quarter of a time fault. Jack Doyle took the Puissance and Con Power won the Slalom, thus making for a reasonably good home performance at the RDS.

Meanwhile, however, fortune seemed to favour the team of Tom Duggan, Michael Walsh, Vincent Burke and Vina Lyons who won the Junior European silver medal in 1983 — the first time since Mandy Lyons, Anne Hatton, Declan McGarry and Trevor McConnell did the same back in 1978. A respectable conclusion to a year that was sparse in terms of classic wins was supplied by Eddie Macken who was Leading Rider in St Gallen, and in Munich, and also took the £10,000 first prize in the Hennessy Puissance Championship in Bordeaux.

Eddie at Bordeaux

During the celebrations after Eddie Macken won the £10,000 Hennessy Puissance Championship at Bordeaux in 1983, it was announced that the first person to jump the wall at the same height would get a cart-load of vintage wine. Eddie ran for the stables where he and groom Fiona Dowley quickly saddled up Royal Lion. However, by the time he got back to the arena, Austria's Hugo Simon had already pole-vaulted over the wall. He got the wine since nobody had said he had to do it on horseback. Eddie grumbled so much that the following year he was invited back and was given the same wine prize for being nominated the Most Stylish Rider in the show.

Developments in 1984

With sixty wins to their credit, 1984 was a far better year for the Irish riders. It began with a superb one-two victory by Gerry Mullins on Rockbarton and Eddie Macken on El Paso in the Volvo World Cup in Dortmund. No one could match Gerry's opening round in the jump-off, not even Eddie who came within a second of catching him but had to settle for the runner-up position. However, Eddie was back in front the following week when he went top of the line in the next round of the Cup, in Milan; his riding at a very difficult double in that event will be remembered for a long time to come.

Both Gerry Mullins and Eddie Macken qualified for the World Cup final in Gothenburg, in 1984. Although there was no luck in the Cup itself, Eddie scored a unique double on the final day of the show. At breakfast he told rival Hugo Simon, 'I will win both of them today,' and he was right. With El Paso, he took the Grand Prix and won the speed championship on Wendy. It was a fulfilment of Eddie's supreme confidence, reminiscent of Tommy Wade's triple gold win in 1962.

Professional riders were still barred from the Olympics in 1984, so Ireland's only representative in Los Angeles was Gerry Mullins on Rockbarton. Unfortunately they missed a place in the final by just a quarter of a time fault. While they were away, Jack Doyle on Kerrygold Island, George Stewart on Leapy Lad, and John Ledingham on Gabhran teamed up with Eddie Macken on El Paso, to score Ireland's fourteenth win of the Aga Khan Trophy. Just a few weeks prior to that, the Equestrian Federation of Ireland finally faced reality and removed its ban on the use of foreign-bred horses by Irish riders. It is worth noting that the applause for Eddie Macken, at the RDS, was just as loud when he won two classes and delivered a cup on the German-bred El Paso as it had been when he triumphed there on Irish horses. Once again in Irish showjumping, the sport itself had won out over ideology.

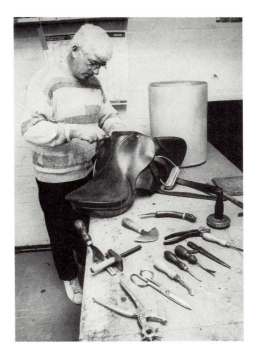

Getting ready for the World Championships — Rockbarton's saddle gets a final check.
(Army Press Office)

With Sean Daly as Chef d'Équipe the Irish team of Jack Doyle, George Stewart, John Ledingham and Eddie Macken won the 1984 Aga Khan Trophy. (RDS Archive)

Further lifts from the Irish showjumping depression were to follow. The very next week, Captain John Ledingham, and the nimble Gabhran, superbly won the Hickstead Derby after a tense three-way jump-off with Paul Schockemohle, on the European champion Deister, and Nick Skelton, with Apollo. His first prize was £20,000 — a long way from the £400 that Seamus Hayes received after taking the first Derby there, back in 1962. Before that year ended, Leonard Cave, from Newtownards, won the Salzburg Grand Prix on Monsanta, his best horse. Also that autumn, former Golden Saddle award winner, Paul Duffy of Galway, made his presence felt by winning the Bicton Derby, in Wales, with a horse called Paddy's Son. This promising young horse was later sold abroad for a reported £250,000. Superb Aga Khan Trophy performer, Leapy Lad, made about the same amount when he was sold to the USA within weeks after the Irish victory at the 1984 Dublin Horse Show. It was the story of the time — offers from abroad for potential team horses were made that could not be refused; other countries could hold onto their stock but it was difficult to do here when international demand for the Irish horse was so great.

The end of that season also saw a turning point in Eddie Macken's career. Over the previous twenty-four months, while still very much lacking Grand Prix horses, he, and a recovered Royal Lion, contested and won a number of well-endowed Puissance classes; but at Olympia in 1984, Eddie's Puissance career ended with a crashing fall at the wall. From then on he decided to concentrate his talents on Grand Prix competition.

Salute to the Grooms

The trip across the Alps from Dortmund to Milan in early 1984 is an example of what riders, horses, grooms and lorry drivers have to cope with on a long international tour. On this occasion, the Irish grooms included Viv Mulden for Paul Darragh's horses, Fiona Dowley for Eddie Macken's and Philip Brady for the army mounts. As always, on trips like this, all of them proved adept at finding fresh grazing where the horses could taste a bit of home between shows. At the shows themselves, the grooms set up a home-from-home for the horses and it was their care and attention that, on so many occasions, made the difference between a good or bad performance in the ring.

The skill of lorry driver, Denis Savage, was also called into play on this trip across the Alps. While negotiating icy roads on an overnight run through Switzerland with Paul Darragh's articulated lorry, the vehicle jack-knifed and the grooms awoke to find themselves hanging out over the edge of a cliff. It was only Denis's quick reflexes and pure expertise that saved the lives of all aboard on that occasion.

This is but one of many thousands of stories that could be recounted by the resourceful and dedicated Irish grooms who have provided the support that has helped to ply the world with Irish riders down through the decades. So good have they been at their jobs, that the Irish have been head-hunted by the best yards all over the world. From this particular group, both Viv and Fiona now work in the USA. They and Philip are representative of hundreds who have done, and continue to do, this difficult work for the horses of the international showjumping circuit. They are the heart and soul of it — fun-loving, informed, enthusiastic, but above all else, self-giving to the horses under their care. I salute all of them in this book.

Chef d'Équipe Row

Irish international wins dipped by 50 per cent in 1985 but that was not the worst story of that year. That sad saga emerged from an internal showjumping row over the appointment of the team's Chef d'Équipe. This issue burst into the news bulletins as a result of a riders' strike at the Dublin Horse Show. The controversy grew out of some unfinished business left over from 1960s, when civilian riders were allowed to be part of Nations' Cup teams for the first time. By some 'gentleman's agreement' one restrictive measure did remain — whenever there were two or more army riders on a team, the Chef d'Équipe *had* to be appointed from the military. Thus, when both John Ledingham and Gerry Mullins became eligible for team selection during the mid-1980s, this nagging problem reared its head again.

The civilian riders wanted an open selection process whereby the best person for the job on a particular occasion could be named by the SJAI. However, the RDS, Equestrian Federation of Ireland and the army wanted to retain the status quo. This may have been partly because of the financial consideration — if the situation remained as it was, the cost of sending the team manager abroad could more often be born by the military. The matter had simmered through 1984, and finally came to a head in 1995 when the civilian riders wanted the then retired Colonel Sean Daly to be given the post. While the Equestrian Federation of Ireland appeared to dither over the issue, the army would not give way and the RDS remained very much in favour of matters staying as they were.

Eddie Macken, James Kernan, Paul Darragh and Paul Duffy were selected to join the two military men (Gerry Mullins and John Ledingham), on that year's official Irish team for the Dublin Horse Show. All four of these civilians were in favour of Colonel Sean Daly being appointed Chef d'Équipe. *The Irish Field* commented at the time that both sides in the controversy misjudged each other's willingness to go to the brink with their convictions on the issue; and it was an accurate assessment of the situation.

Vina Lyons of Gilford County Down — 1986 Irish
Champion and winner of the Irish Field senior
showjumping trophy for that year. Shown here in a
happy moment after the presentation of the award
at Castletown House, County Kildare.
(Irish Field)

As it turned out, nothing had been decided by the time of the opening day of that year's Dublin Horse Show. Consequently, the four civilian riders on the Irish team, went on strike. The sad fact about it all was the degree to which the general public could not understand the problem. Most had never heard of a Chef d'Équipe, and why his appointment should cause such a problem was a mystery. Not so for those involved, to whom it was a bitter and emotive issue. (The author can remember trying to explain the controversy, in what he thought was an objective way, on RTÉ's Marian Finucane Programme but that evening was attacked by representatives of both camps for having sided with the other.) Through the intervention of Paddy O'Keeffe, the Chairman of Bord na gCapall at that time, some degree of peace was achieved and the whole team jumped on the second day of the show. However, the matter was by no means solved by his efforts — nor indeed was a satisfactory resolution found by the end of that year. Although new SJAI Chairman Dr Alec Lyons almost brokered agreement in 1986, the matter still lingered on in the background for the following two years. Colonel Sean Daly died suddenly in June 1987, before the final solution was achieved.

(At the time of Sean's death, his daughter Louise had already been selected to compete for Ireland in the Junior European Championships and in what has to be seen as a brave move, she travelled with the team of Tom Moloney, Ronnie Morton and Philip Gaw only a week after her family's bereavement. The team brought back a bronze medal from the Championships and that would have pleased Sean enormously.)

Soon after Sean Daly's death, the selection of both team and Chef d'Équipe was completely passed over to the SJAI from the Equestrian Federation of Ireland, and there the matter has rested ever since. On some occasions, an army Chef d'Équipe is appointed, and on others, a civilian is given the job. While this is viewed as a more logical approach to the situation, it is also felt that it could have been applied at a much earlier time, to the benefit of all involved. At the time of the main controversy, Sean Daly openly said that he never sought the post for his own glory.[1] That is a known fact and it was the riders themselves who felt he should be freely appointed. When the matter was finally settled, Irish showjumping was all the better for the freedom that the solution afforded it. As a sport, it had in a sense, reached a new level of maturity with no more falsely constructed restrictive bridges to be crossed.

With the Chef d'Équipe row still simmering, there was very little international team participation in 1986 as the Irish withdrew from Lucerne, Aachen and Hickstead. Concentration then focused on the national scene as a league covering eighteen Grand Prix shows was sponsored that year and the Irish Championships took up permanent residence in Salthill, County Galway. This had been won the previous year, at its inauguration in Galway, by Harry Marshall, and Vina

Lyons won it in 1986. She was then selected for the Irish team to compete at the Dublin Horse Show along with Gerry Mullins, Paul Darragh, Paul Duffy, Eddie Macken and John Hall. Paul Darragh jumped a double clear, on Carroll's For Sure, but Ireland still only managed to take third. The high point of the event was when Gerry Mullins won the Grand Prix — Ireland's first time since Diana Conolly-Carew took it twenty years earlier, in 1966. In 1987, Paul Darragh matched Gerry's achievement, on Trigger, but Ireland would not secure it again until 1997.

In 1986, the International Olympic Committee eventually allowed professional showjumping riders to compete in Olympic competitions and Ireland began preparing a team for Seoul, in 1988. Alwin Schockemohle's horse, Piquet, provided Eddie Macken with a potential Olympic performer, taking some good World Cup placings early the following year. However, the partnership was not to last as the gelding was sold for £400,000 to a former pupil of Eddie's — Belgian rider Jean Claude van Geensberghe. Eddie then took on Tom Moloney's stallion, Flight, with which he won the 1987 Irish Championship, and was second to the great Milton and John Whitaker in Dublin.

The year of 1987 was a good one for the Irish on their home ground as the side of Macken, Jack Doyle, John Ledingham and Gerry Mullins beat the British European Championship side in Dublin. Mullins and Macken were second and third behind Paul Darragh in the Grand Prix, and few weeks later, Eddie on Welfenkrone, Paul on Trigger, Gerry with Rockbarton, and John Ledingham on Gabhran, took the Belgian Nations' Cup at Chaudfontaine. This was to be Ireland's last foreign Nations' Cup win for another seven years. The year 1987 finished on a strong note with Gerry Mullins taking the Grand Prix in Helsinki on the grey Glendalough, and Eddie Macken winning his first classic at Olympia with the young German mare, Welfenkrone.

The following year, 1988, was memorable for the changes it brought. The SJAI moved its headquarters from the Irish Farm Centre to its current home at the RDS. Former showjumper Michael Stone took over as Secretary General of the Equestrian Federation of Ireland and the great Rockbarton was retired. Also that year, after quality performances in Aachen, and at the RDS (where, despite being third in the Aga Khan Trophy, the Irish had five wins), it was decided to send a full team to the Seoul Olympics. However, immediately after the decision had been made, problems began. Top candidate, Trevor Coyle, had to drop out after a brilliant outing in Aachen when his mount, True Blue, was sold to Paul Schockemohle for a reported £250,000. Soon after the Dublin Horse Show, Eddie Macken went out as well, when Flight was hurt. The side of Jack Doyle with Hardly, Gerry Mullins with Glendalough, John Ledingham with Kilcoltrim, and Paul Darragh with For Sure, did make the trip but finished eleventh out of a field of sixteen. Individually, Jack Doyle fared the best being twentieth out of a total of seventy-four.

Captain John Ledingham rose to prominence on the Irish team during the 1980s with Hickstead Derby winner, Gabhran, and Kilcoltrim. He is seen here winning the Dublin Puissance with the latter good jumper. (RDS Archive)

A group of showjumping personalities from the SJAI Leinster Region, who featured in the showjumping history of the 1980s — left to right. Committee member and future Director General Tony Kelly; Leinster Chairman Paddy Stone; Eddie Macken, Con Power, showjumping owner Joe McGrath and early teacher of Eddie Macken, Brian Gormley, who served two terms as National Chairman of the SJAI.
(Show Jumping Association of Ireland)

The year 1989 must be recorded as being one of transition — one that set the ground for better things in the 1990s.

Kerrygold announced a three-year sponsorship of £500,000 in total for the Dublin Horse Show, while Ned Campion was appointed Officer Commanding of the Army Equitation School and it was announced that National Lottery money was to be made available for McKee Barracks. The Bill to dissolve Bord na gCapall finally was read and a new Equine Advisory Committee to the Minister for Agriculture was put in place. Noel C. Duggan began a £3.5 million development programme at the Millstreet ground and the Clarke family initiated a £2 million project at their Cavan Equestrian Centre. P.J. Carroll and Company ended their twelve-year showjumping sponsorship and Eddie Macken moved back to Germany. The SJAI re-emerged from debt, Ado Kenny was appointed as its new Chairman and, for the first time, all four of the Association's regions were given equal representation of five members each on the National Executive. The Irish pony team of Tammy Twomey, Fiona Finn, Raymond McNamara and Cameron Hanley, won European Pony Team bronze in Millstreet, while future senior team member Hanley took individual silver there. There was fresh hope in all of these developments and hope as well in a statement by the future SJAI Director General, Tony Kelly:

> *Now that we have the internal disputes of recent years behind us, we must set about a development programme which will allow us to service shows, sponsors and competitors better than ever before.*[2]

Footnotes to Chapter Ten

[1]   *The Irish Field*, 5 August 1985: p. 19.

[2]   *SJAI Leinster Region Chairman's Report*, November 1989.

CHAPTER ELEVEN

THE DECADE OF DIASPORA

The Irish are the hottest showjumping team in the world right now.
— Helen Dolik, Calgary Herald, September 1995

The Irish jumping team fielded for the 1996 Olympics in Atlanta included Eddie Macken (originally from Longford but based in Germany), on the Dutch-bred horse FAN Schalkhaar; Peter Charles (born of Irish parents in Liverpool and based in Hampshire), on the Belgian-bred La Ina; Jessica Chesney (from County Antrim but based in Germany), on the Irish-bred Diamond Exchange and Damien Gardiner (born in Mayo and based in California), on the German-bred Orthos. The past twenty years have witnessed an unprecedented internationalisation of Irish showjumping which has resulted mainly from two factors — a world-wide shortage of showjumping horses, and a lack of the appropriate home funding required to keep a competitive team on the circuit. During the 1990s, these factors have either kept our bright young riders out of international competition altogether, or sent them away to seek financial backing and the opportunity to exercise their talent elsewhere. This period has also seen internationals such as Peter Charles from Britain, and Kevin Babbington of the USA, use their Irish ancestry to bestow on them the right to jump for Ireland.

Thus, the days of diaspora in Irish showjumping have dawned — and have brought their benefits. To date, in the 1990s, the Irish team has had ten Nations' Cup wins, more than in any decade since the 1930s. They began the decade in twenty-second place on the international table, but by 1997, had climbed back to fifth position. During the same period, Irish riders have also secured twenty-five Grand Prix or classic wins — success comparable to that of the booming 1970s. It is quite an achievement that a small country, such as Ireland, has managed to maintain its place in the ever more competitive and expensive world of modern showjumping.

The rebuilding of Ireland's international team began early in the 1990s. Despite the loss of Carroll's sponsorship, Paul Darragh was able to acquire the excellent Grand Prix horse, Killylea, and by 1994, he was riding a string of horses provided by the daughter of Jordan's King Hussein, HRH Princess Haya. Having moved back to Germany, Eddie Macken now had sponsorship from German millionaire Michael Nixdorf and was putting together a new team that was to include the mare La Bamba, the Irish-bred Sky View, and the Dutch horse Schalkhaar. In the meantime, back in Ireland, home-based riders were teaming up with fresh and talented mounts — future Irish champion Edward Doyle with Love Me Do; Jessica Chesney on Diamond Exchange; young Waterford rider, Francis Connors on the stallion Spring Elegance; James Kernan with Touchdown, a stallion which he had bred himself. There was also Robert Splaine with Jimmy Flynn's mare, Heather Blaze, Marion Hughes of Kilkenny, who was bringing along the mare Flo Jo (sired by Clover Hill), and the army which had bought the promising gelding, Kilbaha (sired by Tudor Rocket). As the 1990s progressed, the hallmark style and talent of Irish showjumping began to re-emerge once again.

The showman of Irish showjumping Harry Marshall, who combines a busy international circuit with winning performances in the Land Rover Irish League. Seen here on Burbank having taken the 1997 Stepaside Grand Prix in Dublin. (Parkes/Show Jumping Association of Ireland)

The first taste of major success came for Paul Darragh and Killylea when they won four Grand Prix events in a row in Frankfurt, Oslo, Royal International Birmingham and Helsinki. In the meantime, he and For Sure teamed up with Edward Doyle on Love Me Do, Gerry Mullins on Glendalough, and Eddie Macken on Welfenkrone, to bring Britain to a jump-off at the 1990 Hickstead Nations' Cup. A few months later, but with John Ledingham replacing Paul Darragh, the same side were in a three-way tie-breaker for the Aga Khan Trophy in Dublin. They were beaten into second place, but when the British side was eliminated on a technicality, the Irish were awarded the Trophy. Also, at the Kerrygold Dublin Horse Show that year, Harry Marshall had a superb show when scoring a hat-trick of wins, including the Puissance and two speed events.

Soon after Dublin, with Paul Darragh back on the side, the Irish had a very disappointing outing at the inauguration of the World Equestrian Games in Stockholm. They came eleventh out of sixteen teams and their highest-placed individual was Eddie Macken who came nineteenth on Welfenkrone.

Although 1991 was somewhat victory-starved throughout, it ended on a heart-warming note back in Ireland. Noel C. Duggan fulfilled his determination of previous years by organising the first Millstreet Indoor International, where Gerry Mullins, the reigning Irish champion at the time, put on a heart-stopping performance on Lismore. This innovative event was the climax of the four-day fixture. In a darkened arena, a packed house quietly watched as Noel C. Duggan oversaw the creation of a course, which reproduced many features from outdoor Derby events, and had been masterminded by Noel himself. Sergeant Major Steve Hickey put together gates, ditches, the Duggan Dyke, and even a controversial indoor bank followed by rails, on a fourteen-fence track. When the lights went on and the competition got under way, it quickly became obvious that clear rounds would be very few and that those who could manage the bank and rails would be even fewer. In order to add an extra bit of tension, Noel announced a £500 bonus for the first rider to jump the bank, and finish the course. Then, a little later on, he put up a further £500 for the first clear round of the competition.

Combination after combination attempted the course but after twenty-nine had jumped, there was still no clear round. The thirtieth competitor, and last to go, was Captain Gerry Mullins on Lismore. There was an expectant hush as he saluted and headed for the first fence, and as he continued, little intakes of breath and gasps accompanied him over every obstacle. At the centre of the arena, Steve Hickey lifted a hopeful leg as he helped him up and over every pole and gate. Clear all the way to the bank, Gerry and Lismore climbed up and, as they eased down the slope, Gerry checked back and saw that the rails were still in place. The tension burst into a muffled cheer which was then followed by warning shushing from those who wanted absolute quiet for the last four fences. Straining every muscle, rider and horse breathtakingly cleared the eleventh, twelfth, thirteenth and fourteenth fences to be greeted by an eruption of joyful noise from 5,000 delighted fans. Steve Hickey hugged Noel C. Duggan and Noel C. Duggan hugged Gerry Mullins; Steve almost leapt on Lismore before falling back with laughter in the middle of the gleeful arena. It was a superb moment of raucous noise that lasted a full ten minutes and extended itself out of the arena and into the pubs of the town where equally packed houses had been watching on television. Many of them came rushing down the streets and into Green Glens to congratulate Gerry and Lismore. This was Irish showjumping fever at its best — when the people of the countryside become involved in a moment of Irish triumph on horseback. Moments like this happen only intermittently but when they do, they fuel the sport with legend.

There were indeed to be further legendary performances in Millstreet by both Jessica Chesney and Trevor Coyle. However, before that there was to be another in the 1992 Aga Khan Trophy contest at the Dublin Horse Show. The previous year, sad history had been made at the RDS when, for the first time since this competition began back in 1926, there was no army rider on the Irish team. The new side of Harry Marshall, Francis Connors, Robert Splaine and Eddie Macken did not have a good run and finished last behind Britain. However, in 1992 it was to be very different. Gerry Mullins was back on the side with his Millstreet winner Lismore; also back after a long absence was James Kernan with Touchdown, and adding new strength to the squad was previous British team member, Peter Charles. A former student with both Iris Kellett and Eddie Macken, Peter had had eighteen Nations' Cup appearances for Britain before declaring for Ireland in May of that year. For this, his first performance on the Irish team in Dublin, he rode his former Royal Windsor and Hickstead Derby Trial winner, Kruger.

Showing just what a world-class rider he is, Peter delivered a double clear that day which carried all the hallmarks of greatness. Also going clear in the first round was a delighted James Kernan on the big-jumping Touchdown, while Gerry had four faults first time out. However, he returned to go clear in the second round, putting Ireland in with a realistic chance. That chance, like so many before, then depended on the captain Eddie Macken; first time out he had a disappointing eight faults on the flighty mare, Welfenkrone, so the pressure was really on as he went last to attempt the win for Ireland. Half way around, the crowd itself was almost Ireland's undoing as they greeted two big jumps near the Anglesea stand with muffled applause. The mare did not like the sound behind her as she headed across the arena to the last two obstacles, but with Macken's mighty and balanced grip soothing her, they flew the double for a superbly received home victory. Adding to the Irish score that year were

Noel C. Duggan, whose outdoor and indoor arenas at Millstreet have helped to expand the Irish home international season. (Patrick Casey)

Francis Connors, who took the Puissance on Jim Costigan's Cullohill Castle, as well as Paul Darragh and Marion Hughes, who teamed up to win the pairs competition.

Unfortunately, Eddie Macken, Peter Charles and James Kernan did not have a happy first Olympic outing at Barcelona that year. Joined by Seoul veteran Paul Darragh, the best they could manage was fourteenth out of nineteen teams. Individually, none of them qualified for the final in which twenty riders competed for the medals. The Olympic event had a double sting in it for Paul; his horse, Killylea, died from colic on the way home from the Games.

Matters improved though as Robert Splaine won the Irish Showjumping Derby that year. Then it was on to more home drama, as Noel C. Duggan hosted Ireland's first Volvo World Cup round since 1982 — the master of Millstreet had kept his promise to bring it back to a permanent home. What a homecoming it was, as new Irish queen of the sport, Jessica Chesney, won it on the Irish-bred Diamond Exchange.

Jessica, who hails from Cullybacky, County Antrim, grew up in a home environment filled with horses. Her father, George, had jumped at the RDS during the Second World War, and her mother regularly rode out on hunters. The distinctive blonde youngster combined these two sections of equestrian sport early on when winning both the 148 cm Pony Jumping Championship, and the Ridden Pony Championship in the same year, at the RDS. She was among the first graduates in the new Diploma in Equine Science at Limerick University, and has since been rider in residence there. In the run-up to her great moment in Millstreet, Jessica and Diamond Exchange won in Glasgow, Balmoral and the Spring Show in Dublin, where she said of her big generous gelding, 'If he was a fella I would marry him.'

In the inaugural World Cup in Millstreet, she and Diamond Exchange, had one of eleven clears out of a total of thirty-nine starters. Mid-way through the competition, she took over the lead by all of three seconds from Philip Guerdat of Switzerland and, despite determined efforts by the other riders, such as Britain's Robert Smith and future World Champion Franke Sloothaak, she held on to win. Adding to the elation in Green Glens that year, Francis Connors took second on Spring Elegance. In one quoted comment from the night of celebration it was declared, 'Just like John Kennedy said, the torch has well and truly been passed to a new generation of Irish at this Millstreet.'

Earlier that year, new blood had also come into the administration of the sport, when Ned Campion retired and handed the job of SJAI Director General on to Tony Kelly. In contrast to Ned, who took a cool, objective view of the work, Tony was himself very much involved with the sport. Over a number of years he had served as Secretary to the Leinster Region, and then as its Chairman, before being elected National Chairman in 1992.

Opposite: Winner of the first Indoor Derby at Millstreet in 1991 — Gerry Mullins, seen here on Lismore, taking the bank on their lap of honour. (Maymes Ansell)

Shortly after Ned's retirement became effective, Tony resigned the post as National Chairman and took over as Director General. The vacancy he left was filled by Brian Gormley of Granard, who then began his second term as National Chairman. Ned Campion had brought the Association into the professional and technical age; Tony has further progressed it and, in close co-operation with the new Irish Horse Board, has blended registration with horse-performance testing very successfully. He brought a hands-on approach to the job which kept both the committees and the 6,000 members in touch with the everyday demands of the sport.

The following two years were seasons of transition as Irish showjumping prepared for one of the best seasons of wins in its history. Eddie Macken, with Schalkhaar and Sky View, was second in the 1993 Paris Masters and won the 1994 Grand Prix in both Gothenburg, Germany, and s'Hertogenbosch in Holland. Francis Connors was Irish champion in 1993 and went on to take the Cana Cup at Calgary on Spring Elegance. Peter Charles won the Millstreet Derby and ended the 1993 season by taking the Grand Prix at Olympia in London. In the meantime, Trevor Coyle successfully took the reins on Mary McCann's fine young stallion, Cruising, winning the Grand Prix events in both Bourg en Bresse and Bremen.

As the 1994 season gathered pace the Irish felt strong enough to take on even greater challenges. Jessica Chesney joined the team for Aachen, and along with John Ledingham, Peter Charles and Eddie Macken, brought the British to a jump-off there. The same side went on to win the French Nations' Cup for the first time since 1961. From there it was on to a respectable performance in the World Equestrian Games, in The Hague, where Eddie won the opening leg and Jessica was the highest placed lady rider, finishing in tenth place.

What then appeared to be a happy event for Ireland also occurred in The Hague, as it was announced that the Equestrian Federation of Ireland would be running the next World Games in 1998. The projected cost at the time was £6 million, and that soon grew to £9.5 million. With adequate television coverage a major problem, and a host of other setbacks intervening, the needed funding was not available and the whole ill-advised project foundered. Finally, in 1997, it had to be embarrassingly abandoned and passed on to Rome. The episode was another salutary lesson that modern-day equestrian sport has, in reality, grown beyond the purse strings of our small island.

Nevertheless, while all of this was going on at the administrative level, much that was promising and fulfilling happened within the sport itself. During the terms of both Ado Kenny and Cyril Burke as SJAI Chairman, the most detailed young rider-training program, yet attempted within the Association was initiated. Bursaries to study with top riders, at home and abroad, were distributed to some twenty candidates. Under this scheme the amount made available to each individual ranged from £200 to £500.

Irish course builder, Paul Duffy of Galway, was also to benefit that year by getting additional experience abroad when, in the autumn of 1994, he was invited to build the courses at the two richest shows in the world — Calgary and Pavarotti International in Italy. At the former, Ireland placed a good third with its A team, but one week later, the B team of Francis Connors, Jessica Chesney, Robert Splaine and Trevor Coyle emerged the winners at Pavarotti International. Also coming out on top at that time was young Patrick Hanlon, of Longford, as he took Ireland's first ever Individual European Championship gold medal on Shalom Outlaw.

In addition, at Hickstead that year, Captain John Ledingham truly came into his own. With a speed horse, bred by the Gormleys of Granard, he won the Speed Derby for the second year in a row and, with the well-maturing Kilbaha, he took the Derby itself for the second time after a two-way jump-off with the USA's Katie Monahan. John is the quiet, stylish rider of Irish showjumping, he has empathy with his horses and displays great patience with their development. Born in Waterford to a family deeply involved with horses, he had his first taste of international jumping when he travelled with an SJAI pony team to Toronto in 1968. His sister, Christine, was also involved in the sport and rode for Bord na gCapall during the 1970s. John came to McKee Barracks in December 1977 and, having first made the international team with Gabhran, he then began slowly building Kilbaha to take his place. This he did on that occasion in 1994 when they took the Hickstead Derby for a purse of £45,000 — double the amount of prize money that Gabhran had taken back in 1984.

John was to achieve the double again at Hickstead in 1995 during a year of Irish showjumping glory that will not be forgotten for a long time. It began well with the announcement that Paul Darragh would be riding horses for HRH Princess Haya, while also acting as the Jordanian team member's trainer. This was followed by the good news that Michael Nixdorf had acquired the world silver medalist, Miss FAN, for Eddie Macken and that Peter Charles had bought the Belgian-bred gelding, La Ina; team strength was growing again.

That power quickly showed as Macken won the £100,000 European Classic in Zurich, and when Ireland emerged again at the top of the world in the Aachen Nations' Cup — not won by Ireland since 1979. In the first round, Charles on La Ina, Ledingham with Kilbaha, and Coyle on Cruising, all went clear and Eddie did not have to jump. They held the advantage in the second round, leaving Ireland the winners over Britain, Holland and world champions Germany. In addition, the Irish won three other classes, including the mini-Grand Prix by Jessica Chesney.

King's Cup winner, Robert Splaine, has had a long international which began on the Irish team at the 1978 World Championships. He is shown with his Irish Show Jumper of the Year Trophy, won in 1990. Six times winner of the title, Francis Connors, was runner-up that year. (Author)

The magic held as Gerry Mullins took the Falsterbo Grand Prix on the Millstreet Ruby, which had been bred by Noel C. Duggan. Then in Hickstead, on the same day in July, Robert Splaine won the King's Cup on Heather Blaze, and Marion Hughes took the Queen's Cup on Flo Jo — the first such double by Ireland since Iris Kellett and Kevin Barry back in 1951. There was more gold in store the week after that, when Belfast's Emma Wilson scored Ireland's second European Pony Championship in a row.

There was still more to come; having come a close second in the Nations' Cup in Luxembourg, the Irish team came home to scoop the Aga Khan Trophy in a close battle with the British and the French. Macken, Charles and Coyle, all jumped clears to put Ireland even with France, but when Hervé Godignon put a foot in the water, Ireland had the Cup for the seventeenth time. John Ledingham, who had four faults in each round at the (now-named) Kerrygold Horse Show, was not knocking fences at the Hickstead show. He took the Speed Derby for a record third year in a row and then delivered a double clear in the Derby, to beat John Whitaker on Grannusch.

There was no time for rest as the Irish took the plane to western Canada, and the showjumping venue in Calgary. There, against the top teams from Europe and America, they were victorious again. Charles, Ledingham and Coyle all had clear rounds, and once again, Macken did not have to jump his second round as they took the Bank of Montreal Cup ahead of Britain, Germany, the USA and six other teams. In the *Calgary Herald*, they were termed, 'The hottest team in the world,' a title that they would soon have to live up to at a rain-soaked European Championships in St Gallen.

They very nearly did and were beaten for a medal only after a jump-off with France. Recompense came when Peter Charles won Ireland's first individual European gold medal since Iris Kellett took the Ladies' Championship in 1969. After three dour days of jumping, Peter and La Ina were into a jump-off for the gold medal against Michael Whitaker on Two Step — Peter finally beat them on time, by all of a second. It was yet another great Irish showjumping moment. Still on the trail of gold, Jessica Chesney ended that brilliant year by winning the Grand Prix at the Christmas show in Mechelen, and Robert Splaine was awarded the gold medal from Hickstead for the most points scored during the year.

When Max Ammann's team ratings were published in that year's *L'Année Hippique*, he rated Ireland Number One for the first time since he began his table in 1959. Acknowledgement indeed that the Irish had battled their way back to the top.

That would be a good point at which to end this book of legends but there is more, as there is always more where the Irish on horseback are concerned.

Sadly, 1996 began with the death of a legend as Major Ged O'Dwyer passed away. As if in tribute to his memory, the Irish opened

Then termed the 'Hottest Showjumping team in the World' — the Irish side of Peter Charles, Eddie Macken, Trevor Coyle and John Ledingham with the Bank of Montreal Cup, won at Spruce Meadows, in 1995.
(Whitehouse Publishing/Dr Jan White)

the season with a spate of wins — two for Eddie Macken in Hamburg, two for Peter Charles at Wiesbaden, and for Trevor Coyle and Cruising, the Grand Prix in Wolfsburg.

Alas, this optimistic start was dampened by more unfortunate news. For reasons of health, neither Trevor's mount, the valuable stallion, Cruising, nor Eddie's horse, Miss FAN, would be fit for the 1996 Olympic Games in Atlanta. As if that wasn't bad enough, Paul Darragh's horses were not eligible either, having tested positive to for bug they had picked up in Spain. Then at the very last moment, John Ledingham's army mount, Kilbaha, had to be taken off the plane for Atlanta when he began showing signs of a temperature.

As a result, reserve rider Damien Gardiner, from County Mayo, was called in to join Jessica Chesney, Peter Charles and Eddie Macken. A former pupil of Iris Kellett's, Damien had moved to California three years earlier. In the intervening years, he worked for Pinon Farms in the most prestigious stable-rider's job on the West Coast of America. A host of Grand Prix wins, over the past five seasons, has also made him one of the leading riders on the circuit there.

However, at this late stage, no effort could undo the devastating blows that had undermined Ireland's hopes of winning their first ever Olympic medal. The potential to realise this aspiration at this time was painfully demonstrated in later events. Cruising won the Grand Prix at the Pavarotti International; the Irish side took second in the Aga Khan Trophy in Dublin, beaten by just half a time-fault; and the team of Darragh, Coyle, Charles and Macken went on to win the Nations' Cup in Rotterdam. Surely such success could have been theirs in the heat of the Equestrian Park in Atlanta.

Further successes during the months after the Games made the regrets even more poignant. Eddie Macken won the Dublin Grand Prix on Schalkhaar — his first win in this event in eighteen years of trying. Peter Charles scored the richest win of his career against the Olympic champions, in the $500,000 du Maurier Classic at Calgary, on La Ina. Paul Darragh and Princess Haya's team rampaged through the autumn in Donaueschingen, Brussels, Maastrict, Olympia and Seville, where he won his first Volvo World Cup qualifier on Cera. So ended an eventful 1996.

Marion Hughes began and ended 1997 with Grand Prix wins on Flo Jo — first on the Spanish Sunshine Tour in Vejer, and then at the Nations' Cup meeting in Athens. In the meantime, Ireland's team goal of the year was to qualify for the new Samsung Nations' Cup Championship at Calgary. With Tom Slattery and the Irish Draught stallion, Coille Mor Hill, drafted onto the side, and 1960s hero Tommy Wade as Chef d'Équipe, they took second at the Royal Windsor Horse Show. Then they finished third in Aachen, and the Irish bid for qualification for the finals wavered after a disappointing result in Falsterbo where they came sixth.

Thus, qualification for Calgary rested on the results of both a very tough Aga Khan Trophy challenge, in Dublin, and the Nations' Cup in

From Tynagh in County Galway, Tom Slattery joined the Irish Team on Coille Mor Hill, by Clover Hill, in 1996 — the first Approved Irish Draught stallion ever to jump for Ireland.
(Showjumping Association of Ireland)

The current bar-coded and computerised ticket used for over 6,000 animals now on the SJAI books. Also shown is the very first form devised by George Hanbury Robinson at the beginning of the Horse Jumping and Riding Encouragement Association in 1944. In the first year fewer than 100 horses were registered.
(Show Jumping Association of Ireland)

A group of Northern Region SJAI members, working at the 1994 National Championships in Balmoral along with UK course-builder Bob Ellis (centre) — Louis Lowry (current EFI chairman), Dr Ernie Logan, Harold Lusk and Paddy McEvoy. (J. Kirkpatrick)

Rotterdam. With Paul Darragh delivering two pulsating clear rounds on Princess Haya's Scandal, and both John Ledingham and Trevor Coyle contributing one clear each, they won the Aga Khan Trophy. This win, combined with third place in the Dutch Cup, gave the Irish their place in the final. Winning was not necessarily the goal on this occasion but being there was very important for Irish morale. 'We have a mountain to climb,' Tommy Wade declared at the beginning of the competition. They climbed it though, and with wins from Peter Charles on T'Aime, Trevor Coyle on Cruising, and John Ledingham on Millstreet Ruby, they took a healthy share of the prizes from the total fund of over one million pounds, which was on offer.

That autumn, the Irish pony team of Elizabeth Power, Sara Kate Quinlivan, Shane Sweetnam and Carl Hanley also performed well, taking the European Championship bronze medal, while the wonderfully fresh side of Cameron Hanley, Captain Gerry Flynn, Marion Hughes and John Ledingham won the Nations' Cup in Zagreb. The Chef d'Équipe on that occasion was Lieutenant Colonel Ronnie McMahon, who had just taken over from Ned Campion as Officer Commanding of the Army Equitation School — now more secure in its funding than ever, as a result of revived Government interest.

The Irish reaped rich rewards toward the end of 1997, when Captain John Ledingham won the $100,000 Monterey Derby, on Millstreet Ruby, and Eddie Macken maintained his place near the top of the BCM computer ranking list with his second win of the Aarhus Volvo World Cup, in Denmark, on La Bamba.

During the closing months of 1997, there were flashbacks for Irish showjumping as the sport experienced financial encouragement reminiscent of that which had originally helped to develop it during the latter half of the last century. The RDS, the grand old mother of the international sport, announced a £1 million refurbishment programme for its Ballsbridge show grounds, while at the same time, Kerrygold pledged its tenth year of sponsorship for the 125th Dublin Horse Show.

Also, during that year of expansion and investment, there were over 500 showjumping competition days on the national circuit, with close on £1 million in prize money on offer; SJAI membership topped 6,000 for the first time — at least 1,000 of the new members in the new and growing amateur section.

Mid-way through the 1997 season, Edward Doyle took over the Irish Championship Crown from Conor Swail, in Ballinasloe, the town where the very first moves to form an Irish Showjumping Association had taken place back in 1939.

At the end of 1997, the first lady was elected to the SJAI Chair, as Bernie Brennan, of Galway, took over from Dr Alec Lyons who had completed his second full term. Up to the time of writing this book, the Association has thought and acted purely as a representative sporting body. However, modern times, and changes in its structure, have dictated that the SJAI fall into line with company law. The transition from a representative association to a fully commercial entity is still in bitter process. As this book goes to press it is difficult to assess just how the situation will evolve. However, in keeping with its history to date, the demands of the sport must surely eventually prove to be the dominant deciding factor.

Despite the apparent difficulties of these transitional times, the SJAI continues with its main business in the world of Irish showjumping. Since taking the chair, Bernie Brennan has endorsed a further expansion of the young rider programme under the direction of Jack Doyle. This scheme provides support for equestrian students while they are training abroad. The programme proved its worth when the side of James Hogg, Richie Moloney, Peter McEntee and Shane McFadden won a bronze medal at the 1998 European Junior Championships in Lisbon.

During 1998, with the much respected former international rider Colonel Ned Campion, at the helm, the Equestrian Federation of Ireland produced the most comprehensive programme ever devised for this body. Its evolution will also have a profound bearing on how Irish showjumping will develop from here.

This Odyessy through the world of Irish showjumping now draws to a close and it does so to the beat of more Irish winners at home and abroad. In the Volvo World Cup, in Millstreet, November 1997, Trevor Coyle rode two rounds of a lifetime on the Irish-bred stallion, Cruising, to win ahead of a quality field flown in from all around the world. Just as it did on the night Gerry Mullins won the Indoor Derby, or when Jessica Chesney took the inaugural Cup there in 1992, the arena came alive with joyous lilting laughter and applause born of the love of the equine, which roots the sport of showjumping solidly in the heart of this nation of the horse.

Afterwards, Cruising went on to win the Grand Prix at Lucerne CSIO in early 1998 and in June, Kilbaha and John Ledingham scored a similar victory at Drammen CSIO in Norway. This was followed by another Irish victory by the young Eric Holstein at the Hickstead Royal International Horse Show, in July.

Thus I end my reflection and reminiscence on the legends of Irish showjumping secure in the knowledge that they will be repeated again and again in the century to come.

Twice National SJAI Chairman Dr Alec Lyons receiving an FEI award from President Hillery. In background is former EFI chairman Bill Buller, who competed on the Irish international three-day-eventing team and whose son Alfie is married to Dr Lyons' daughter, 1986 Irish champion, Vina. (Irish Field)

Swapping the riding togs and Chef d'Équipe uniform for a business suit, Colonel Ned Campion has now taken on the duties of Secretary General of the Equestrian Federation of Ireland. Under his leadership it has put together the most progressive programme since its foundation, almost seventy years ago. (Show Jumping Association of Ireland)

APPENDIX

Ireland's Nations' Cup Wins

1928	Dublin	1961	Nice — Enschede
1931	Lucerne	1963	Dublin
1932	Dublin — Boston	1967	Dublin
1933	Toronto	1971	Ostend
1935	Lucerne — Dublin — New York — Toronto	1975	Ostend
1936	Nice — Amsterdam — Lucerne — Dublin	1976	Dublin
1937	London — Lucerne — Dublin — Aachen	1977	Dublin
1938	Dublin — New York — Toronto	1978	Dublin — Aachen
1939	Lucerne	1983	Dublin
1946	Dublin	1986	Dublin — Chaudefontaine
1949	Dublin — Harrisburg	1989	Dublin
1950	Nice	1991	Dublin
1951	Toronto	1993	Pavarotti — La Baule
1953	New York	1994	Aachen — Dublin — Calgary
1954	Rotterdam	1995	Rotterdam
1955	Harrisburg — Toronto	1996	Dublin — Zagreb
1960	Enschede		

Ireland's Major Grand Prix Wins

1930	Dublin	Dan Corry	Slievenamon
1932	Dublin	Ged O'Dwyer	Limerick Lace
1934	Dublin	Ged O'Dwyer	Limerick Lace
1935	King's Cup	John Lewis	Tramore Bay
1936	King's Cup	Ged O'Dwyer	Limerick Lace
1937	Dublin	Jack Bamber	Silver Mist
	Lucerne	Dan Corry	Red Hugh
1938	Dublin	Fred Ahern	Blarney Castle
	Lucerne	John Lewis	Limerick Lace
	Rome	John Lewis	Limerick Lace
1939	Amsterdam	Ged O'Dwyer	Limerick Lace
	Dublin	Dan Corry	Red Hugh
1946	Dublin	Michael Tubridy	Kilkenny
1948	Dublin	Iris Kellett	Rusty
	Queen's Cup	Iris Kellett	Rusty
1950	Dublin	Ian Dudgeon	Go Lightly
	New York	Michael Tubridy	Rostrevor
1951	Dublin	John Lewis	Hack On
	King's Cup	Kevin Barry	Ballyneety
	Queen's Cup	Iris Kellett	Rusty
1952	Dublin	Ian Dudgeon	Go Lightly
1953	Dublin	Michael Tubridy	Ballynonty
	Rotterdam	Kevin Barry	Hollyford
1955	Dublin	Patrick Kernan	Glenamaddy
1956	Dublin	Joe Hume-Dudgeon	Sea Spray
	New York	Billy Ringrose	Ballynonty
1959	Dublin	Seamus Hayes	Kilrush
1961	Dublin	Tommy Wade	Dundrum
	Rome	Billy Ringrose	Loch an Easpaig
1963	King's Cup	Tommy Wade	Dundrum
	Brussels	Tommy Wade	Dundrum
	Wiesbaden	Tommy Brennan	Kilbrack
1964	Harrisburg	Billy Ringrose	Loch an Easpaig
	Rotterdam	Seamus Hayes	Goodbye
1966	Dublin	Diana Conolly-Carew	Barrymore
1967	s'Hertogenbosch	Seamus Hayes	Doneraile
1975	Wiesbaden	Eddie Macken	Boomerang
	Royal International	Eddie Macken	Boomerang
	St Gallen	Eddie Macken	Boomerang
	Horse of the Year Show	Eddie Macken	Boomerang

Ireland's Major Grand Prix Wins (continued)

Year	Location	Rider	Horse
1976	Hickstead	Eddie Macken	Pele
	Horse of the Year Show	Eddie Macken	Boomerang
	New York	Eddie Macken	Boomerang
1977	Brussels	Eddie Macken	Boomerang
	La Baule	Eddie Macken	Boomerang
	Hickstead	Eddie Macken	Boomerang
	Horse of the Year Show	Eddie Macken	Boomerang
1978	Aachen	Eddie Macken	Boomerang
	Gothenburg	Eddie Macken	Boomerang
	Nice	Eddie Macken	Boomerang
	Rome	Eddie Macken	Boomerang
1979	Calgary	Eddie Macken	Boomerang
	Royal International	Eddie Macken	Boomerang
1982	La Baule	Gerry Mullins	Rockbarton
	Bordeaux World Cup	Gerry Mullins	Rockbarton
	Helsinki	Paul Darragh	Ballycullen
1983	Dortmund	Eddie Macken	Royal Lion
	Royal International	Eddie Macken	Royal Lion
1984	Gothenburg	Eddie Macken	El Paso
	Salzburg	Leonard Cave	Monsanta
	Dortmund World Cup	Gerry Mullins	Rockbarton
	Milan World Cup	Eddie Macken	El Paso
1986	Dublin	Gerry Mullins	Rockbarton
1987	Dublin	Paul Darragh	Carroll's Trigger
	Helsinki	Gerry Mullins	Glendalough
	Olympia	Eddie Macken	Welfenkrone
1990	Frankfurt	Paul Darragh	Killylea
1991	Royal International	Paul Darragh	Killylea
	Oslo	Paul Darragh	Killylea
1992	Millstreet World Cup	Jessica Chesney	Diamond Exchange
1993	Olympia	Peter Charles	Impulse
1994	s'Hertogenbosch	Eddie Macken	Sky View
	Gothenburg	Eddie Macken	Sky View
	Aarhus	Peter Charles	La Ina
	Hickstead	Gerry Mullins	Pallas Green
1995	Zurich	Eddie Macken	Miss FAN
	Royan	Peter Charles	La Ina
	Falsterbi	Gerry Mullins	Millstreet Ruby
	Pavarotti International	Trevor Coyle	Cruising
	Aarhus World Cup	Eddie Macken	Miss FAN
	Mechelen	Jessica Chesney	Diamond Exchange
1996	Barcelona	Paul Darragh	Cera
	Calgary	Peter Charles	La Ina
	Brussels	Paul Darragh	Cera
	Dublin	Eddie Macken	Schalkaar
	Denver	Damien Gardiner	Pinon Finnegan
	Wolfsburg	Trevor Coyle	Cruising
	Seville World Cup	Paul Darragh	Cera
	Helsinki	Jessica Chesney	Diamond Exchange
1997	Biarritz	Harry Marshall	Cruisline
	Denver	Damien Gardiner	Pinon Finnegan
	Aarhus World Cup	Eddie Macken	La Bamba
	Millstreet World Cup	Trevor Coyle	Cruising

Ireland's Derby Wins

1962	Hickstead	Seamus Hayes	Goodbye
1964	Hickstead	Seamus Hayes	Goodbye
1975	Hickstead	Paul Darragh	Pele
1976	Hickstead	Eddie Macken	Boomerang
	Hamburg	Eddie Macken	Boomerang
1977	Hickstead	Eddie Macken	Boomerang
1978	Hickstead	Eddie Macken	Boomerang
	Hamburg	Eddie Macken	Boy
1979	Hickstead	Eddie Macken	Boomerang
	Millstreet	Paul Darragh	Heather Honey
1980	Millstreet	Eddie Macken	Onward Bound
1981	Millstreet	Paul Darragh	Doreen
	Hamburg	Eddie Macken	Spotlight
1983	Millstreet	James Kernan	Condy
1984	Hickstead	John Ledingham	Gabhran
1988	Millstreet	John Ledingham	Gabhran
1992	Millstreet	Robert Splaine	Heather Blaze
1993	Millstreet	Peter Charles	Impulse
1995	Falsterbo	Gerry Mullins	Millstreet Ruby
	Hickstead	John Ledingham	Kilbaha
1996	Hickstead	John Ledingham	Kilbaha

Irish Champions

1985	Harry Marshall	Avalon	1992	James Kernan	IJM Touchdown
1986	Vina Lyons	Giltspur	1993	Francis Connors	Spring Elegance
1987	Eddie Macken	Flight	1994	Gerry Mullins	Millstreet Ruby
1988	Eddie Macken	Flight	1995	Edward Doyle	Flex
1989	Paul Darragh	Forsure	1996	Conor Swail	Lisna Tutor
1990	John Ledingham	Gabhran	1997	Edward Doyle	Windgates King Koal
1991	Gerry Mullins	Glendalough			

Irish Showjumper of the Year

1980	Eddie Macken	1986	Con Power	1992	Francis Connors
1981	Paul Darragh	1987	Jack Doyle	1993	Francis Connors
1982	Eddie Macken	1988	Paul Darragh	1994	Francis Connors
1983	Con Power	1989	Robert Splaine	1995	Francis Connors
1984	Con Power	1990	Francis Connors	1996	Marion Hughes
1985	Con Power	1991	Francis Connors	1997	Francis Connors (outdoor); Clement McMahon (indoor)

The Irish Field Award Winners

1974	Eddie Macken	1982	Gerry Mullins	1990	Robert Splaine
1975	Paul Darragh	1983	Eddie Macken	1991	Gerry Mullins
1976	Eddie Macken	1984	John Ledingham	1992	Robert Splaine
1977	Eddie Macken	1985	Con Power	1993	Francis Connors
1978	Eddie Macken	1986	Gerry Mullins	1994	John Ledingham
1979	Eddie Macken	1987	Eddie Macken	1995	Peter Charles
1980	Eddie Macken	1988	Jack Doyle	1996	Peter Charles
1981	Eddie Macken	1989	Paul Darragh	1997	Trevor Coyle

SJAI Chairmanships

1954–1963	Colonel Joe Hume-Dudgeon	1982–1984	Brian Gormley
1964–1965	Dermot V. Buchanan	1985–1986	Donal Johnson
1966–1967	Colonel John J. Lewis	1987–1988	Dr Alec Lyons
1968	Dr Tom McNab	1989–1991	Ado Kenny
1969	William McLernon	1992	Tony Kelly
1969–1972	Sir Robert Lowry	1992–1993	Brian Gormley
1973–1974	Philip O'Connor	1994–1995	Cyril Burke
1975–1977	Aidan Doyle	1996–1997	Dr Alec Lyons
1978–1979	George Monson	1998	Bernie Brennan
1980–1981	John Moore		

BIBLIOGRAPHY

Ammann, M. (ed.) *Volvo World Cup Media Guide, 1982–1990*, Gothenburg: Reklam Poolen AB.

Ammann, M. (ed.), *Volvo World Cup Media Guide*, Gothenburg: Reklam Poolen AB, 1983 and 1984.

Ansell, M.P. *Showjumping Obstacles and Courses*, Glasgow: Collins Sons & Co. Ltd., 1951.

Ansell, M.P., *Showjumping — Obstacles and Courses*, London: W. Collins Sons & Co, London, 1951.

Barker, D., *One Thing and Another*, London: Pelham Books, 1964.

Beker, A., *Woman on a Horse*, London: William Kimber, 1956.

Berry, H.F., *A History of the Royal Dublin Society*, London: Longmans Green and Co., 1915.

Brooke, G., *The Way of Man with a Horse*, London: Seeley, Service & Co., 1929.

Browne, N.P., *The Horse in Ireland*, London: Pelham Books, 1967.

C. Hallam-Gordan (ed.), *International Showjumping Book*, London: Souvenir Press Ltd, 1968.

Churchill, P., *Practical Showjumping*, London: David and Charles, 1990.

Clayton, M. and S., *The Complete Book of Showjumping*, London: Heinemann, 1975.

Clayton, M., and Tracy, D., *Hickstead, The First Twelve Years*, London: Pelham Books, 1972.

Coldrey, C., *Courses for Horses (revised edition)*, London: J.A. Allen, 1991.

D'Orgeix, J., *Horse in the Blood*, London: Nicholas Kaye, 1951.

De Nemethy, B., *The de Nemethy Method*, New York: Doubleday, 1988.

De Vere White, T., *The Story of the Royal Dublin Society*, Tralee: The Kerryman, 1955.

Doran O'Reilly, Q. (ed.), *Horses of Ireland*, Dublin: Agri Books, 1982.

Dossenbach, M. and H., *Irish Horses*, Dublin: Gill and Macmillan, 1975.

Dreaper, J., *Showjumping Records Facts and Champions*, London: Guinness Books, 1987.

Dreaper, J., *The Stars of Showjumping*, London: Stanley Paul, 1990.

Fell, A., *The Irish Draught Horse*, London: J.A. Allen, 1991.

Foster, C. (ed.), *The Complete Book of the Horse*, Surrey: Colour Library Books, 1991.

Fritz, J.H. (ed.), *Designing Courses and Obstacles*, London: Pelham Books, 1978.

Gerard, H., *Souvenir of Dublin Horse Show 1934*, Dublin: Royal Dublin Society.

Hallam-Gordon, C. (ed.), *International Showjumping Book*, London: Souvenir Press, 1968.

Hartley, E. and Edwards, D. (eds), *The Encyclopaedia of the Horse*, London: Octopus Books, 1977.

Horse and Hound Year Book 1951–1952, London: Odlams Press.

Horse and Hound Yearbook 1962–1963, London: Longacre, 1963.

Horse and Hound Yearbook, London: IPC, 1971 and 1972.

Irish Showjumping Annual, Dublin: Merit Publications, 1978 and 1979.

Le Chevalier, D., *Horse in the Blood — A Show Jumper's Working Notebook*, London: Nicholas Kaye, 1951.

Lewis, C., *Horse Breeding in Ireland*, London: J.A. Allen, 1980.

Lewis, C., *Horse Breeding In Ireland*, London: J.A. Allen, 1980.

Light Horse, The, London: D. J. Murphy Publishers, 1956.

Lyon, W.E. (ed.), *The Horseman's Year*, London: Collins, 1953.

MacGregor Moris, P., *Great Show Jumpers, Past, Present and To Come*, London: George Allen & Unwin Ltd., 1950.

MacGregor Morris, P., *Great Show Jumpers, Past, Present and To Come*, London: George Allen & Unwin Ltd., 1950.

Meenan, J. and Clarke, D. (eds), *The Royal Dublin Society 1731–1981*, Dublin: Gill and Macmillan, 1981.

Meenan, J. and Clarke, D. (eds), *The Royal Dublin Society 1731–1981*, Dublin: Gill and Macmillan, 1981: p. 123.

Murphy, G., *British Showjumpers*, London: Stanley Paul, 1968.

O'Hare, N. and Slavin, M., *The Irish Draught Horse from the Earliest Times to the Present Day*, Dublin: Irish Draught Horse Society, 1989.

Pollard, H.B.C., *Riding and Hunting*, London: Eyre and Spottiswoode, 1938.

Shedden, Lady D. and Lady A., *To Whom the Goddess — Hunting and Riding for Women*, London: Hutchinson & Co. Ltd., 1932.

Smith, B., *The Horse in Ireland*, Dublin: Wolfhound Press, 1991.

Smith, B., *The Horse in Ireland*, Dublin: Wolfhound Press, 1991.

Smith, H., *Harvey Smith on Showjumping*, London: Pelham Books, 1984.

Smyth, P., *Leaping Life's Fences*, London: Sportsman Press, 1992.

Tapani, Count, *Modern Showjumping*, London: Stanley Paul, 1954.

Thoms Directory of Ireland, Dublin: Alex Thom & Co, 1931.

Tinsley, M.E. *The Aga Khan Trophy – 50 Years On*, Dublin: Pontoon Press, 1979.

Toomey, T., *Forgotten Dreams*, Limerick: O'Brien–Toomey, 1995.

Treasury of Irish Songs and Ballads, Dublin: Waltons, 1947.

Williams, D., *Showjumping*, London: Faber and Faber, 1968.

Willis, G., *The World of the Irish Horse*, London: Weidenfeld and Nicolson, 1992.

Wylie, The Hon. W.E., *The Development of Horse Jumping at the Royal Dublin Society's Shows*, Dublin: 1939

Wylie, W. E., *The Development of Horse Jumping at the Royal Dublin Society's Shows*, Dublin: Royal Dublin Society, 2nd. Ed., 1952.

An Cosantóir, the Irish Defence Journal, Dublin: Irish Army, August 1978: vol. XXXVI, no 8.

Bord na gCapall Reports and Accounts, 1978.

Horse and Hound Yearbook, The, London: Odhams Press, 1951–1952.

Horse and Hound, London: 1940–1954.

Horse and Pony Yearbook, The, Dublin: Farmstock Press, 1993.

Horse Show Annual, The, Dublin: Royal Dublin Society, 1900–1910.

Irish Field, The, Dublin: 1940–1954.

Irish Field, The, January–December 1944, July 1991.

Irish Field, The, Dublin: 1980–1990.

Irish Horse Yearbook 1981, Dublin: Bord na gCapall.

Irish Horse Yearbook, Dublin: Bord na gCapall, 1978.

Irish Horse, The, Dublin: Bloodstock Breeders and Horse Owners Association of Ireland, 1944: vol. XII.

Irish Horse, The, Dublin: The Bloodstock Breeders and Horse Owners' Association of Ireland, 1953.

Irish Press, August 1944.

Irish Times, The, August 1944.

Irish Times, The, Dublin: 1980–1990.

L'Année Hippique, 1982–1985, Holland: BCM.

Official Report on Ireland's Participation, XIVth Olympiad, Dublin: Irish Olympic Council, 1948.

Official Report on Ireland's Participation in XVth Olympiad, Dublin: Irish Olympic Council, 1952.

Personal Archive of Poet and Journalist Stanislaus Lynch (RIP) with grateful thanks to his wife Margaret.

Personal Archive provided by Billy McCully, Carrowdore, County Down.

Personal Archive provided by James Bryson, Bambridge, County Down.

Proceedings of the Royal Dublin Society 1930–1939, Dublin: Royal Dublin Society.

Proceedings of the Royal Dublin Society, Dublin: Royal Dublin Society 1866–1880: vols 110–120.

Proceedings of the Royal Dublin Society, Dublin: Royal Dublin Society, 1967–1968: vol. 104, p. 100.

Royal Agricultural Society Proceedings, Dublin: Royal Dublin Society, 1877.

Royal Dublin Society Library Archive.

SJAI Archive, Dublin.

SJAI Rule Book, 1954.

Standard Jumping Rules, Dublin: Royal Dublin Society and Irish Shows Association, 1948.

Standard Rules of Jumping, The, Dublin: Royal Dublin Society, 1948.

*Tuam Herald.*Saturday, 26 May 1900.

INDEX

GLOSSARY

Puissance	A high-jump competition featuring a wall.
Derby	A rustic course of up to sixteen fences.
Classic	Another name for a major jumping competition.
Grand Prix	The most important event at a show.
Three-day-eventing	A competition that includes dressage, cross country and show-jumping.
Nations' Cup Competition	A competition in which teams from different countries compete over two rounds. Whichever has the least amount of total faults after the two rounds is the winner. In the event of a tie after two rounds, all four riders from the tying teams jump again against the clock. The winner is then determined by the least amount of faults in the fastest time. Each team consists of four riders and only the best three scores from each round are counted.
Olympic Games	In Olympic competition there is a preliminary speed round, then a team round and then a final. Riders carry their scores forward and the final usually has twenty or so riders competing in it.
World Championship	In this competition there is a speed round, a team round and a semi-final out of which only the best four riders go forward to the final. In the final each rider must jump one round on each of the four finalists' horses — their own and the other three.
European Championship	European competition consists of a speed round, team round and final which comprises two rounds. If there is a tie for a medal, the competitors jump-off against the clock.
Leading Rider	The rider with best overall performance at a show.
Pocket	The area where horse and rider wait immediately before going into the ring to jump.
Dam	Equine mother.
Sire	Equine father.
Time Fault	A penalty received for taking longer than the time allowed to complete a round.
BCM World Computer Ranking	Scores from international competitions throughout the world are recorded on a central computer and a list maintained in descending order of rider results. Points are awarded for placings in such competitions and input to the computer which then compiles the list. The points are awarded to varying degrees depending on the competitors taking part — thus a second or third placing in a major competition may earn more points in this ranking system than a win at a minor show.
CSIO	Concours Saut International Officiel. (An international show which includes a Nations' Cup Competition)
CHIO	Concours Hippique International Officiel. (The old form of CSIO)
CSI	Concours Saut International. (An international show which does not include a Nations' Cup Competition)
CHI	Concours Hippique International. (The old form of CSI)